PLAYED UP POMPEY 4

NEIL ALLEN

verticaleditions.com

First published in the United Kingdom in 2024 by Vertical
Editions, Unit 41 Regency Court, Sheffield, S35 9ZQ

www.verticaleditions.com

Follow us on Twitter:
@VerticalEds
@pn_neil_allen

Cover images courtesy
of the *Portsmouth News*

ISBN 978-1-917117-00-5

1

A CIP catalogue record for this book is available from the British Library

Printed and bound by Jellyfish
Print Solutions, Swanmore, Hants

*Dedicated to Basher Benfield,
Bobby Kellard, John Mortimore,
Ian St John, Alan McLoughlin,
Joyce Tynan, Frank Burrows,
Terry Harwood, Pat Symes,
Pete Blackman, Dave Dodson
and John McClelland.*

*Their contributions to Pompey
should never be forgotten.*

CONTENTS

HARRY REDKNAPP

243 games, 108 wins (March 2002 - November 2004
and December 2005 - October 2008)

I am a very impulsive person; during my younger days especially I would re-act, then look at it in the cold light of day a little while later and realise how I shouldn't have done something. I'm not condoning it, it's just how I was. I regret quitting Pompey. I do tend to do stupid things — and going to South-ampton was the biggest stupid thing.

We were at Leicester City for our penultimate game of the 2003/04 season, when Milan Mandaric asked to see me in his hotel room at 11.45am on the day of the match. Basically, he was keen to recruit another coach, a foreign coach, and didn't want Jim Smith. With Jim by my side, we'd won promotion and then remained in the Premier League. We had performed an amazing job together. Me and Milan started to get into a bad argument and then, God's honest truth, the fire alarm went off, so we had to leave the room with the issue unresolved. The match ended in a 3-1 defeat for us and, afterwards, I took part in a *Sky Sports* interview with Alan Smith. Three other TV cameras were set up nearby, none of which were being used. Once we'd finished, Alan said: "What's the matter Harry? You're not your normal self." So, I went into one off the record, giving some al-mighty grief about Milan like you wouldn't believe — not realising that the three unmanned cameras were filming.

On the Monday morning I received a phone call from the late Steve Curry, a football writer with *the Daily Mail* and a good friend of mine. "You've done it this time Harry, haven't you?" he said. When I asked what he was referring to, he replied: "Three TV companies have footage of you slagging your chairman off!" I contacted Gary Newbon, who got rid of it at *Sky Sports*, but Milan still found out.

The Jim Smith issue also hadn't gone away, and Milan still wanted to get rid of him the following season. Then, in November 2004, he requested to see me in London. It was a general meeting, so I drove there with our chief executive Peter Storrie, and, at the end of it, Peter stayed while I set off home. On the journey back, I received a phone call from a reporter: "Harry, you've got a director of football coming tomorrow." When I asked what he was talking about, he added: "Velimir Zajec is arriving." I'd left Milan 10 minutes earlier and he never mentioned it. "No chance," I responded. A few minutes later, another reporter called, then another — that was three people now telling me the same thing. So, I rang Milan and asked what was going on. "This is rubbish," he assured me. "It's people trying to cause a problem between us. No way."

The next day I arrived at training, and he was there — Zajec. Not that I knew who he was, even though I was aware he'd been a great player for Yugoslavia. As you can imagine, Milan and I had another argument. Our coaching staff consisted of Jim Smith, Joe Jordan and Kevin Bond, so why did we need somebody else telling us about football? We were 15th in the Premier League, so it wasn't like we were fighting relegation or stuck at the bottom. I wanted Jim to stay — and told Milan precisely that — so it became heated again. He never said Jim had to go, but had now brought this guy in.

Until that point, I'd never told Jim what we had been arguing about. I didn't want him to know the chairman wanted rid, I didn't want to hurt his feelings. As far as he was concerned, it was a usual bust-up. When I'd brought Joe Jordan to the club in the summer of 2004, Milan wasn't keen and really wanted a foreign coach. We were going along well as we were; we had a lovely atmosphere, a fantastic feeling around the place, I couldn't see any reason to change it. As executive director, I suppose Zajec would have brought new players in, but I had no idea about his exact role. I didn't stay long enough to find out either, I was gone pretty quickly. I never spoke to the guy — and within no time had left.

It was difficult, a strange time. There were a couple of articles Milan put into the 'papers having a pop at me, then we had a mass fall-out and I walked. People think I left Pompey because I had a job lined up at Southampton, but I didn't. No way. I never, ever spoke to anyone at St Mary's about leaving to join them. I packed up at Pompey and then, not long after, received a phone call from the agent Dennis Roach, saying: "Harry, Rupert Lowe wants you to go to Southampton. Would you be interested?" I thought: "Well, I haven't done anything wrong, am I not going to work again?"

Looking back, it was like a rebound; your girlfriend leaves so you marry someone else. It was silly. Milan had brought in Zajec and wanted to get rid of Jim, so I decided to leave. It was a bit impulsive. I didn't have to leave over it, but I'd got the hump. I wasn't clever behaving that way, but that's me. "Milan can stick it." After I left, Southampton made an approach. I lived on the south coast, it was convenient, they trained up the road. Why shouldn't I go to work? Southampton was never two fingers up at Milan. I just wanted a job — and at another Premier League club.

I loved Milan, I enjoyed his company and he loved me. He's the favourite chairman of my managerial career — and the reason why I came to Pompey as director of football in June 2001. I'm not a big drinker, but we often had a couple of glasses of wine together, regularly going for dinner at The Pizza House restaurant in Hilsea. We also go way back to 1976, when I moved to North American Soccer League side Seattle Sounders as player-coach, with Milan one of the biggest owners over there. He had the San Jose Earthquakes and a few other clubs, and everybody knew him. I argued with all my chairmen and, looking back, it wasn't a clever thing to do. If someone said something I didn't agree with, I'd let them know in no uncertain terms. I shouldn't have, I realise that, but I couldn't sit there and say nothing. I was the same at West Ham United. I used to be terrible. They'd say something in a board meeting, and I'd jump on them, which cost me my job at Upton Park in May 2001 — and led me to Pompey.

I had been at West Ham for seven seasons and a new four-year contract was waiting to be signed. Mick McGuire from the PFA was negotiating my deal, he always did, and it dragged on and on. But there was no rush, things were good. Then I did an interview for a Hammers fanzine, with the guy mentioning how the chairman, Terry Brown, claimed we'd spent £9m of the money from Rio Ferdinand's £18m sale to Leeds United. Well, I responded by going on one about how he was supposed to be an accountant and couldn't even add up. Terry later told Mick not to bother about the contract — he'd read that interview. That was that. I was gone. I absolutely regret that.

Now out of work in the summer of 2001, Milan asked to meet for a cup of coffee and a chat. Graham Rix was Pompey's manager — and I was offered the chance to become the club's director of football. It was meant to be a stopover after West Ham, a new position to keep me involved in the game in the meantime. I found it the most difficult few months I've ever spent in football. It wasn't a role I knew anything about, and I didn't even understand what the job entailed. After a while, I had no intention of carrying on and my mind was made up to leave at the end of the season. It was also difficult for Graham. I like Graham, he's an excellent coach, but I didn't know him, and I don't believe he wanted a director of football any more than I did when Velimir Zajec was later brought in. I was effectively a chauffeur for Milan. We drove to away games together, often with Fred Dinenage. Every morning, me and Milan would meet for a cup of coffee and chat for hours, wasting the day away, talking about the club and everything.

During that period, I was offered the Leicester City job in October 2001, but didn't fancy it. The chairman, John Elsom, made me a fantastic offer, but the Friday drive home following talks took about four-and-a-half hours, putting doubts in my mind. I wasn't going to move up there permanently, so the alternative was spending all week in Leicester and popping back to the south coast, where the quality of our life is great, and my family are around me. Maybe if I sat tight for a bit, another opportunity would come up. I was certainly getting one or two people ringing up. Being the manager of Pompey was never, ever, ever on my mind or agenda. It wasn't something I could ever see happening or, to be truthful, even wanted to happen at the time.

Then, in March 2002, Milan asked me to take over until the end of the season. His relationship with Graham wasn't great, he'd have the hump with the playing style or the team tactically — and eventually decided to sack him. I told him I didn't want the job and that I'd be leaving at the season's end anyway. After a year of doing nothing, it was time for me to move on. Milan insisted Graham was going anyway; whatever my decision, he was still getting rid of him. Eventually I decided to give it a go, signing a three-year deal. I'm not saying it because I'm talking to you, but it became the best time of my life.

Days after becoming manager, we sold Peter Crouch to Aston Villa for £5m. It was a club record for Pompey and presented us with the finances to strengthen the squad. Milan was never going to splash the cash — it was only when Sacha Gaydamak came in when things changed in that department. That Crouchie fee was crucial in rebuilding the team for the forthcoming 2002/03 promotion season, firstly allowing me to bring in Svetoslav Todorov and Eddie Howe. Toddy was a great buy. I previously recruited him at West Ham from Bulgarian side Litex Lovech and knew he could score goals, especially in Division One. Eddie would have been amazing had he not picked up a serious knee injury and could have played in the Premier League. He could pass the ball and was a good reader of the game.

My best signing, though, was Jim Smith. Ahead of my first full season as Pompey boss, I called him in June 2002 and said: "Jim, will you come and work with me?" I didn't even mention it involved being my assistant. He replied that he'd love to, so now I was fortunate to have someone onside who had been a great manager — not only at Pompey but also at clubs like Oxford United, QPR and Newcastle United. Between us, I felt we could make something happen. Milan ran a tight ship, he wasn't going to spend money unless he could help it, so we built carefully and, with Jim around, we had fun. We laughed; the atmosphere was amazing. He was special around the place, and the lads loved him. Jim was an amazing character and once told Teddy Sheringham how he had scored 120 goals in a season as a player. "You mean you played in a team which got 120 goals in a season?" I asked. No, he insisted — he got them for Sheffield United in their local leagues. You can imagine the teams they were playing, can't you! Teddy was laughing with me.

Jim was a manager, he knew the game, and was great company. The job of a manager is often lonely, yet here was someone I could talk to. I look at some young managers these days and they surround themselves with kids rather than experience, which I don't understand. I always employed good people. I took Steve McClaren and then Glenn Hoddle, both former England managers, to QPR. I also recruited Joe Jordan, Kevin Bond and Frank Lampard Snr. Whereas too many of these young managers take kids and yes men with them — and Jim was no way a yes man! We'd have rows, he had his own opinions, I'd bounce things off him, and he would be honest: "He's useless, I wouldn't play him." Jim never messed about. I took on the challenge at Pompey, but never thought we'd get promoted in 2002/03. It was going to be a hard job, yet, with Jim alongside me, I had a lot more confidence. He knew the club, people loved him and with Kevin Bond also coming in, things suddenly took off.

In the summer of 2002, I set about improving the team I had inherited. I'd been watching Matty Taylor at Luton Town, with their first-team coach Mick Harford telling me: "Matt's all right, but he isn't a left winger and isn't a left-back." Considering I planned on playing three in defence with wingbacks, he was exactly what I wanted. Absolutely perfect. He was such a super player. What he achieved at the club was amazing, and a smashing boy as well. Arjan de Zeeuw had done well at Wigan Athletic, where John Bond — Kevin's dad — was involved. He mentioned to Kevin: "Tell Harry, he's got to take this fella, he's fantastic … a leader, a great man. You've got to get him." Arjan was such an amazing man and special player. I loved him. Not long before the start of the season, I was watching a non-league player turning out in a match at Bournemouth's training ground when I received a phone call from Paul Merson's agent. He asked whether I would be interested in signing him for Pompey — of course I was, but we wouldn't be able to afford him. It turned out he would be a free transfer as Villa wanted rid of him and would accept whatever wages we offered. I rang Merse that same night. I never thought he'd come but had to try. "I want to bring you to Pompey," I told him. "I will make you captain, the number 10, and will build a team around you. He replied: "I like that. I want to play for you." That was it.

I love Merse, I'm great friends with him even now. He's had his issues, and I probably treated him a bit differently to the rest of the squad, but they didn't mind because he was special. He was living in Birmingham, so he'd come in for three days a week. I wouldn't drag him down for the sake of a warm-down on a Monday. What was the point of driving two-and-a-half hours for a 30-minute stretch? Although there was that time when he was supposed to be recovering at Tony Adams' Sporting Chance clinic in January 2003 – only to return from a week in Liphook with the best suntan I'd ever seen. It was so stupid. He had actually been to Barbados and a mate of mine, Michael Taybor, had seen him out there! I had the right hump, but never said anything to Merse. If it had been anyone else, I'd have booted them out. But I knew the only chance we had of getting promoted was with him in the team.

At the end of the season, Merse told me he didn't think he could play in the Premier League anymore. Obviously, he'd dropped down a level, now he was going back a year later. He added: "You're going to need all hands on deck next year to try to stay up, you can't afford a luxury like me who's only going to play when I've got the ball. You need everybody grafting." I had given him a free role when we won the title, and he was fantastic that year. From the moment Merse walked into Fratton Park in August 2002, things took off. He was that good. He changed everything. Before I'd even signed him, a mate of mine rang and announced he was going to have a grand each way on us at 33-1. I told him: "Alan, don't waste your money, we haven't got a chance. Listen, if we could finish halfway then I'd be pleased, it would be a big improvement." We won the Division One title against Rotherham United in April 2003 and finished with 98 points and 97 goals. Alan never spoke to me again. That was the end of our friendship!

We were the bookies' promotion outsiders ahead of my first full Pompey season yet had no expectations of going up whatsoever. Our opening match in August 2002 was against Nottingham Forest and we'd lost our centre-forward the previous day. There we were on the Friday, doing a bit of shape with the team, and Rory Allen told us he wasn't fit to play — which wasn't great when he was meant to be starting! He was a lovely boy, but he got nervous and couldn't face playing. We didn't know too much about mental issues at the time, and he obviously had a problem. He later quit Pompey to watch the Ashes in Australia. Mark Burchill was not yet ready after long-term injury and we were without the suspended Svetoslav Todorov, leaving just Vincent Pericard. Jim's solution was Deon Burton, who he'd previously managed at Derby and Pompey. He quickly engineered a loan deal for Deon and the first time he met the players was 1.30pm in the Fratton Park dressing room on the day of the match. Then he scored eight minutes into his debut as we beat Forest 2-0, with Pericard getting the other.

Following a 1-1 draw at Sheffield United, in which Deon netted again, we headed to Crystal Palace and found ourselves 2-0 down at half-time. Milan tells the story that when he entered their boardroom at the interval, their chairman Simon Jordan came up to him and said: "Oh well, we'll see how clever your big-shot manager is now, won't we." Really mouthing off. When it finished 3-2 to us, Milan went up to him and said: "What did I tell you? That's my big-shot manager!" I had changed to a back three at half-time, a system I previously used at West Ham when we finished fifth in the Premier League in 1998/99, with Eyal Berkovic playing behind the two up front, just as Merson would do for us. Implementing that formation was my long-term plan anyway. It suited Merse, Matty Taylor was a left wing-back in my mind, while Steve Stone later came in and it was perfect for right wing-back. The tactical switch worked that day at Selhurst Park, and, in the second half, substitute Jason Crowe scored twice and Hayden Foxe the other as we fought back to win it.

That first year would see Linvoy Primus named as *The News/Sports Mail's* player of the season but, being truthful, when I took over as manager, he was the first one I was looking to get rid of. To me, he was a good lad, but not good enough. Then Eddie Howe collected an injury after nine minutes in that first game against Forest and Linvoy came off the bench, was fantastic and never looked back. The next thing I know he's marking Thierry Henry and the Premier League was no problem for him. What a person. At first, Linvoy wasn't my type of player. I love people who can play and are comfortable on the ball, which he wasn't. I thought his feet didn't belong to him! But I came to realise what a competitor he was. Linvoy was like a rash, stopping people playing, defending for his life, and became better with better players around him.

That first full season at Pompey was a special time for me, and getting the club into the Premier League was my favourite year in management. Better than winning the FA Cup in 2008. That was a great group. You loved being around them, they were the best I have ever been with. No Billy Bigheads, no-one causing a problem. They got on with that awful training ground, no-one moaned, they loved what they were doing and there was a lovely chemistry. The crowd would sing "Harry and Jim," which gave Milan the hump as they were no longer chanting "There's only one Milan!"

I got on so well with Milan, although we had our arguments. Having beaten Aston Villa in our first Premier League match in August 2003, we were in Manchester on the Friday night ahead of playing at the City of Manchester Stadium. I was trying to sign a left-back from Italy, who ended up playing in the World Cup some years later. I was having dinner with Milan, Terry Brady, Jim Smith and Peter Storrie. I had been to watch this Italian the previous Sunday and was keen, so Milan turned to me and said: "Harry, this player, he's not really a full-back. He's a centre-back." I replied: "No, he's a full-back, a left-back", only for Milan to argue back how he wasn't. When I asked how he knew, he said: "Well, Peter Storrie's stepson has looked him up on *Championship Manager*." At that point, I went into one. We have a row like you cannot believe. The next day we were playing Manchester City. I used to go in the directors' box then, but that match Milan wouldn't sit next to me or speak to me.

On the Monday, I received a letter informing me of an official warning — for the first and only time in my career. It stated I had used a very, very, very bad word to Milan 16 times while giving him grief that Friday night. The word was four letters; you work out the rest. The following day we had Bolton Wanderers at Fratton Park for a midweek game, with Milan still not talking to me. He had the right hump. We beat them 4-0, Teddy Sheringham got a second-half hat-trick and we were top of the Premier League after three games. At the final whistle, Milan came straight up to me, saying: "Harry, come on, you're my friend." All forgotten. I said to him: "Did I only use that word 16 times? I thought it was more than that."

I could have easily been sacked after giving Milan some abuse that night, but it was me standing my ground. We'd often argue — and then forget all about it. I would hear the way he'd talk to Graham Rix: "What is this system you are playing? A Christmas tree? It's not Christmas, why are you playing with a Christmas tree when it's not Christmas?" I was in the car when Milan instructed Rix he had to play Yoshi Kawaguchi instead of Dave Beasant at Sheffield Wednesday in November 2001. I felt for Graham and told Milan he couldn't do that, but he was adamant. He'd spent a club record £1.8m on a Japanese keeper who had yet to play. Pompey had brought him over thinking they were going to get millions of pounds worth of sponsorship out of it. He had been sold this story by someone, but it never came off.

As director of football, I went over to watch Yoshi play for Yokohama Marinos. What a journey, oh my goodness. After the flight, I took a two-hour train journey, with somebody then picking me up and driving me straight to the ground in Tokyo. Yoshi didn't touch the ball for the opening 40 minutes and then, five minutes into the second half, I fell asleep. I mean a proper deep sleep. I was wiped out after the journey and, when I woke up, it was 4-0 — and Yoshi still hasn't touched the ball. I told Milan: "He was all right, but I can't really offer an opinion … he didn't have anything to do." They wanted him so badly because of the financial potential and signed him anyway.

As previously mentioned, I walked out on Pompey in November 2004 and 15 days later joined Southampton, who were struggling in the Premier League, taking Jim Smith and Kevin Bond with me. I knew the rivalry between the clubs was bad, but I didn't realise how personal it would get. I'd receive horrendous phone calls, really nasty things like "I hope your wife gets cancer," or "I hope you get killed in a car crash." All kinds of things. Evil, evil messages all day, hundreds of them, so I had to change my mobile number. Driving to Southampton's training ground in Marchwood on my first day, I arrived at a crossroads and, with roadworks going on, I had to stop at temporary traffic lights. There were eight blokes digging the road — all Pompey boys — who spotted me and shouted: "You Judas so and so." Every morning for three weeks they were there giving me grief. Even at home in Sandbanks, fishermen coming past in their boats would shout things when I was in my garden. It was hard, I'd never had that before and found it horrendous.

I went back to Fratton Park with Southampton in April 2005 for a Premier League match — and Pompey battered us 4-1. The whole build-up was scary. We had four SAS men on the team coach with a helicopter flying above throughout the journey along the M27 because they'd heard fans would be dropping concrete blocks off the bridges. It was like entering a war zone — and the Southampton players absolutely bricked themselves. That was the most intimidating football atmosphere I came across in my life. Thankfully, Lomana LuaLua had to come off after 28 minutes, taking pity on us after scoring twice and winning a penalty, otherwise it would have been about nine. We had Manchester United at St Mary's for the final home game and still had a chance of staying up. It was a week before they were meant to play Arsenal in the 2005 FA Cup final, so we thought that perhaps could help us. Well, Sir Alex Ferguson put out his best team because he's mates with West Bromwich Albion boss Bryan Robson — while the Baggies hosted Pompey and won 2-0. We went down to the Championship.

Moves to bring me back to Fratton Park as manager began in November 2005, when Frank Lampard Snr attended Pompey's 2-0 defeat to Chelsea. At the end of the game, he was invited into the boardroom, where Milan came over and admitted: "We're struggling, the team is useless. We're getting relegated." Frank suggested they brought me back, but Milan replied: "No, Harry wouldn't return. He doesn't like me anymore; we're no longer friends." Yet he asked Frank whether he could broach the issue with me — and when he did, I was interested. We met at Milan's Port Solent apartment at night so nobody could see us — after all, I was the Southampton manager. It was quite bizarre, though, because the following day Peter White wrote in *the Daily Express* about the encounter. I hadn't told a soul, but I could hardly go back to Southampton after that had come out!

Funnily enough, I got a phone call from Chris Kamara and, while chatting generally, he told me that Neil Warnock was going to be Pompey manager: "He's done a deal with Milan, it's all been sorted." I didn't like to tell him that I was now getting the job. I wasn't unhappy at Southampton — it was fine, I had no problems there — but once Pompey came up, I decided I had to come back. I hadn't spoken to Milan for a year, yet once we opened up a bottle of wine and got chatting, we were mates again, which made up my mind. I'd had such a great time at Fratton Park in my first spell and I didn't want them to go down. Pompey were third from bottom, three points adrift from safety, but I felt I could keep them in the Premier League — then when I returned and saw that team I thought: "No, I probably can't!" Dejan Stefanovic, one of the few remaining faces from my first spell, told me: "Gaffer, you must be crazy coming back here. This is the worst team you've ever seen; all the good players have gone. You've got no chance." Now I was thinking: "What have I done?"

I had been back at Pompey four weeks when Sacha Gaydamak came in, initially as joint-owner — and I didn't have a clue it was happening. I had returned for Milan, now someone else was in charge. Someone I never really got to know during our time together at Pompey. In January 2006 we were smashed 5-0 at Birmingham City and, for the first time, I thought we'd be relegated. We were among four teams cut adrift at the bottom and Birmingham had just murdered a struggling rival. Our new signings Pedro Mendes and Sean Davis weren't fit because they hadn't been playing at Tottenham Hotspur and went down with cramp during that match.

After that defeat, Gaydamak wanted to meet me – and John Gregory was being lined up to take the job. Gaydamak said: "Why do the players not try?" I replied: "They do try, they're just not good enough." He added: "That's not good enough," so I answered: "I agree with you, the players are not good enough. It was a good team before I left and now it's a rubbish team." I know for a fact that Gregory was lined up to come back. Absolutely 100 per cent he was waiting to come in – then we beat Manchester City. Lost and I would have got the sack. I had only just come back, Milan had gone, now there was a new owner with no allegiance to me. He was well connected in Israel and friends with Pini Zahavi, with Pini also very close to John Gregory. I didn't know Sacha and I didn't get to know him at all. I don't even know if he had any interest in football. It was a strange situation. But if I had lost against Manchester City, Gregory would have come in. That was how it was. New owner comes in, doesn't know me, doesn't want me, Milan's gone – and I'm now going with him.

We won 2-1 that day, with Pedro scoring twice, and it was incredible. At the end of the game, it was like we'd won the cup. The atmosphere in that dressing room was amazing, everyone singing and dancing around. That win gave us lift off and, from there, we stayed in the Premier League. *The Great Escape*. Although I had heard about John Gregory coming in, I never mentioned it to the players. We needed a win to stay up, and that's all I was concerned about. Had I been sacked, it could have finished me. I'd put my neck on the line going back to Pompey and if we didn't stay up, I was finished. I knew that. But I'm a gambler and took the gamble I could keep them up. And we won.

After Manchester City, we won 4-2 at West Ham and then, in April 2006, the night before our match with Fulham, I took the players to see *Movin' Out* at the Apollo Victoria Theatre in London, a show featuring the songs of Billy Joel. On the coach to the game the next day, our head of performance analysis Michael Edwards, who would later become Liverpool's sporting director, put on a video containing Al Pacino's famous motivational speech from the film *Any Given Sunday*. We won 3-1 and ended up getting 20 points from a possible 27 to stay up at Wigan, with a game to spare. We had recruited better players in the January window, there was a great atmosphere around the place, and the crowd was incredible, lifting us when we needed it most during that run in. The fans were ready to turn, though, and there were obviously mixed feelings about my return. Aston Villa was the game before Manchester City and we lost 1-0 there, with a group in the away end giving me grief. Winning Division One was incredible but keeping Pompey up was close to it. It was unbelievable. Following that 2-1 win at Wigan, I shed a tear on the pitch when I heard Birmingham had drawn against Newcastle to ensure our safety. Dejan Stefanovic came up and cuddled me. Such a special day, a mixture of relief and joy.

My relationship with Gaydamak over time didn't improve. I never got to know him, he was a distant figure — and I missed Milan. Milan was a big draw for me coming back. I loved his company, and the times we had were just incredible. After keeping Pompey in the Premier League, I travelled to Israel for a meeting with Sacha Gaydamak over dinner. He said: "Mr Redknapp, what do you think about bringing in a coach who understands tactics in football?" I replied: "What do you think me, Joe Jordan and Tony Adams do?" He responded: "Yes, but this man is very clever. He understands the diamond formation." I said: "The diamond formation, very good. I saw an under-10s team playing like that over the park on Sunday and it was very good. It's a good formation." When I asked who this man was, I was told Avram Grant. Gaydamak was informed I didn't want him. I didn't need anybody else.

So, I left this meeting, I'd only just arrived in Israel, and I was ready to go home — and I was ready to quit Pompey. Then a very close friend of mine called.

I explained what was going on and he told me: "Harry, if he's going to bring in Grant, why would you walk out? You've done a miracle and kept Pompey up; you shouldn't leave over this." The next day I had another meeting with Gaydamak, who said: "Listen, if we take Avram Grant, we can take one, maybe two players on loan from Chelsea. Would you like Glen Johnson?" Of course I would. The owner continued: "Mr Abramovich will let us have Johnson if you give Avram Grant a job." Now how does that work? The owner of Chelsea is telling Pompey who to employ. Incredible, isn't it? I replied: "So why doesn't Mr Abramovich give Avram a job?" Gaydamak responded: "He wants him to come to England to work at Portsmouth." It was basically give Avram a job, and we get a player like Glen Johnson on loan for nothing. Yes, I changed my mind!

Gaydamak added: "Even if he sits on the PlayStation all day, you can do what you want with Avram." The owner himself was something to do with Abramovich, through business or whatever, and just wanted to please him. I loved Avram, I enjoyed having him there and he was no threat to me. He was there as support. We would chat away; he wasn't taking training sessions or anything. Glen Johnson signed on a season-long loan in June 2006, and, from that point, we built a team with incredible players. Sol Campbell had a fall-out at Arsenal and didn't have a club, so I rang to see what the situation was and was told: "I've had enough of football." He agreed to hear what I had to say, and we met at a coffee shop near where he lived in London, sitting outside chatting. We did the deal, and he earned a third of what he had at Arsenal. Sol wasn't happy at the Emirates and just wanted to play.

Ahead of our first game of the 2006/07 season, there were injuries up front and knew Toddy could play only half a game, with the fitness guys warning any more and he would break down. We had Benjani Mwaruwari, but that was it. So, I suggested Kanu to Tony Adams, who had played with him at Arsenal, winning the Premier League title together in 2001/02. "Kanu? Harry, he's got to be about 48!" he replied, mentioning how he had spoken to Arsenal's physios about him. I had seen Kanu at West Brom when they were relegated and now, he was a free agent, unable to find a club at that late stage, so I rang him. It turned out he'd just come back from a run at the park across the road, so had been keeping himself fit. He'd been on the free transfer list for weeks and weeks and there was no offer, so we asked him to come down for a medical with a view to having a game that Saturday against Blackburn Rovers.

We put him up in a hotel and I was thinking: "Have I made a ricket here? Is Tony right?" So, I decided to play him in a Tuesday afternoon reserve game against Cardiff City at our training ground. I gave Kanu the excuse that I couldn't get the doctor there for a medical, so it would be good for him to have 60 minutes under his belt ahead of Blackburn. Really, I was having a look at him — and if he wasn't any good, I would have failed him on the medical, saying he had a dodgy knee or something. Well, Kanu scored twice that day and I have never seen two goals like it in all my life. They were incredible. After an hour, I turned to Tony and said: "Look at that" — and we signed him on a 12-month deal. After passing a medical, of course. We hosted Blackburn, Kanu replaced Toddy on 59 minutes, scored a header with his first touch, got another goal, and then missed a stoppage-time penalty for his hat-trick in a 3-0 win. He was still at Pompey five-and-a-half years later, yet didn't have a single offer before we signed him. He may never have played again.

We paid £5m for Lassana Diarra in January 2008, and he was an incredible player. His third Premier League match for us was a 1-1 draw with Chelsea and he ran the game. Frank Lampard told me he hated playing practice matches against Diarra at Chelsea: "I can't get near him," he said. "He's that good." He went to Arsenal, and we watched him in a Carling Cup game at Blackburn, with the Gunners winning 3-2, and he was their best player. Arsenal played Spurs the following weekend, but Diarra was left out, so his agent rang and asked whether I would be interested in meeting a £5m buy-out clause.

Now I didn't think it was possible, but the agent assured me the lad wanted to play and Arsenal had told him he could go. It turned out he'd said to Arsene Wenger: "I'm not happy, I think I should be in the team, and I want a move." The manager replied: "You want a move? No problem, you can go." The next day, Arsene called him in and said: "Listen, I didn't mean that, I don't want you to go. You are going to be in the team." Diarra responded: "No, you said I can go. I'm going." That was how he was, a very strong character. After he joined us, apparently his agent hadn't been paid money owed and Lassie insisted: "If he doesn't get paid by Friday, I don't play." And he wasn't messing about. He wouldn't budge. In the end, the club paid up.

Sylvain Distin joined on a free transfer from Manchester City in May 2007, and we'd been talking since Christmas. We initially held talks in a room on the 12th floor of a Manchester hotel because we couldn't be seen together, even arriving at different entrances. But as we were chatting with Sylvain and his agent, the hotel's fire alarm went off and wouldn't stop. There were staff banging on the doors and shouting: "Everybody out." We had to go down the fire escape and into the lobby, with about 300 people standing there as we came down with Sylvain. "We'll be in trouble here," I thought — but no-one found out.

David James arrived the previous summer from Manchester City for £1.2m as they had just bought Joe Hart. Their manager, Stuart Pearce, wanted to shift Jamo to make room, so we got this great goalkeeper. Then there was Niko Kranjcar, who arrived from Hajduk Split and was such a fantastic player — just a class act. He was always a bit heavy at times with his weight, but a classy player. They were all great players for me and part of the 2008 FA Cup-winning team, which also ended up eighth in the Premier League — the club's highest finish in more than half a century.

We stopped Manchester United doing the treble that year, winning at Old Trafford in the FA Cup quarter-finals in March 2008 through Sully Muntari's penalty. I had never seen Alex Ferguson so upset at being beaten. He was bad news that day, not very friendly at all. The pace of Sylvain, the power and strength of Sol; they could get into any team in the world at that point. It was a great side full of amazing players. Hermann Hreidarsson, what a character. The night before the FA Cup final, I took them to an Italian restaurant in Bray, near our Windsor hotel, with karaoke afterwards. Hermann brought his Elvis outfit and belted out Blue Suede Shoes and An American Trilogy. I'd asked my mate Kenny Lynch to come along and give us some songs. After he watched Hermann, he said: "Harry, there's no way I can follow that," — and wouldn't do it! Then we had John Utaka and Kanu doing Bob Marley's No Woman, No Cry on the karaoke. It was a good, fun night to relax them – and we won the FA Cup the next day.

In January 2008 — five months before we got the FA Cup — I agreed a deal to become Newcastle manager following the sacking of Sam Allardyce. I was approached by Paul Kemsley, a former vice-chairman of Spurs but also very close to Newcastle owner Mike Ashley. Now Ashley wouldn't meet me because he didn't want to break any rules, so I met with Kemsley and Tony Jimenez, vice-president at St James' Park, at some London offices. They were offering me crazy money, an amazing deal, and we had a second meeting the following evening — at which I verbally agreed to become the next Newcastle manager. I didn't have a great relationship with Gaydamak, so it appealed. But, on the Friday, I had a change of heart. I was happy where I was and I loved it at Fratton Park, so turned them down.

I had also rejected Spurs about 18 months before I eventually took the job in October 2008, which people probably don't know. I met Daniel Levy at his house, and we spent five hours chatting. But what I couldn't understand was why they wanted to get rid of their manager at the time, Martin Jol. "He's a good manager, you're doing okay," I said. Levy replied: "We are doing okay, but I want you to be manager, coming in for Saturday." We met again the next evening, with director of football Daniel Comolli this time present, but I had decided it wasn't for me. I was happy at Pompey. Levy replied: "Let's leave it, who knows what will happen in the future".

In October 2008, we were on the coach returning to the airport following a 3-0 defeat at Braga in the UEFA Cup when my phone rang — it was Paul Kemsley again. This time he was representing Spurs and told me: "Daniel wants to speak to you." I told him to ring me back in 20 minutes when I'd be at the airport as I needed to find somewhere out of earshot. It turned out they wanted me to replace Juande Ramos as manager, inviting me for talks that evening. So, I returned home to Sandbanks, got changed and began the drive to Daniel Levy's house — only to receive a call from an agent called Phil Smith, who somehow knew all about where I was heading and asked: "Who's doing your deal?" I replied: "Well there isn't a deal, I don't know whether I'm going to join them." He was urging me to talk to Spurs and see the offer.

Then I pulled into a lay-by. I'd had second thoughts and called Peter Storrie, who had been informed of Spurs' interest. "Peter, I'm not going to this meeting," I said. "I've decided to turn around." His response was "The chairman thinks it would be a great move for you. You'd be crazy not to go." Do you know what? I wouldn't have gone that night if Peter had reassured me Gaydamak wanted me to stay. Instead, it convinced me I should leave Pompey. They'd been offered £5m compensation from Spurs, which was a lot of money in those days, and wanted the cash more than me staying as their manager. I said to Peter: "Really? Okay, he doesn't want me anyway," and started my car up again. Gaydamak had £5m and thought Tony Adams could do the job instead, so that was that.

At Pompey, I never had a clue about the finances. I didn't know Gaydamak and as far as I knew he was richer than Roman Abramovich. They told me he was Abramovich's pal and that his dad Arkadi was incredibly rich in Israel, a billionaire many times over. Pompey was his dad's club and apparently, he was quite a ruthless man. Ossie Ardiles managed under him at Beitar Jerusalem and lasted three-and-a-half months. As a manager, you're relying on the owner; you don't know details about his bank account. Should an owner not have the money, he would say to me: "We can't afford that player, Harry. We can't get him," yet Gaydamak was saying: "Go and get him. Get him as well. What about him?" He wanted players all the time. In my view, he was on a par with Abramovich in terms of wealth, yet I didn't have a clue about him.

There were great plans about building a new stadium in Portsmouth Harbour, yet people I knew from Portsmouth were telling me: "Harry, there's no way they can build that stadium there. If it caught fire, there's no escape." They bought acres of land in Titchfield for a training ground, but never built anything. It was a load of cobblers. At the time, though, as far as I was aware, this was one of the richest men in the world. If he had said: "We can't afford Diarra, we haven't got the money, don't get him," that would have been fine, but that never happened. When I worked at Tottenham, and Daniel Levy didn't want to buy anybody, I'd have to take two or three free transfers until the end of the season. That's how it works — you can only do what your chairman tells you.

Without doubt, Pompey was the best time of my life. I absolutely loved it there. The rats running about the changing rooms in the early days, Linvoy Primus making the Fratton Park boot room into a prayer room. Big Kev McCormack doing the kit, moaning about everything and being my golf partner, taking on Jim Smith and Kevin Bond; the Harry and Jim song; my friendship with Milan, the favourite chairman of my career; and the last day of the title season at Bradford City.

Nowhere else did I have the feeling I had at Pompey. I can't remember having a bad day there: it was all up, up, up. Okay, when I came back for a second spell we had a couple of iffy results, but, in the main, it was a fun time. I started my playing career at West Ham, making 175 appearances, and later managed them for seven years, but I enjoyed it more as Pompey boss. At Upton Park it was always pressure, pressure, pressure, and I got low there at times. Really low, especially when I first arrived, and we struggled. I could have easily suffered a breakdown. I didn't realise at the time, but it was scary how low I'd get on a Saturday night after a Hammers game, such was the pressure of the job. But at Pompey, I hit the ground running. We won the Division One title in 2002/03 and off we went, never looking back. I loved it. It was such an incredible time.

SOL CAMPBELL

111 games, two goals (August 2006 — July 2009)

Manchester United 0
Pompey 1 (Muntari)

FA Cup quarter-final, Old Trafford, Saturday, March 8, 2008

Pompey: James, Johnson, Campbell, Distin, Hreidarsson, Muntari, Diarra, Diop, Kranjcar (81 mins, Hughes), Utaka (74 mins, Lauren), Kanu (54 mins, Baros). Subs not used: Ashdown, Mvuemba.

Attendance; 75,463

Everyone was saying: "Sol is finished, he's done. He has gone to Pompey. There's nothing happening at Pompey." Yet they didn't realise my character — and completely overlooked that it was Harry Redknapp building this team. I'm a winner, I want to do well whenever I put my hands to anything, so there was absolutely no way I saw it as an opportunity to play for at least three more years and do nothing. I wanted to get something out of my Fratton Park move and I'd be trying everything in my powers to ensure I did.

That's my philosophy, that's my mentality; giving it my best shot to the team, to my teammates, to the club, the fans — that's me. People seem to think that when you go down to clubs like Pompey you're usually done, it's a payday, keep ticking over and occasionally turn up a few results. No, it's not. Winning never gets blasé. You have a short career, but you want to keep running to the very end, not slowing down. It's not like a singer who makes so many amazing songs in the opening 10 years, before chilling out for four or five years to get the artistic juices flowing again and then releasing another album. In football, you can do well for a decade and, should you then want to chill, you're out of the game. See you later. You cannot rest, you must keep going. For 10, 15, 20 years. Don't stop. Just don't stop.

Certain clubs in the Premier League are historically big with big budgets, so everyone saw Pompey as a step down for me — it turned out it wasn't. I won the FA Cup for a fourth time, regained my England place and played in the Premier League for another three seasons there. Football's all about passion – and I loved that passion at Pompey. Such a fantastic club. It was a fresh beginning for me after Arsenal, but also reconnected me with people, with players, with supporters. With football.

I'd had lots of problems at Arsenal and 2005/06 wasn't a particularly easy season for me. I wanted a fresh start. For that reason, I was keen to leave the country and play abroad because the whole situation of being in London was no longer right for me. I wanted to concentrate on broadening my horizons in football — but it just didn't materialise. Inter Milan and Fenerbahçe were interested, and Juventus was the closest and nearly happened, however it fell through at the last hurdle. The deal was done but Didier Deschamps, who had recently been appointed head coach, didn't want me. Juve had just been relegated to Serie B for the first time in their history after being found guilty of match-fixing, while they were also forced to start the next season with minus-30 points, reduced to nine upon appeal. Nonetheless, I was happy to go there, with their hierarchy setting up a move which would involve Arsenal cancelling the final 12 months of my contract by mutual consent and me joining Juve on a three-year deal. The wages were done, the terms were done, I was in Milan waiting for the call to go over and complete everything — but Deschamps told them he didn't want me. It was off.

I really wanted to go abroad, and I tried everything to get that deal done. I was aged 31, it was perfect, but the head coach had other ideas. They subsequently won Serie B that season, immediately bouncing back with promotion, and Deschamps resigned weeks later. Juve probably saw me winning the FA Cup and back in the England team two years later and thought: "Do you know what, he's alive!"

I was on England duty at the 2006 World Cup finals in Germany that same summer when Pompey first made their move, albeit through my international teammate Frank Lampard. He asked: "Do you fancy having a chat with my uncle?" — and it went from there. Following the World Cup, I had a meeting with Harry Redknapp in a cafe in Chelsea and continued talking to the chief executive Peter Storrie after that. It was all completed pretty quickly. The great thing about Harry is he gets you thinking you've still got a job to do. He's capable of stoking that fire again in players who'd had long careers, squeezing some more talent out of them. Sometimes they'd gone off the boil, others were coming back from injury, but he could draw out that extra bit of quality, getting them reconnected with the sport, playing top, top football. He got a lot of those sorts of characters into Pompey and was proven right because many went off to bigger clubs for massive fees, the likes of Lassana Diarra and Glen Johnson in particular.

I joined Pompey because of Harry and maybe if it had been anyone else, I wouldn't have gone there. I loved the fact this was a manager who had your back, he knew how you thought and felt. I had something still in the tank but needed the right person to get it out of me in the right environment. Harry's a top man-manager and, while he can sometimes blow his top, I don't mind that because that's passion. He cares about the game and is a typical East Londoner, quick with his comments. Some of them are legendary. He's definitely up there among the best managers I came across because he can handle players, he can handle egos — and so many managers really can't handle egos.

I arrived at Pompey in August 2006, six weeks short of my 32nd birthday, yet while I was able to play week in, week out, including midweek fixtures, I needed recovery days, which Harry completely understood. We weren't 18-year-olds any more, some of us were in our early thirties going into the mid-thirties and we needed need a little time to recover. Physically the body was not the same as it was at 25. Mentally we're stronger but physically you needed another 24 hours to recharge — and Harry managed us properly. These days you have 20-year-olds who physically can't play 30 games in a season, yet I made 111 appearances during three years at Fratton Park. That's a lot of matches at the back end of my career, working my backside off while winning trophies at the same time. Pound for pound, Pompey got a lot from those guys who played for them, regardless of what happened in the club's future.

What I found at Fratton Park was a good bunch of lads who were top, top footballers, yet requiring the right environment to progress in — and that environment was amazing. The training ground had cold showers and if it rained, the pitches became a mud pile. Sometimes we had to train on the University of Southampton's astroturf if it got too bad, but it was never about the training ground. It was about the people. That's the thing about football, if the people are right then you're going to play right. I could have been snooty about the facilities, but no. I'm from East London, I appreciate everything I get and I work for everything I've had. I don't care about how much I earn, I still put in 100 per cent and don't drop off. The training ground showers may have been cold, but I still bust a gut defending for my life and playing good football, while attempting to get the team going in the right direction. I just got on with it.

Pompey was a fresh beginning, but it also reconnected me with football. I wasn't the only one coming down trying to make it happen, Pedro Mendes had won the Champions League with Porto and was later at Tottenham Hotspur; Kanu had achieved footballing gold at the 1996 Olympics in Atlanta and done some unbelievable stuff with Arsenal. Jermain Defoe was a fantastic centre-forward, Peter Crouch, Glen Johnson, Sulley Muntari, Lassana Diarra … these guys came in and, all of a sudden, were springboarded to big clubs because we played so well. If those guys don't perform then we were not winning the FA Cup and they weren't moving to Liverpool, Real Madrid, Inter Milan, back to Tottenham. No chance.

As for myself, within a week of arriving at Fratton Park, I was left out of new England manager Steve McClaren's first squad for a friendly against Greece, despite featuring once in that summer's World Cup finals in Germany. I never gave up on England, but it would take another 16 months before my Pompey form earned me a recall. In October 2007 I was back, partnering Rio Ferdinand in the centre of defence against Estonia for a Euro 2008 qualifier. The qualification campaign was going a bit iffy, so McClaren brought me in for four games to help us go through, and we nearly did — but for that 3-2 home defeat to Croatia in November 2007. I never represented my country again, finishing on 73 caps.

In my first Pompey season in 2006/07, we narrowly missed out on Europe after failing to beat Arsenal on the final day and instead the goalless draw saw us finish ninth in the Premier League. Sides didn't like coming to Fratton Park, it's such a tight ground and can be intimidating, with the fans right on top of you. If you aren't ready for it, you can be done over quite easily. It's a proper, old-school stadium and I loved playing there. The fans are firmly behind you, singing, ringing that bell. Everybody's up for it and I loved it, I loved the passion. Those supporters are incredible, they love football and they have your back, even singing after the final whistle, regardless of the score. They are amazing fans – and that's what it's all about, that's why football can be wonderful. Winning the FA Cup and travelling on an open-top bus across Southsea with 250,000 coming out to cheer us over the course of the day … it's amazing what that does for the city.

My regular central-defensive partner in that first season was Linvoy Primus, who I had previously come up against while growing up in London. I'm from Stratford, with Linvoy living 10 minutes away in Leyton, and some of my close friends knew him, although Pompey was the first time we'd played together at any level. Another face from my past was former Arsenal teammate Kanu, who arrived at Fratton Park two days after me on a free transfer having been released by West Bromwich Albion. He had this ability to bring players into the game and his hold-up play was tremendous, you couldn't get it off him. He also possessed these extendable legs which got everywhere, and an amazing touch. He was a special player — they call him the King of Nigeria and he remains an incredible human being, born to play football and a great, great guy. Of course, the following season he would become an absolute legend at Pompey for his goals in the FA Cup semi-final and then the final.

The summer of 2007 would see the arrivals of Muntari, John Utaka, Glen Johnson, on a permanent deal, and Papa Bouba Diop and it would be a season in which we finished eighth and claimed silverware at Wembley. There were some tough games along the way in that FA Cup run, including a 1-0 win at Preston North End secured through a Darren Carter own goal in stoppage time — and a quarter-final trip to Old Trafford. Manchester United had beaten us there 2-0 just five weeks earlier, with Cristiano Ronaldo scoring twice, including that fantastic 30-yard free-kick which swerved away from David James. Now we were back and they must have been thinking: "Job done, just stay in the game." But it's a special competition and if you disrespect the FA Cup, it disrespects you. It does so time and time again, with so many giant killings. I didn't taste victory at Old Trafford many times, but enough to possess the understanding of what you needed to win the game. Everybody turned up that day and it was amazing. We won 1-0 through Sulley Muntari's 78th-minute penalty.

The performances from every single one of our players were heroic. At one point in the first half they had a breakaway and I was up for our corner and had to run from their box to our box. We are talking about 60-70 yards and I was behind

Wayne Rooney, but I knew he wanted to walk the goal in. It was just him and David James, so I still had a chance. He went around Jamo and I got a touch to block the ball, it bounced up to Carlos Tevez and his shot was headed off the line by Glen Johnson. Another moment involved Nani crossing from the right and I managed to hook it away for a corner with Ronaldo looking like he was going to finish it. Time stood still for a second. I don't even know how I did it. There was also Jamo pushing Patrice Evra's shot against the post, Sylvain Distin blocking the ball on the line from Michael Carrick — these moments win you cups.

What you have to realise is we had big-game players in there who knew what to do. We weren't novices, but we all went to another level that day at Old Trafford. A level we'd played at before in our careers — at places like Old Trafford and others. We were in it together, a team.

In the tunnel afterwards I was crying, the emotions were too much. The feeling of achievement engulfed me. It was unbelievable. The Theatre Of Dreams — Pompey were there to be fodder. We were the sideshow, there to please the Mancunians who were thinking: "It's going to be 5-0, let's eat our sandwiches and go home really happy." We weren't expected to win, but they didn't reckon on our team showing a bit about us, producing a heroic performance across the board. This is what it's all about, this is football. When you look at the finances, the gulf between the talent, sometimes the machine of Manchester United can almost beat players in the tunnel, but we had a bit about us and could handle that. Boy the bookies must have lost a lot of money that day. The treble was gone, *poof*, and I keep on saying heroic, but it really was. Pompey's performance was mesmerising, unbelievable. Everyone played in a different universe that game: the team, the subs, everyone. You are at Manchester United to lose, you're there for the entertainment of 75,463 people, you're there to pick up the cheque for 50 per cent of the gate receipts to take home. Bye. But no, now we were in the semi-finals of the FA Cup.

The semi-final against West Brom and the final against Cardiff were both tight games which finished 1-0, but we had a squad which possessed the experience and we were able to ensure the occasion didn't run away from us. It's easy to lose your focus in big games like that, become distracted from what you're there to achieve. Let everyone else party, but you have a job to do and — on May 17, 2008 — Pompey were FA Cup winners.

There are a lot of clubs in the Premier League who haven't been in a cup final of any sort for 30 years, yet spent 10 times – 20 times – more money than Pompey over that period. They've never reached a final, let alone won a final. It's usually the top-six Premier League teams winning things, yet we did it at Pompey. We got to a final and then, after I had gone, reached another FA Cup final two years later in 2010 and lost against Chelsea. That's an amazing feat for Pompey. You have to appreciate the quality of that team Harry built; the whole ethos and philosophy, young players, experienced players. We all got the best out of each other for that period of time and that's key. People in football have to realise the accomplishment at Pompey during that time. It was unbelievable, incredible. That's a special thing. Not everyone can win the FA Cup, it's the oldest cup competition in the world and it's a special team which achieves that. For players and management – it's special.

When I look back on that FA Cup-winning side and some of those players — wow. Sylvain Distin has to be up there with my best central-defensive partners. He was an excellent player — quick, strong and, being left footed, complemented my right foot, so we had balance at the back. He was always in the gym, had tremendous physicality and movement, and it's no surprise he's now a personal trainer after retiring from football.

Lassana Diarra dropped off after going to Real Madrid. He needed the Sol man there, motivating him on the pitch! He was 21 and had gone from Chelsea to Arsenal and then joined us for £5m, all within six months. You look at that and think: "Where do you go from there, mate?" If you're intelligent, you watch the good players. If you are not intelligent you do what you want. Diarra was intelligent. He looked around that dressing room, saw what we did and how we did it, how we conducted ourselves, not only on the field but off it — and that's how he became an amazing player. That's why Real Madrid came in and said: "We need you." Diarra's energy levels were incredible. He was quicker than Claude Makelele, the same kind of pace as N'Golo Kante, maybe a little faster in some instances, and a top, top player. He'd close things down with his energy, release it and play.

Hermann Hreidarsson is one of my big muckers. I've come up against him in Iceland in an England international and played alongside him at Pompey. He's an honest character, willing to do anything — and he does it well. Obviously he has tons of banter, sometimes too much, but he's a great character in the changing room. As a defender, Hermann was athletic, his physical attributes were incredible but he could put his foot in and play football. In the nicest way, he's one of the craziest players I have ever come across, capable of having fun but working incredibly hard, and was my assistant when I became Southend United manager in October 2019.

As for David James, he's one of the best goalkeepers I played with, certainly the most athletic I've ever seen. Incredible. His attitude was second-to-none as well because he always wanted to train, always wanted to get better. His whole attitude towards playing in goal was amazing and infectious. You need to love the game, you must be obsessed with the game, and he went on until he was 44, which is testament to him. At Pompey, he was also up there with the long-distance running, in the top three, which is incredible for the size of the man. Jamo is a top, top bloke — his physicality, electricity, the way he could stretch his arms — yet the only thing against him were mistakes in major moments. Regardless, he's the best. Unbelievable.

When Glen Johnson initially arrived on loan from Chelsea in the 2006/07 season I remember thinking: "What's happening here?" This was his second chance and he stayed for three seasons, then was sold for £18.5m to Liverpool and did really well for them. Some players came, did really well, then secured some fantastic moves that their performances warranted — and I love all that. You work hard, try your best, someone recognises it and says: "Hey, they're really at it. Let's have some of that, sign here."

Everything was fantastic on the pitch, and if only Pompey's hierarchy had been a bit more savvy in making sure the foundations were secure. I met the owner Sacha Gaydamak, but his money got stuck, he couldn't get any more in and that's when the financial troubles really hit. Before then, I remember going to a press conference at the Carlton Tower Jumeirah Hotel in Knightsbridge, where plans for a new £600m, 36,000-capacity stadium in The Hard were unveiled in April 2007. It's a shame the finances weren't managed properly, because who knows where the club could be now? They just needed a bit more management off the field, somebody astute in the business and finance area to do it properly, guiding the club, proper, safe investment — it just wasn't managed properly. As a player, even though I was captain, you never truly know the full situation. I wasn't the one running the finances. The only thing I recognised was how quality players eventually began to leave for big money and to further their careers, which was understandable. But when that's happening, you're questioning whether you can bring in others of the same ability range to replace them. The answer was no.

Harry Redknapp had rejected the Newcastle United job in January 2008 and I knew another club would come in sooner or later — it turned out to be nine months down the road. He never confided in me that he was considering the Spurs offer, yet I had that sense he wouldn't be at Pompey for much longer. When he moved to this big Premier League club in October 2008, I wasn't surprised because football's all about seeing how far you can go. It's such a short career. Even with management, you don't know whether you're going to be a manager for 20 years or five years, so you have to make the most of your opportunities.

His replacement was our assistant manager, Tony Adams, who I had played alongside at Arsenal for a season and also in England colours. I could understand the attraction of the job; Tony had his own ideas and this was the opportunity to take the club on, representing a fantastic chance for a young manager. As a coach, he focused on work and analysis and Harry did most of the talking, although Tony stepped in when he could influence things. He was good at that. Regardless of our new manager, when you've got players moving on, it gets difficult. It's like the water is being drained out of the bathtub, the talent's going out and nothing's coming in, so it makes your job more difficult. The talent you saw the previous year is no longer there, so how are we going to replenish that? You have to work extra hard, be even cleverer in the transfer market, but when you get players coming in who aren't really at the level or are injured, it disturbs the whole flow of the club. The mentality changed and for a manager attempting to maintain a good philosophy, it's difficult. If you wish to be stable and competitive in the Premier League, you need good footballers to share the burden. You can't have three or four players carrying the team. It was unravelling.

Paul Hart stepped up from the academy to take over from Tony in February 2009, initially as caretaker boss, and was a stand-up guy. He was very serious but could also have a laugh. He was probably suited to the players remaining at the club or being recruited, so it was perfect for him to be on that level. It was hairy for a while, but we stayed up with two games to spare, finishing 14th in the Premier League, while I had made 40 appearances in my third — and what proved to be final — season.

The point I knew I was leaving Pompey was when there was no new contract offer. As it turned out, the club didn't have the money. You have to accept it. I was older, 34 by that point, although they could have offered me something else, like player-manager. Why not? I'm one of the best players this country has ever produced. Okay, I hadn't done my coaching badges by then, but why not? The owner was looking to sell the club, administration was close, it was a house of cards. One of the reasons Kanu stayed for such a long time was because they renegotiated his contract as they could no longer afford to pay him as much, so it was split over three years and all of sudden he was there for six seasons. If they had said: "Hey Sol, fancy being a player-manager, a player-coach, whatever?" then I would have looked at that. We'd won the FA Cup, I was captain of the club, the fans knew me. They could have told me: "We like you Sol, the finances aren't here, so do you fancy doing another job here?"

I wasn't in decline. I subsequently joined Notts County for a month, then returned to Arsenal, scored in the Champions League and produced one of my best performances against Porto when Hulk was trying to run the show, putting him in my pocket at the age of 35. I'll tell you what, if something was offered by Pompey in the summer of 2009, I would definitely have had a look. Speak to me, it's quite simple. I can appreciate the situation was dire behind the scenes, so obviously they're not going to talk to you if they can't pay you. However, Tony Adams previously got the job, so why couldn't I be a player-manager? I was in the club, I was in the house, I was right there. I could have been seriously thinking about management, yet Pompey never asked and no new contract was offered. You want to play for as long as possible, but someone has to make an offer for you to think about. "Sol, we want you to stay at the club, what about this? What about the youth-team? What about the reserves?" There was nothing and I became a free agent in the summer of 2009.

Pompey went into administration twice in two years after I left and I was owed more than £1.6m, but I didn't want to hamper them moving forward and so I wrote off everything I was entitled to. Another person could have said: "No, I want my money," but I didn't. I've been very generous and perhaps people haven't appreciated that. Regardless of what might have been said about me, I could have stuck to my guns and said I wanted the money, but I didn't. No way. It was actually more bonuses than image rights, but when they said I couldn't get it, I thought: "Fine, I'll walk away." That was out of respect for a fantastic club like Pompey and should be common knowledge. In the end, once I knew of their dire situation, I let it go and took it on the chin. Others wouldn't, they'd have wanted their money, but that's the situation with me. That's what people have to realise.

It was like that at Notts County as well. I could have said: "I want all my money," because I'd signed a five-year deal there, but I had to let that go as well. The trouble is, at Pompey there have been people in the finance and accounts office who have not run the club properly – then you, as a player, get the brunt of it. I believe I did an amazing job there as a footballer, but you guys in the accounts department haven't. I stuck to my part of the agreement, I did everything I was entrusted to do and more. I've kept us in the Premier League, won the FA Cup, took us into Europe, I did everything right – but you guys didn't. Pompey and Notts County were two clubs where I lost my money for the love of football, and people don't talk about that enough. I was honourable and let it go. I let it go. People may say: "You have enough money anyway," but a lot of players would definitely have said: "I want my money." Not me – I didn't take a penny. I've not been perfect, but I have been honourable when it comes to football.

When I arrived at Pompey, it was about finding myself, rediscovering my love of the game, feeling wanted — and it worked. I felt young again, I was fighting for something once more, wanting to play every second. Sure, the environment wasn't perfect, yet it was about stripping yourself down, working from scratch, and getting the best out of yourself and people around you. The love and warmth that Pompey and their incredible supporters gave me and others was exactly what I needed at that stage of my career. I felt alive. I'm a street footballer, I started on the streets of East London, and while I may have a cool persona on the outside, I'm very passionate on the inside. I'm sensitive, I'm strong, and I want to win. On the field I had to be a different animal, a different human being, whereas off it I'm slightly relaxed, observing a little. But I loved that feeling of being alive, which Pompey gave to me and others.

There were rubbish training pitches often waterlogged, but it re-acquainted me with a type of football and lifestyle I'd had as a youngster growing up — and that was the beautiful thing. I rediscovered myself. It was simple, stripped down, not all gleaming and gold, just about football, and I loved it. Once it's about football, I come alive and you can't compete with me. That's it. I fly.

In May 2008, at the age of 33, I walked up the Wembley steps, lifted the FA Cup and said to myself: "You know what, after all the heartache, all the ups and downs, this is so special." It makes a difference in your life and no-one can ever take that away from you. No-one. Whatever anyone around the world says from now on, they cannot take that away from those Pompey players, managers and staff. That's the beautiful thing about winning in that kind of way — you're part of history. That moment is yours, it's unique. Only a few people can have that feeling – and it's so very, very special.

That time in our lives is etched in Pompey fans' hearts, souls, spirits, memories and books. They will continue talking about it for a long, long time — and so will I. Thank you Pompey for giving me back football.

GARETH EVANS

218 games, 38 goals (July 2015 — September 2020)

Pompey 6 (O'Shaughnessy OG, Bennett, Naismith 2, Lowe, Evans)
Cheltenham Town 1 (Dayton)

League Two, Fratton Park, Saturday, May 6, 2017

Pompey: Forde, Evans, Burgess, Clarke, Stevens, Doyle, Rose (71 mins, Aborah),
Baker (60 mins, Lowe), Naismith, Bennett, Chaplin (61 mins, Roberts).
Subs not used: O'Brien, Whatmough, Linganzi, Kabamba.

Attendance; 17,956

As I waited behind the temporary stage constructed on Southsea Common, I could hear 'Touchline' Tony Male introducing people who didn't really have a massive part in Pompey's promotion. We were League Two champions, the trophy had finally arrived that morning and the city's celebrations had continued into a second day, yet councillors and other faceless dignitaries were first in line to meet the 15,000 crowd, with everyone half-heartedly clapping in response. "Blimey, this is supposed to be a party," I thought. "What's going on?" I told Michael Doyle I'd get the things going. Not that he believed me.

The idea popped into my head. When it was my turn, I'd go on stage, steal a microphone and sing a song. I mentioned the plan to the lads and they laughed. Players were announced according to squad numbers, starting from David Forde, with me, as number 26, standing there for ages — enough time to get a little nervous over what I intended to carry out. Then it was my turn. I entered the stage, grabbed the mike off Tony and sang: "If you all hate Scummers, clap your hands." I wanted to liven up the crowd and, as it happened, that was the only thing I could think of. Obviously it was well received. I wasn't hammered, I think I'd had five pints by that point. Certainly I wouldn't have done it unless I'd had a drink, but I wasn't falling over drunk. Although, thinking back, it could well have reignited the booze from the previous night.

Earlier that morning, some of us had met at the Royal Beach Hotel, although I was without my girlfriend Hazel, later to be my wife, who was hungover after the Saturday evening festivities to mark winning the title, which also coincided with her 30th birthday. By the time I turned up at the hotel, six or seven of the lads were there and Cookie put a pint in front of me with the words: "Well done son, congratulations." After two or three pints, we caught taxis back to Fratton Park, where players' families were around and a bus was waiting to take us to the official celebrations on the seafront. The Victory Lounge was shut, so me and Michael Smith, who also didn't have any family there, went behind the bar there, pouring ourselves a few lagers, while the other players were on the bus. I don't think anyone had a clue where we'd been. When we eventually boarded, the pair of us sat at the back singing: "Up the Football League we go," "Play Up Pompey," or anything else which popped into our heads. A few hours later, I was performing in front of thousands on Southsea Common. That May 2017 weekend will forever remain the favourite time of my football career.

Just two years earlier, while sitting on a beach in Lagos, Portugal, I agonised over my footballing future. Aged 27, I had just helped Fleetwood Town finish 10th in League One, earning the offer of a new two-year deal — yet there was a spark missing. I'd previously been at Bradford City, while my time with Rotherham United coincided with the move to the New York Stadium and subsequently attracting 8,000 supporters for every home fixture. However, after two-and-a-half years at the Highbury Stadium, I was craving the adrenaline buzz of performing in front of bigger crowds. I wanted something more from football. As it turned out, the next move presented me with the best times of my playing career. Pompey.

Having returned from holiday and turned Fleetwood down, among others, the summer was dragging and I was getting a little concerned over my options. Then Paul Cook contacted my agent, asking me to drive down to the south coast to spend a few days with his League Two side. Pre-season had already begun and Pompey's boss was eager to assess my fitness. I ended up training for three weeks, playing four friendlies, scoring twice, and still waiting to discover whether I would get a contract! Eventually, I was handed a 12-month deal with an option, representing a pay cut compared to my Fleetwood salary. But the financial hit was worth it, because I wanted to be part of where this club was going.

My first Pompey game was against Dagenham & Redbridge on the opening day of the 2015/16 season, among nine debutants. I walked onto that pitch with the sun beating down, the playing surface amazing, not a free seat at Fratton Park, and the fans were singing non-stop — the excitement of this new Paul Cook era had captured the city. This was the buzz I wanted. I absolutely loved it, and even scored with a far-post header from Kyle Bennett's left-wing corner in a 3-0 win.

I loved Cookie, he was really good for me and my career — and the best manager I played under. During that first season, we headed to Mansfield Town in March 2016 and drew 1-1, which did little to help our promotion aspirations, and, in the dressing room afterwards, Cook went mad about our performance. Yet he possesses this clever knack of knowing when the team requires a lift and, with the players realising the automatics had now all but gone, he initiated a boost to the squad morale. We were on the team bus, ready to leave, when he came on and instructed: "Right, everyone off." We thought one of the tyres were flat or something, but instead he took us into one of the Field Mill lounges and told us to order a drink from the bar. Ben Davies and a few of the lads started getting them in and, at that point we saw a totally different side to the manager. Until that point, he'd been pretty professional. Certainly he didn't mind the lads going out for a drink around Portsmouth, but always reminded us not to get carried away with it. Now, an hour following a League Two match, he was encouraging us to have a beer, even putting a pint into the hands of the younger lads and saying: "Get that down you." Alex Bass was there and even to this day he doesn't really drink. Cook noticed he'd had just one sip, so encouraged him to have another.

When Bass obeyed, the manager told him: "No, down it or you're getting back on the bus." So the lad did — then Cook shouted: "Get him another!"

We must have spent almost three hours in that lounge and some of the lads had consumed eight or nine pints by the time we returned to the bus. Danny Hollands stumbled on, fell onto the steps, then made his way to the back of the bus and performed a roly-poly over a table with a seating area, crashing into everyone, while shouting: "Waheyy." As we'd got the taste for drink, we ended up stopping off for more beers on the long journey back, completing a strange day. Arriving in for training on the Monday, it was all everyone was talking about — the drinking, the roly-poly over the table, the laughter — and no inquest into how the home goalkeeper's punt down the middle had created Mansfield's goal. That was clever. The mood had been on the floor and Cook had turned it around. The following match we won 4-0 against Notts County.

Considering our team, it was a travesty we didn't get promoted in 2015/16. I know we finished sixth and lost in the play-offs to Plymouth Argyle, but injuries meant we eventually ran out of steam. Look at the talent in that squad, people like Adam Webster and Enda Stevens, who reached the Premier League, so it was a huge shame that we fell short. In February 2016, we were positioned sixth and travelled to Morecambe, taking a first-half lead through my seventh goal of the season after Kal Naismith played it out to the right to me, although it was actually a bad shot and went straight through their keeper Barry Roche. He made amends, though, heading home a corner for a 94th-minute equaliser in a 1-1 draw. Victory would have put us fourth, but we got sloppy after absolutely battering them and there was a big inquest afterwards, Cook was rightly furious. The fact the keeper scored was embarrassing, with *Soccer AM* laughing about it the following week and it being regularly replayed on *Sky Sports News*. Our season didn't really recover after that, we never found the consistency required to challenge for the three automatic spots, even losing 3-1 at a relegation-bound York City as we ended up in the play-off semi-finals against Argyle.

During that Fratton Park first leg, Jamille Matt should have been sent off. I've watched that incident when he headbutted Michael Doyle from behind loads of times. I also know him, I played with him at Fleetwood, and a year or so after that match he admitted to me that he deserved a red card. He'd lost his head, steam was coming out his ears, Doyley had been winding him up like Doyley does — he was the master of it, pinching him and that sort of stuff — and Jamille reacted. The atmosphere when Marc McNulty gave us a third-minute lead was amazing, you felt something really good was going to happen beyond that, but the game was a disaster and Matt scored twice, not that we should have conceded. All season Cook couldn't nail down a proper goalkeeper capable of performing week in, week out, and it was an ongoing problem. We used five of them. Bournemouth's Ryan Allsop was recruited as an emergency loan for the play-offs — and it was something of a calamity. The guy was thrown in, didn't know anything about the club or the dressing room, made his debut in front of a packed Fratton Park, and was a rabbit in the headlights. I don't want to be too derogatory, but he should have saved both goals in the first leg and flapped at the one in the second leg, which saw us lose 3-2 on aggregate in stoppage time.

We had a lot of injury problems over the course of that season, but I felt one of the biggest issues was the goalkeeper. The following summer David Forde arrived from Millwall on a season-long loan and he was massive — someone you could look up to, an elder statesman in the dressing room working alongside Michael Doyle. He was like an enforcer. Everyone was a little scared of him because he was quite an imposing character who had a switch. He could get angry, so nobody really wanted to let him down or disappoint. In the previous campaign, the goalkeepers we used were feeble. I played right-back in Fordey's season at Fratton Park and if you misplaced a pass he would let you know. If you were out of position and not covering Christian Burgess well enough, he'd rip into me, and it was an influence we missed previously. Not only did he organise the back four superbly but he'd claim anything around the six-yard box and penalty spot, on occasions not having to face that many shots in matches on account of us being so organised.

Play-off elimination at Plymouth was twice as painful for me as I had to come off in the 31st minute after Carl McHugh's challenge damaged medial ligaments in my left knee and tore deltoid ligaments in my ankle. I was on the left-hand side of our penalty box when I received the ball and, seeing McHugh behind, went to turn and move away, only for him to go straight through me, with my foot planted. I knew immediately it was bad because there was a crack, like a pop, and I couldn't even stand, with Adam McGurk replacing me. It was a bad challenge and he was booked, but, as he had gone through me and managed to get a toe on the ball, it wasn't a sending-off. I left the stadium on crutches and faced the prospect of League Two football for another season.

Having fallen in the play-offs, a few new faces were required to strengthen the team, with the likes of Carl Baker and Danny Rose arriving, along with Milan Lalkovic, Curtis Main, Tom Davies and Drew Talbot. During my injury rehabilitation, I'd train in the gym on my own and see them arrive, thinking: "That's another good signing." However, the recruitment of MK Dons' Baker disappointed me at the time. I had been a first-team regular during my maiden Pompey season and the manager's favoured 4-2-3-1 system suited me. I felt 10 goals was a pretty good return, while I also weighed in with plenty of assists and the League One player of the month award for December. To me, I'd had a pretty good year, yet was now injured, with another right winger arriving at the club having made 34 appearances in the Championship the previous campaign. I had triggered a contract extension after making 23 starts, for no wage rise, and wasn't on massive amounts — yet here was Carl Baker, on decent money and surely likely to play every week as a consequence. I looked around the team wondering where else I could play. There was Kyle Bennett on the left who was really good mates with Cook, and Gary Roberts in the number 10 role was also very close to our manager. It occurred I'd have to see how things went — only to end up in a position which had never crossed my mind.

Our regular right-back Ben Davies left in the summer of 2016, so Cook moved to fill the hole by recruiting Drew Talbot, whose abilities he knew all about during their time at Chesterfield together. Then, on the eve of the season, Adam Buxton joined from Accrington Stanley after turning down a new contract. However, I don't think Drew was a good fit — personality-wise he didn't match the club — and, having not performed particularly well in his opening five league games, did his hamstring. Ahead of Crawley Town's visit in September 2016, the manager called me into his office and asked how I was feeling after my injury return. He then added: "Well, you're playing right-back on Saturday. We'll go through a few things Friday with you and you'll be fine." That was it — for the first time in my career, I had been selected to play at right-back! We won 3-0 through a Curtis Main double and Gary Roberts and I played really well, although perhaps too well as it crossed my mind I may remain in this position I didn't want to be in. After a while, I thought: "Do you know what? I'm playing for Pompey, so just go with it." Bakes was obviously preferred on the right wing, so if it was a choice between sitting on the bench and playing 20 minutes here and there, or featuring for 90 minutes every week at right-back for an amazing club, I should just go for it.

I was never a conventional right-back, of course. Under Cook, we were so possession-based that I never really had to defend, which I always felt was a weak part of my game, despite being required to at times. By and large, the version of a right-back in that Pompey team involved me giving the ball to Bakes, running around him, receiving it back and then delivering it into the box, almost like a second winger. Certainly I wasn't standing next to Burge all game — instead I was attacking way more than defending and ended up buying into it massively. I remained there for the rest of the season — and came to love it.

In November 2016, Stevenage visited Fratton Park and, with the game goalless at half-time, we returned to our dressing room. I've seen fights among teammates before, a bit of pushing or a punch to the head before those involved are separated, but never to the extreme that I witnessed between Michael Doyle and Christian Burgess. Perhaps it was a shock because, on this occasion, blood was involved. It had started on the pitch, with something said about a mistake which led to Stevenage almost scoring just before the break. I was sitting next to Burge, who was on my left, and to the left of him was Doyley, and suddenly words were exchanged: "Don't you ever speak to me like that again." Burge responded with: "Shut up, I can say what I want." Doyle, who had a plastic bottle in his hand, punched him, so our central defender tried to pick him up and throw him to the floor. Everyone jumped in, trying to separate them, with Doyle on his back and Burge trying to lean into our skipper to get at him. Then Doyle's leg connected with his head — and blood spurted out. I hadn't got up, I was still sitting there, but trying to split them, while Burge's hair was everywhere, like The Undertaker from WWE, with blood spilling down his face.

Once it had calmed down, Cook and Leam Richardson left the room to talk, before returning, with our manager announcing: "You're both coming off, we can't have that. That's not happening in my changing room." There was blood all over the place, all over Burge, all over Doyley's sock and boot. It was just a mess. The crowd must have been wondering why two of our big players had been taken off at the interval — and we ended up losing 2-1. We had organised a Christmas night out in Cardiff that evening, a fancy dress theme, with a bus and hotels booked, only for a furious Cook to instruct its cancellation. What he didn't know, of course, was that we'd decided to go out anyway, meeting at the Solent Hotel & Spa in Whiteley before heading to Southampton, ending up in Oceania nightclub. It was either going two ways: either the whole squad would fold, with everyone drifting off into their own groups and it getting bitchy, or we came together as a team, using it as a bonding exercise, and moving on. Thankfully it was the latter, with Doyle and Burgess making up that evening. Plenty of times you'd see the pair of them at the bar together having a drink and a chat. Afterwards, it was never awkward between them.

The following day, Leam put a message on the team WhatsApp group: "As you didn't go out last night, have a few drinks today. I'll see you Tuesday and enjoy yourselves." He probably felt bad about stopping us going out on Saturday evening, without realising we actually had! Anyhow, as an impromptu decision, we then headed to Winter Wonderland in Hyde Park, staying over that night. When we returned to training on Tuesday morning, Leam entered the dressing room and instructed us to gather in the communal area as the manager wanted to talk to us. We thought he was going to address the Doyley and Burgess fight, but, when he walked in shaking with anger with the cup of tea he was holding spilling over the edges, it was obvious this was something more.

"Who went out on Saturday night?" he demanded, yet no-one really knew what to do as we all had. I put my hand up, followed by Enda Stevens, and then it went around the room, like some Mexican Wave. He replied: "Right, everyone onto the pitch. Now. No-one had their kit on at that point, so firstly we had to get changed. Then he ran us into the ground — and the incident was never mentioned by him again. It actually brought the lads closer together, almost an us against them mentality. The spirit had become stronger, although not intentionally initiated by the manager.

Some three months later, In March 2017, we faced a struggling Crewe Alexandra side at home — and they won 1-0. As I was playing right-back, whenever I took throw-ins I could hear every word from the stands, not solely aimed at me, but all the players. The supporters were furious at a terrible team performance. We lacked energy, and the atmosphere became toxic, culminating in us being booed off at the final whistle. I thought Cookie would quit after that match. There was no coming back for him, the disappointment of the play-offs the previous year combined with being fifth in the current season. Once again, it didn't appear we'd be getting into the automatics. He didn't say much after the game, more subdued and quiet. There were the usual cliches, such as we'll pick up again next week, try to work on it, yet this was no typical Cookie rollicking — and I thought he was off. By all accounts, it had become very unpleasant around the home bench, and he was receiving all sorts of abuse during the match. I expected him to walk, he was four hours from home and would be thinking: "I don't need this stick." In the aftermath, he was visibly deflated and at rock bottom. Cookie was trying to make things happen with the team, yet they weren't coming to fruition and it didn't really feel like anything was paying off.

The following Monday morning, before training, Doyley called a players' meeting and a few home truths were aired. This couldn't be brushed under the carpet, we had to discuss what went wrong and how we could change it. Our captain started the discussion, standing in front of everyone for 10 minutes, saying his piece, then David Forde contributed, Gary Roberts spoke a few words, and then it went around the room, some voicing their views while sitting down, with the whole process lasting about 45 minutes. At one point, the manager came to the door and looked through the window. It was clear we were talking, but he had no idea what it consisted of. He afterwards had Doyley in his office, wanting to know the outcome. We had the option to swiftly make amends, with a trip to Crawley the following evening. That became the spark to our season, and we absolutely battered then, winning 2-0 through second-half goals from Christian Burgess and Kyle Bennett. The Crawley players came off the pitch at the final whistle telling us: "You lads are the best team in this league by a country mile."

From there it escalated. We knew we had the ingredients to do it: we had the players, we had the manager, we had the supporters. Everything was there — and we were just waiting for it to click. We won six of our next seven matches as we finally broke into the top three, while a 3-1 victory against Yeovil Town saw me become our latest penalty taker. Roberts and Eoin Doyle had previously missed, and I was often in the gaffer's ear about taking over, having previously done the job at other clubs. Once I put mine away against Yeovil, I was staying on them, scoring three spot-kicks in the final six matches, including at Notts County in April 2017 when we secured promotion. Admittedly I slipped as I took it, with my shot ending up in the top corner, yet still to my right-hand side, where I'd planned it. That opened the scoring, although we relied on Jamal Lowe coming off the bench to earn us a 3-1 victory to clinch League One football for the following season. The fans invaded the Meadow Lane pitch and afterwards we celebrated with them at Fratton Park in the Victory Lounge, absolutely filling our boots with alcohol. Everything we'd been working towards over the past two years had paid off.

I didn't think for a minute we'd be able to win League Two; no chance. We had our automatic promotion, the heartbreak of the previous campaign had been put behind us, everything was done. Ahead of the final match against Cheltenham Town, the manager told us: "Listen, we'll win this game, don't worry about anything elsewhere. In the final home match, we want to give our fans something to cheer about, but in football you never know what's going to happen." Capturing the title was never mentioned, because there was such a small chance of achieving it. We were relying on both Plymouth and Doncaster Rovers failing to win, and what subsequently unfolded was my favourite Pompey match. We knew we were going to steamroll Cheltenham, I expected to beat them by three or four, and I've watched that match back three times since.

All the positives about playing for Pompey were there that day: the atmosphere, the style of football. It was perfect. After winning 6-1, in which I scored a penalty, there was a pitch invasion and we headed back to the dressing room still awaiting results from other matches not yet completed — then they came through on *Sky Sports*. We afterwards went home, got changed, and the squad met at Bar 69 in Gunwharf, with a private area cordoned off upstairs. Then it was onto Tiger Tiger, where once again we had table reservations. It was fantastic that our wives and girlfriends had been included, reward for their constant support, and we stayed out until about two or three in the morning, partying for a brilliant night.

In the aftermath of claiming the League Two title, there were no individual end-of-season meetings with the manager, as was customary. Instead Cooky and his backroom staff holidayed in Portugal together. Besides, the players had gone to Marbella for four days, paid for by chairman Iain McInnes. Regardless, despite being one of those out of contract, I was relaxed, having already been assured by Cook that a new deal would be forthcoming. There was also no chance I wanted to leave. Upon returning from Spain, I called Leam Richardson to ask what was happening with the contract and, probably over the course of the week, there were four or five phone calls, with him delivering the same message: "Don't sign, don't sign. Don't sign anything. The club are going to offer you a new contract, but don't sign." Whenever I questioned what he meant, he responded with: "We'll get you what you want." I had been pushing for a two-year contract, with the club coming back with a lesser deal, and now the assistant manager was advising me not to sign it. Eventually, Pompey returned with a figure I was happy with, so I rang Leam, who reiterated not to sign it before finishing the conversation mysteriously by saying: "That's all I can say." I thought it was really weird.

The following day, Kyle Bennett signed a new three-year deal and, two days later, I went to Fratton Park and also pledged my future to the Blues — only I never heard anything from the manager. Certainly, I was expecting a call from Cookie to say: "Brilliant Gaz, fantastic, it's great to have you on board again. We're delighted you've signed." Instead, there was silence, which was strange. Obviously, I didn't know the politics going on between the club and the manager at that time, then rumours emerged that he was off to Wigan Athletic. I had signed a contract on the back of Cook being Pompey's manager, I was under the impression I was playing for him, so what exactly was going on? I called Leam, but he didn't pick up. A few of the lads also tried without success, so I asked Gary Roberts, who was very close to the manager, and he didn't know either. Then it came out he had left — and I was gutted.

As it turned out, while I was helping physio Nick Meace move out of his Knowle home to join Cook in Wigan, he admitted: "You know why the manager told you not to sign, don't you? He knew he was going to Wigan and wanted to take you with him." I wouldn't have gone; I was so happy at Pompey, settled with my fiancée in Knowle village. There's no way I would have left.

To this day, nobody has really got to the bottom of why Paul Cook left Fratton Park. I certainly don't know the truth. He never said goodbye to the players, and, thinking about it, the last time he spoke to the group was at half-time of the Cheltenham game. Even after winning 6-1 to take the League Two title, he never got everyone together to say: "Brilliant lads, our hard work has paid off. What a fantastic achievement, congratulations to everyone." After the final whistle, everyone piled in the dressing room, bottles of beer and champagne were sprayed everywhere, yet the manager didn't address any of us. Not so much as a WhatsApp message. Considering the achievement, he really should have done. Aside from buying me a drink at the Royal Beach Hotel on the day of the Southsea Common celebrations, the next time I spoke to him was in August 2017, when I was sent off in a 1-1 draw at Wigan. As I left the DW Stadium pitch, he came over, shook my hand and said: "Top man, Gaz. Unlucky." A token of his appreciation, I suppose, but that was it.

Cook's May 2017 departure would inevitably spark massive change. As ever when a new manager comes in, they have their own ideas, their own people they want to work with, and players they're keen to sign which they may previously have worked with. Kenny Jackett was now in charge, and I found a lot of it all so unnecessary. It's easy to say he inherited an ageing squad, yet the subsequent overhaul frustrated me — I just felt it was a massive anti-climax to what was a really good team. Doyle and Stevens had left when Cook was still manager, while David Forde returned to Millwall, but then, under the new regime, Gary Roberts and Carl Baker were moved on, while Benno departed in January. Suddenly the spine of a successful team had been ripped out.

Without a shadow of a doubt, Cook's approach to fitness got the best out of me. There might be a six-mile run along Southsea seafront, which no-one enjoyed, and there was a lot of gym stuff, such as boxing, while training sessions were an hour-and-a-half long. But, by the time it came to Saturday's game, I was flying physically. Under Jackett, I didn't feel we trained enough. We didn't have to be in until 9.30am, then it was out on the training pitch at 10.30am, but sometimes I'd be back sitting on my sofa at 11.50am, with a cup of tea, and thinking: "I've not done anything." There were times I'd go straight up to the Roko gym after training and spend another 45 minutes on the treadmill, then do pull ups and press ups. An extra hour overall because I needed more fitness work than Jackett provided in training.

Cook had individual binders focused on each player's fitness and you'd speak to the fitness coach about what you wanted to work on, followed by a weekly programme to follow. There was none of that with Jackett, which I felt affected performance. It was pretty obvious those things were essential in the modern era, strength and conditioning is a massive part of the game, yet Jackett was quite old school in a way. As a consequence, I was probably 90 per cent fit under him. Sometimes training wasn't even an hour, whereas Cook's could span two hours, then everyone went off to lunch. Sitting together, socialising.

Now training was finishing well before lunch and the lads didn't want to sit around for more than an hour waiting to be fed at 12pm, so instead they went home without eating, often putting the canteen food into Tupperware to have later. You'd walk around the training ground at 1pm and there would be no-one there. Previously it was a social thing. We had the communal area so, after training under Cook and doing extras in the gym until 2pm, you'd walk into the room and Kal Naismith and Christian Burgess would be playing table tennis, having a laugh and a joke. Under Jackett the place would be dead.

For the 2017/18 campaign, Jackett's first as manager, Drew Talbot started at right-back, before I replaced him, yet it soon became clear that wasn't my position. I was effectively a second winger in that role under Cook, yet, bearing in mind the way Kenny set his team up, both in terms of formation and personnel, I was definitely more exposed as a right-back — and in a better standard of league. I just wasn't comfortable and my inability to defend was particularly exposed in a 1-1 draw at Wigan in our fourth League One match, when I was troubled by Michael Jacobs, eventually being sent off after earning a second yellow for pulling him back when through on goal. I started another five games in that position, but needed somewhere else to play in Kenny's team and, towards the end of the season, operated as a number 10 at Walsall, scoring the winner in a 1-0 victory to nail that position down.

During his time at Pompey, Kenny had no relationship with any of the players. Previously, Paul Cook would be seen drinking with Gary Roberts on a Sunday, which didn't bother the lads, but Jackett definitely distanced himself from the squad. In the summer of 2018, ahead of his second campaign at the Pompey helm, the manager took us for a pre-season training camp to Fota Island, Cork, in the Republic of Ireland, and it was like a prison. We weren't even allowed to play golf. Normally on such trips, you'd work double or triple sessions for five days and then, at the end of it, receive permission to have a knees-up, with the squad going out together for a drink — only Kenny wouldn't allow it. During that tour, England played Columbia in the last 16 of the 2018 World Cup finals and, while we could watch it, we weren't allowed a drink. Now that isn't really a big thing, but I'd like to believe all the lads watching the England game together and having a few pints opens up conversation a bit.

The following night, me and roommate Christian Burgess rebelled — by attending an Alanis Morissette concert! We'd finished training at 2pm and there was nothing to do until you went to bed, so Burge suggested watching her at The Marquee in Cork, obviously without asking the manager's permission. Outside the window of our room was a hedgerow trailing down the side of the hotel, so we scaled down it, out of sight of everyone, then made our way down the resort's massive driveway and jumped into a waiting cab at the entrance which we'd pre-booked. After a few drinks, we made our way to the gig, but it had already started and sold out — and we didn't have any tickets. We tried to persuade the ticket office to let us in, offering £50 each, and eventually the sales assistant pressed a button and admitted us for free. After the stress of getting there, we were willing to pay double. There was no way we were giving up to return to the hotel room and sleep. It was a really good night too, with a few more drinks in Cork afterwards — and we had training the next morning! Mind you, we invited Danny Rose and Dion Donohue to come with us, as we knew they had sneaked out to a club the previous evening with *The News'* Will Rooney, but they couldn't manage two consecutive nights of drinking!

We should have won promotion to the Championship in 2018/19 and one of the downfalls was Kenny's desire to stay in all the cup competitions, unlike many managers. Whether it was the FA Cup, the Carabao Cup or the Checkatrade Trophy, we were still in two of them by early February 2019, along with competing for promotion. That season we played a club-record 62 matches and the starting XI was pretty much fixed. The same players featured in virtually every game, he didn't rotate the squad and, ultimately, we ran out of steam. I was definitely feeling it towards the end of March and start of April. I was fatigued, it was Saturday-Tuesday-Saturday with no respite, and certainly we didn't get enough recovery time between fixtures. Jamal Lowe and Ronan Curtis were explosive players, direct wingers, yet operating on tough pitches and training every day. It builds up and, come the finale, they were understandably shattered.

Of course, there were other reasons for our collapse from five points clear after 26 games to finishing fourth and having to make do with the play-offs. Ben Thompson was a massive player and unfortunately recalled from his loan spell by Millwall, and, although we still possessed the quality to be able to see it through, we probably needed two or three really good new additions in the January transfer window. Okay, they might not start every game because we had a settled XI who were doing the business, but, should there be fatigue and muscle injuries, they could step right in. Instead that window was a disaster, simply not good enough. Without wanting to be derogatory about the lads who did sign, Bryn Morris couldn't stay fit, Andy Cannon was out injured for the rest of the season after 40 minutes of action and others didn't perform, so the manager continued relying on his regulars. Six of us each made 51 or more appearances.

We didn't perform well enough in those League One play-off semi-finals and were eliminated by Sunderland 1-0 on aggregate over two legs. At the Stadium of Light for the first leg, we were trailing to Chris Maguire's second-half goal when

I ran clean through — only to be taken down by Alim Ozturk, who was deservedly shown the red card. I hit the bar from the resulting free-kick as we failed to find an equaliser against 10 men for the final 23 minutes, leaving us requiring to beat them at Fratton Park to go through. The team Jackett picked for the decisive match was bizarre, however. We had played 4-2-3-1 all season, with me largely in the number 10 role, yet when working on shape the day before the game, he declared: "Right, we're going to be 4-4-2." I was on the right of a midfield four, where I hadn't played all season; Brett featured when not fully fit after missing the first leg through injury; our leading scorer Jamal Lowe was a substitute. Viv Solomon-Otabor started, and Ronan subsequently didn't even come off the bench. Come on. Surely in the second leg of the play-offs you put your best 11 players out there, using the formation which had worked all season and earned 88 points? Before the game, some of the lads were looking around thinking: "Why are we playing 4-4-2?" We had lost 1-0 at the Stadium of Light, which wasn't too bad. It was salvageable, especially in the play-off situation. Just score in the opening five minutes at Fratton Park and it would be fine. But the manager changed everything.

Regardless, I should have scored in the first half — something I still think about to this day. Lee Brown's cross from the left was headed down by Oli Hawkins and I timed my run to instinctively meet it with a flying header from five yards out, but it went straight at keeper Jon McLaughlin. If I had half-sliced the header then it's 1-1 on aggregate, the atmosphere would have gone through the roof and perhaps we could have gone on to reach the play-off final. You can't live with regrets, but there are moments which stick out where you look back and think: "If only I had finished that." Having said that, Jackett made just two of his three available substitutions against Sunderland, despite the game fizzling out, with the last 15-20 minutes a non-event. What have you got to lose? Bring off Burgess or Matt Clarke, put a forward on … just do something. You're the manager. Michael Doyle was a guest at the game and afterwards pulled me in the car park and asked: "What the hell was that?" It was the second leg of a play-off semi-final, in front of a crowd of 18,077, with a place at Wembley at stake and he had one unused sub — it was bizarre. Midway through the season, it looked as though we were going up, we were five points clear at the start of January and there was no way we would let that slip. I almost don't feel it was the players' fault. We gave everything, but simply ran out of steam in the end.

During that season, we claimed the Checkatrade Trophy in March 2019. On the road to Wembley I had netted three goals in five matches, while skippering the team in our semi-final win at Bury, so I believed I had contributed more than most towards reaching the final against Sunderland. However, I was left out of the starting XI and absolutely fuming. Ronan Curtis had chopped off the top of a finger in his front door two-and-half weeks earlier and was unable to train until the previous day in case sweat got into the wound and caused infection. He wasn't fit, through no fault of his own, and, when the team was announced on the Saturday, I couldn't understand why the manager had picked him on the left wing ahead of me. I remember coming out of the tunnel ahead of kick-off, wearing my yellow bib, and seeing all these Pompey flags to my right, while Sunderland were to the left. It was a theatre of football and such an amazing sight and noise. How I would have loved to be in that line-up, walking out on to the pitch. Instead I was on the bench, on the periphery of the experience, not feeling part of it. We weren't out of the traps that first half, stuck like rabbits in headlights, and Sunderland could easily have been two or three up at half-time rather than the 1-0 scoreline in their favour. The goalscorer, Aiden McGeady, was running riot, we couldn't live with them — it was a hard watch. All the time I was thinking: "Put me on, I want to make an impact, we can't lose this game. We've put too much into it to play at a packed Wembley for it to fizzle out."

When I eventually came on in the 56th minute, for Ronan who was not at his best, I had a point to prove and the bit between my teeth. I should have been playing. Asked to go on the left, it meant I could cut in, allowing our left-back Lee Brown to overlap and, eight minutes from time, I delivered a right-footed cross to the far post which was headed home by Nathan Thompson for the equaliser. With the match entering extra-time, Jamal Lowe put us in front with six minutes left, only for McGeady to grab his second of the game in the last minute to ensure it finished 2-2. So it was on to penalties, with our captain, Brett Pitman, correctly calling the toss of the coin and choosing for it to take place in front of the Pompey end. Then the manager, holding a piece of paper, asked who wanted to take them. Brett and I put our hands up, but nobody else did. None of them fancied it. I was losing the plot and shouted: "Put your hands up and take a penalty" — and Browny and Jamal stepped forward. Nathan Thompson no, Christian Burgess no. Matt Clarke, no chance. He was massively against it. Then Oli Hawkins said: "Go on then, I'll take one," and ended up being the hero by netting the fifth and final spot kick in a 5-4 victory.

Ahead of Wembley, the club announced they would be selling limited edition Topps memorabilia cards containing match-worn shirts from the final, involving players having their shirts cut into tiny pieces. Now that was no problem if you started the game as you were given a fresh one at half-time, so had two shirts — one to keep and one to give the club. However, considering I came on the 56th minute, I owned just one match-worn shirt — and was instructed to hand it over. No chance. This was one of the best moments of my career and I wasn't giving anyone my shirt. I wanted it framed to put on my lounge wall at home. They went on and on and on about it and I was getting threats that they'd fine me two weeks' wages, then an additional £5,000. It was getting ridiculous, but I was adamant and fully prepared to take the hit. I fell out with the manager a little, who insisted: "You have no idea of the implications of this." Mark Catlin, the chief executive, was upset with me — and the owners really, really upset. There was so much politics involved that I got the impression I wouldn't play for Pompey again unless I relented, even though they never said it outright — so I gave it to them. That left me with a Wembley final shirt never worn and unframed because I just can't bring myself to look at it. In 20 or 30 years, I want to be able to bring the shirt down off the wall and say to my grandchildren: "I wore this at Wembley." It's a massive thing for me, but that was taken away.

Ahead of the 2019/20 season, we sold Jamal Lowe to Wigan and Matt Clarke to Brighton & Hove Albion, both for big transfer fees, with the money used to recruit John Marquis, Ellis Harrison and Marcus Harness. However, things didn't start well, drawing 3-3 against nine-man Coventry City in August 2019 after being 3-1 up — and the atmosphere afterwards was toxic. The following league match was a trip to Blackpool, after which I had the vice-captaincy taken off me, having held it for two years, while Brett Pitman was stripped of the captaincy. In a 1-1 draw, I was brought off the bench to replace the injured Harness — and then was myself substituted 25 minutes later. I threw my water bottle on the floor and said it was a joke of a decision. Afterwards Jackett claimed it was tactical, which it wasn't. He didn't change the formation, instead replacing me on the right for Ellis Harrison in the same position. It was clearly only a personnel change. It felt like he was teeing me up. This was his perfect opportunity, the chance to remove me as vice-captain. He was looking for an excuse.

On the Monday morning after the Bloomfield Road incident, I arrived early for training and found Brett in the changing room. It turned out he'd been instructed to meet Kenny — and subsequently replaced by Tom Naylor as captain. Then my phone pinged with a text. It was 8am, my phone never goes off at that time, and immediately I knew something was up — sure enough, it was the manager asking to see me in his office. When I arrived, he sat me at the table with Joe Gallen and said: "First and foremost, I want to apologise for what happened at the weekend." I responded: "I don't really think that was an acceptable way to treat me." He continued: "Anyway, we have decided to not go ahead with Brett as captain because he's not playing enough — and we're going with Lee Brown as the vice-captain."

I knew it was coming after what happened with Brett, but I expected a reason — and he didn't have one. He looked at the floor and said: "We think, going forwards, Tom Naylor and Lee Brown are going to be regulars and we want people who are going to play regularly." So I replied: "I'm not going to play regularly then?" and he said: "No, we're not saying that." I told him that wasn't really a reason and that started getting his back up. He wasn't comfortable with the situation, while I told him I wasn't happy with the decision and needed a few days to see where I wanted to go from here. At that point he was getting a bit angry and touchy and, when I walked out, he followed, heading to the gym, where everyone had gathered after getting changed. All I could hear was the manager's voice going: "Right, everybody out," clearing people from the gym and offices and telling them to go to the centre circle of the nearest training pitch. As well as players, some who hadn't the chance to put their boots on, there were our sports scientists, physios, kitman Kev McCormack, all the academy staff, people like head of education and welfare Jon Slater and academy manager Mark Kelly. Everyone — and me and Brett were told to stand in front of them.

Pointing to us in turn, Jackett announced: "That's not your captain or vice-captain any more. We're going with Tom Naylor as captain and Lee Brown as the vice- captain." Me and Brett looked at each other as if to say: "What's going on?" The manager was trying to embarrass us, but it didn't work. The situation was awkward for everyone. People were glancing around, some didn't know where to look or what to say, others weren't comfortable because they had nothing to do with the first-team picture. At the end of it, Kenny said: "Okay, off you go, do whatever you want to do," — and me and Brett walked off laughing at the ridiculousness of it all. Lee Brown was also chuckling alongside us: "So am I the vice-captain now?" That's how the news was broken to him. It had been staged to humiliate us but it actually backfired and even the lads were thinking it was a bit much. Whether we agreed with the decision to take away our roles is irrelevant — the truth is that wasn't the right way to go about it and, in my opinion, the manager probably lost a bit of respect among some of the players. I could actually understand why Jackett removed us — we weren't playing regularly so maybe something needed to be done — but the way he went about it was wrong. He behaved like an idiot.

The following evening we hosted Crawley in the Leasing.com Trophy — and I was captain! I walked into the changing room before the game and the armband was hung up on my peg. I thought one of the lads was having me on, making a joke. Then there was the awkward moment of having to enter the referee's room with Joe Gallen to exchange the team sheets. "What's going on here then?"

I asked Joe. He looked at me and shook his head as if to say: "I have absolutely no idea." It was almost as if the manager had forgotten everything which occurred the previous day. As it turned out, I suffered concussion after 30 minutes when somebody headed the back of my head during an aerial challenge, so I needed to be replaced at half-time. My replacement was Brett — who grabbed the winner in a 1-0 victory!

Jackett's treatment of Brett was very unnecessary and I could never understand where he was coming from because, ultimately, everyone knows what a good striker he was in and around the box. Even if not starting, the majority of the squad would probably agree he would give you something if you brought him on for the last 10 minutes when you needed a goal. Given the strikers we had in that 2019/20 season, with John Marquis and Ellis Harrison on our books, I would have started him anyway. Instead he was told to stay at home, something I've never seen in my career — you don't oust someone from the squad and tell them to stay away on full pay.

I was a bit-part player after the vice-captaincy was removed, starting six league games in the next four months, and then, absolutely out of nowhere, I was selected at Gillingham on New Year's Day, playing well and scoring in a 1-1 draw. I was dropped for the following game at Fleetwood in the FA Cup and never started a league game for the remainder of the season — and Jackett didn't say a word to me to explain why. We played Southampton in the Carabao Cup in September 2019. What a draw; I couldn't wait, I was looking forward to it for weeks and weeks, only to find myself on the bench. The Pompey fans clearly wanted me to start, singing my name as I warmed up, while I believe I should have been on the pitch on merit. But I could never get into Jackett's head, so I can't speak for him.

He wasn't a very good man-manager, he struggled with conversations. If I knocked on his door it wouldn't be appreciated, whereas Paul Cook would sit down, get a laptop out and show clips on why I wasn't playing. Kenny wasn't capable of having those interactions and his treatment of some players was really poor. I think he had a reasonably successful Plan A, but the lack of a Plan B at times didn't help when required and more often than not we instead drew or lost the game. Yet I can't look at it too negatively because I played for Pompey, wore the armband for many games, had success under him at Wembley, featured in two play-off semi-finals and scored a lot of goals. At the same time, I always think it could have been so much more.

In mid-March 2020, Covid-19 curtailed our season, with the table instead decided by unweighted points per game, giving us fifth spot and a League One semi-final play-off against Oxford United. My only involvement was being introduced off the bench in the final minute of stoppage time at the Kassam Stadium in the second leg, which I was furious with. How can you not want to play me for the play-offs, home and away, when we've been dreadful — then bring me on to take a penalty, which I scored, in a 5-4 shoot-out defeat?

As for the decision to drop Tom Naylor for the play-offs, that was bizarre. He was captain and, during Covid, we trained for two months solid leading up to the semi-final — then Nayls wasn't in the team. We didn't have a clue. We would have been aware of any sort of argument or confrontation with the manager, but there wasn't one. Instead it was explained as a tactical decision. Bryn Morris had really looked after himself during Covid. We had an app called Strava and, whenever you did a run or anything, it would register with your Apple Watch and automatically be logged. We could see everyone's activities and Bryn was running himself into the ground. There would be three 5km runs a day — and in really good times. Perhaps that impressed Kenny and Joe? Everyone was working hard, but there's only so much you can do. Bryn was carrying out a ridiculous amount of stuff and everyone was thinking: "He's doing too much … he's going to end up injured or burning himself out."

We all thought Naylor was Kenny's boy, the first name on the teamsheet, and, while Nayls had an issue with being dropped, he didn't really kick up a stink, instead leaving any confrontation with the manager until after the play-offs. It was weird. Everyone was thinking it was Kenny opening the door for Naylor to leave in the summer and we believed it was the end of him, that he was going back up north. Then we returned for the first day of pre-season and it was like nothing had ever happened!

I didn't really know what to expect about my own Pompey career going into the 2020 pre-season. I was braced for the manager to pull me to one side to tell me: "It's time to start looking elsewhere. We're trying to sign other players," yet there wasn't really any dialogue between us. It was the same as usual, wishing each other good morning every now and again. I thought my penalty in the play-off semi-final would be my last Pompey kick, to be honest. I wasn't actively looking to leave, but I didn't believe Kenny would survive the summer having missed out on promotion again — yet nothing changed.

The 2020/21 season opened with a trip to Stevenage in the Carabao Cup and I was back in the starting XI, scoring a spot-kick on the stroke of half-time as we fought back from 3-1 down to draw 3-3, then winning on a penalty shoot-out. I ended up lining up in the opening three matches, which included a goalless League One draw at home to Shrewsbury Town. I was substituted in the 55th minute, although I actually thought I'd played quite well that day. It turned out to be my final Pompey match. I couldn't work out that decision. Surely you had the whole of the summer and pre-season to think about it, getting your recruitment in place, then you start me in the first three games only to deem me surplus to requirements. If you don't think I'm going to be a regular fixture going forwards for the season, then don't start me. Surely for the first game of a campaign, the 11 names on the teamsheet are what the manager considers to be his best side — and I was selected. Then three weeks later I was not even in the squad against Rochdale.

My absence coincided with Michael Jacobs arriving on a free transfer. Then little things started happening, such as Kenny making me do running on my own after Friday's training as I wasn't in the following day's squad, which really wasn't necessary. I'm a professional and on a Saturday without a game I'd go for a run or train with the kids. I wouldn't sit there with my feet up, so there really was no need. Jackett was poking me and I didn't need it. We'd just had our son Atlas, we were living four hours away from home in Macclesfield and without help from anyone, with no family around — so we decided to move back up north. My time at Pompey was up.

I subsequently held talks with Wigan a few times, with Leam Richardson now their manager, and there was also interest from Bolton Wanderers and Salford City. Then Stuart McCall got in touch about going to Bradford and, having played for them before and knowing everything about the club, it just made sense. I didn't want to finish my time at Fratton Park hanging on and not playing, making do with the odd 10 minutes here or there and Papa John's Trophy appearances. I'd had enough of not being treated well by the management, while close mates like Brett and Christian Burgess had moved on. If I was playing every week there's no way that I would have left, but, ultimately, I wasn't, and, in September 2020, I moved to Valley Parade.

A part of me died when I left Fratton Park. I was of an age when I thought it's not going to get any better than what I've just had. I'm not suddenly going to sign for a top Championship club — and if you're not playing in the Championship then you aren't getting any better than Pompey. I knew joining Bradford was a massive step down, this was League Two, and, within a week or two of being there, it was pretty clear we weren't going to get any success. I'm really proud of what I achieved at Pompey over more than five years at the club; scoring in six seasons on the bounce, playing 218 times and walking away with trophies and accolades. I never wanted it to end, but my hand was forced. It was the favourite time of my career, and I loved it.

STEVE FOSTER

127 games, eight goals (August 1974 — June 1979)

Pompey 2 (Green, Foster)
Aldershot 1 (McGregor)

FA Cup first-round replay, Fratton Park, Tuesday, November 23, 1976

Pompey: Lloyd, Piper, Cahill, Foster, Viney, Pullar, Denyer, Kamara, Mellows, Pollock, Green. Sub Not Used: Lawler.

Attendance; 15,089

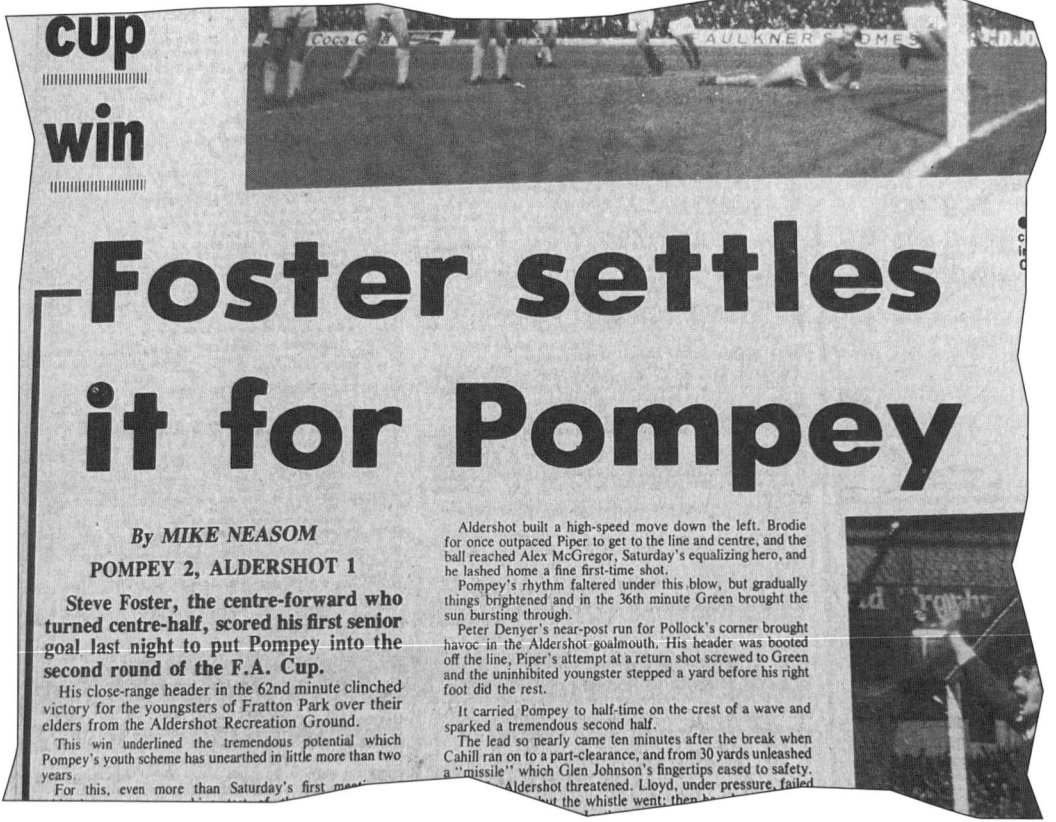

cup win

Foster settles it for Pompey

By *MIKE NEASOM*
POMPEY 2, ALDERSHOT 1

Steve Foster, the centre-forward who turned centre-half, scored his first senior goal last night to put Pompey into the second round of the F.A. Cup.

His close-range header in the 62nd minute clinched victory for the youngsters of Fratton Park over their elders from the Aldershot Recreation Ground.

This win underlined the tremendous potential which Pompey's youth scheme has unearthed in little more than two years.

For this, even more than Saturday's first meeting,

Aldershot built a high-speed move down the left. Brodie for once outpaced Piper to get to the line and centre, and the ball reached Alex McGregor, Saturday's equalizing hero, and he lashed home a fine first-time shot.

Pompey's rhythm faltered under this blow, but gradually things brightened and in the 36th minute Green brought the sun bursting through.

Peter Denyer's near-post run for Pollock's corner brought havoc in the Aldershot goalmouth. His header was booted off the line, Piper's attempt at a return shot screwed to Green and the uninhibited youngster stepped a yard before his right foot did the rest.

It carried Pompey to half-time on the crest of a wave and sparked a tremendous second half.

The lead so nearly came ten minutes after the break when Cahill ran on to a part-clearance, and from 30 yards unleashed a "missile" which Glen Johnson's fingertips eased to safety.

Aldershot threatened. Lloyd, under pressure, failed . . . . . . out the whistle went; then h . . .

Partnering Liverpool's Phil Thompson in the centre of England's defence, we beat Kuwait 1-0 in the 1982 World Cup finals in Spain — yet five-and-a-half years earlier I had been a Third Division centre-forward with Pompey. I was 100 per cent a better central defender than striker. Not only did I find it a lot easier, but I enjoy organising. I wanted to oversee the back four. Whenever I see central defenders on the touchline kicking someone, I don't understand it. This is the goal, they can only score in this area, so let's protect it.

I had featured 17 games up front for my hometown club without scoring when Ian St John decided my playing attributes were best suited as a centre-half, although it would be Frank Burrows who was instrumental in my transformation. He was a tough central defender at Swindon Town and as the Blues' first-team coach he'd take me to Eastney Barracks after training every Thursday, along with a bag of 10 balls. For 45 minutes he'd drop-kick a ball for me to head. I must have headed 80 of them in every session before returning home dizzy, yet it was part of the learning process. As a defender, heading the ball requires different timing. One position requires heading it away from goal, while the striker depends on accuracy to get the ball into the net. There's a huge difference technically.

Until the age of 19, I was a hard-working striker, firstly in Southampton's youth-team and then Pompey, but, in November 1976, the moment arrived which changed my career. The visit of Bury to Fratton Park signalled my first competitive appearance at centre-half — and I marked the occasion by scoring an own goal! Nonetheless, it remained my position for the next 20 years, featuring in the First Division for 10 seasons, playing in the 1983 FA Cup final, winning the 1988 Littlewoods Cup, losing in the 1989 Littlewoods Cup final and, of course, representing England three times.

I'm a Pompey lad, born in St Mary's Hospital in September 1957, and, apart from two years when my dad's job in the Royal Navy took us to Singapore, I lived in the city until joining Brighton & Hove Albion in June 1979 as a 21-year-old. Home was Gladys Avenue, North End, and, with my parents divorced, nan and grandad were upstairs, while later fellow Pompey teammates Steve Piper, Colin Garwood and a few others also lodged there at various times.

I attended St Swithun's Catholic Primary School, Southsea and then, after passing my 11-plus, I went to St John's College. My Uncle Eric, my dad's brother, took me to Pompey matches on a Saturday and we'd stand in the Fratton End, cheering on the likes of Albie McCann, Ray Hiron, Norman Piper, Billy Wilson and Paul Went. When I started to play for Pompey, I'd get my uncle tickets for the South Stand, which was a bit different to what he was used to!

At the age of 14, I made my debut for The Stamshaw pub in Division 7 of the

Dockyard League. I'd play in the morning for St John's College, then mum would drop me off in the car park to meet up with the Stamshaw team. I later turned out for Hilsea Old Boys, where we'd have to wait until our captain Dave Corbin had drunk seven pints of lager before we could leave, with four or five cars in convoy. That was the culture back then and a really good learning process, with senior players kicking lumps out of me. Nowadays club academies are signing kids aged eight, it's unbelievable, whereas I was playing in the Dockyard League until 15.

I also represented Portsmouth Schools and Hampshire Schools, which is where I came to the attention of Southampton, who signed me as a schoolboy aged 14. I'd train there once or twice a week, going on the train after school, while there would also be Southampton summer soccer camps. Being a Pompey fan representing Southampton didn't bother me because I wanted to play football, you've got to take what's there. If I had turned them down, I'm not sure what would have happened. It's about whoever wants you and I would have signed for anyone — even Pompey's biggest rivals. Throughout my career, every time I played against Southampton, I would get slaughtered. Although it was confusing as they'd call me "Scummer" — which is what we call them!

Our youth-team coach was John McGrath, a former centre-half with his sleeves always rolled right up and shorts turned over, with my age group consisting of Steve Williams, Trevor Hebberd and Austin Hayes, who would all progress to represent Southampton's first-team. Like me, Hayes was a striker but, after two years, when apprenticeships were handed out, I was released as they had better players on their books. First-team manager Lawrie McMenemy called us into the changing rooms one-by-one in the summer of 1974, to deliver the decisions and told me: "Will you do me a favour, please? Leave this room and prove me wrong." When I received my first England cap in February 1982 against Northern Ireland, McMenemy sent me a telegram which read: "Well done, you've proved me wrong." I appreciated that.

Fortunately, Pompey's youth-team coach Ray Crawford wanted me and I was asked to appear in a match so they could have a look — against Southampton! I scored twice, but, as Pompey already had 12 apprentices signed up, there was no room, so instead I was put on non-schoolboy terms. Then, a few weeks into the season, one of the players became homesick and left, creating a space for me to become a Fratton Park apprentice in August 1974. Ray was brilliant, I always remember him scoring twice for Colchester United to dump Leeds United out of the FA Cup in 1971 and he would constantly drum into us the importance of hitting the target. It sounds incredibly obvious, but you're not going to get goals unless your attempts are accurate. Should you miss the target in training, Ray instructed you to run around the pitch. It was: "Hit the target, hit the target, hit the target." If the goalkeeper saved, not a problem; let it go and move onto the next goal attempt.

Chris Kamara signed shortly after me, which was hilarious. He was still in the Royal Navy and would turn up for games wearing a sailor's uniform with bell bottoms and a round hat, accompanied by two officers. Eventually, Pompey bought him out of the Navy for £200. Of that youth side, seven reached Pompey's first-team, including myself, Kamara, Keith Viney, Peter Denyer, Billy Eames, Dave Pullar and goalkeeper Paul Bennett.

As a 17-year-old, Ian St John handed me my Pompey debut against Aldershot in a League Cup first round second leg at Fratton Park in August 1975. Although still a scholar, I'd been an unused substitute for the first leg's 1-1 draw, but had now replaced Bobby McGuinness in the starting XI, partnering George Graham in attack as we won 2-1 to progress into the next round 3-2 on aggregate. It would signal three successive starts for me, with my Football League bow arriving three days later at Orient in a Friday night 1-0 win. I was a hard-working centre-forward who got goals for the youth team and reserves, yet I wasn't a natural scorer. I had to work on it, and it took me 20-odd years to score 50 career goals. In that initial burst of appearances, I was in attack with George Graham and Peter Marinello, so you can work out who was doing all the running! I was here, there and everywhere. There's a reason why George was nicknamed "Stroller" during his Arsenal days.

My third Pompey outing was at Luton Town in September 1975, which marked Chris Kamara's debut and another success story for Ray's youth-team. Kammy's work ethic was brilliant. He had such big, long legs that made him ideally suited for a box-to-box midfielder. I was diagnosed with a low active thyroid at one point and needed blood tests every three months as it was worryingly low, with Kammy also having the same issue for a while.

My first Pompey season in 1975/76 consisted of 12 appearances, yet we'd be relegated after finishing bottom of the Second Division. Not that it impacted me that much being young — you don't think too deeply about things like that at the start of your career. I would start the following season in St John's team, with our opening two matches against Terry Venables' Crystal Palace in the League Cup. Although we lost the two-legged tie 3-2 on aggregate, I had once again failed to open my Pompey goal account. Worryingly, I was now slipping out of contention for a striking spot, with three subsequent substitute appearances taking me to a total of 17 games and no goals — I just couldn't break my scoring duck.

Then St John had an idea — he'd play me at centre-half. I had already been tried there for the reserves against Gillingham in April 1976, in a goalless draw which involved their striker Terry Jolley being taken to hospital for concussion after a clash of heads with me. I played five more times in this new position for the second string, but remained a striker until, seven months later, Peter Ellis was ruled out with a knee injury. "But I'm a centre-forward," I told St John. He replied: "No, you head the ball, you're good in the air." Bury visited Fratton Park in November 1976 and I partnered Paul Cahill in the centre of defence — only to score an own goal after 46 minutes. Their midfielder Jimmy McIlwraith fired in a cross-shot, which I tried to clear with a flying header, only for it to find my own net. I was grateful for Peter Denyer thundering one in from the edge of the box with three minutes remaining to make it 1-1 and spare my embarrassment even further.

Yet I had done enough to suggest this positional switch could actually work, keeping my place in the side, and, two weeks later, Aldershot visited in an FA Cup first-round replay — with yours truly the matchwinner. It was the first time back at Fratton Park since that own goal and, on this occasion, I scored in the right end, netting a close-range header on 62 minutes to earn us a 2-1 victory. During the celebrations, I could see my mate Martin Parker jumping around in the Fratton End, a mad, mad Pompey fan who lived around the corner from me — and distinctive because he was the only one wearing glasses! Of my 127 appearances for the Blues, that remains my favourite match. A fantastic way to bounce back after two games earlier.

I had never played centre-half before that 1976/77 season, yet it would become my position for the rest of my career, earning England representation at under-21 and senior levels. Thankfully, St John saw something in me. The manager handed me the opportunity to play in the first-team and, even though it was an unfamiliar role, I took it. It wasn't really that difficult to adjust to. It's a lot easier to destroy than create, and getting rid of the ball into the stand felt absolutely natural.

St John's decision was based on my ability to head the ball. Up until a few years ago, heading was important. Now it's different. The manager was a very fiery character, he loved playing in five-a-sides on Friday mornings, running around and kicking you as much as possible. He wanted it to be as aggressive as the Saturday match. I liked St John. He said it as it was and, having inherited a lot of Pompey players in their 30s, he got rid of them, bringing through us kids. As a consequence, some would be bitter about him. There were older players set in their ways, yet the truth was we didn't have a successful team, suffering one relegation and coming close to another in that 1976/77 campaign.

Stuck in the Third Division relegation zone with three matches remaining, I was sad to see St John sacked in May 1977, with Jimmy Dickinson named as his replacement. We subsequently drew 0-0 at Preston North End before winning 3-1 at home to York City through Clive Green (two) and Dave Kemp to keep us up with a game to spare. I wasn't part of it, however, missing two matches through a throat infection. Jimmy was a lovely, lovely man, but shouldn't have been appointed as manager. For many years he was sitting in a Fratton Park office, and now he was in charge of a Third Division team. Jimmy was a laid-back character, yet you could see he wasn't happy to have taken over. The owner John Deacon persuaded him.

What I am grateful for, however, was the arrival of Frank Burrows as coach under Jimmy. He was appointed in January 1978 from Swindon and somebody who took my game to the next level as a centre-half. Despite surviving under Jimmy, the following season was once again a struggle and, in December 1977, I had a new centre-half partner in Eoin Hand, who had returned to Fratton Park for a second spell having left 20 months earlier. He's a lovely man who really helped me learn the role. He taught me one important thing — to try to knock your opponent out! Basically, stand with the centre-forward and keep hold of him as he jumps, then you also leap. Should you catch him on the back of the head, he won't be jumping after that! Very good advice. Eoin played in contact lenses and hated midweek games as he couldn't see the ball because of the floodlights! I remember going to Fratton Park as a fan aged around 15 and there was a song the crowd had for him. They would chant: "Knock, knock. Who's there?" — with the Fratton End responding with: "Eoin ... Eoin who?" Then it would be: "Oh when the Blues go marching in," and everyone would jump up and down!

Hand was in Pompey's team when I fractured my right cheekbone in three places against Port Vale in January 1978, ruling me out for two-and-a-half months. I was struck by an elbow, causing my face to cave in, with my right eye dropping, and I was operated on straight away after being taken to hospital. They inserted a rod, so the face could knit back together, sidelining me for 12 matches, a period in which I could barely train. I returned for the final nine games, which unfortunately yielded just two wins, as we suffered relegation to the Fourth Division, having finished bottom for the second time in three years. The final match of the campaign saw the lad who cleaned my boots — 16-year-old Alan Knight — replacing Steve Middleton as goalkeeper against Rotherham United for his Pompey debut, with me in defence, as we wrapped up with a 1-0 victory through Denyer's second-half goal.

Ahead of our 1978/79 season in the Fourth Division, the likes of Peter Mellor and Jeff Hemmerman were recruited, while another new face, Jimmy McIlwraith, got in a bit of bother with me, resulting in us being handed a seven-day suspension by Pompey following a breach of club discipline. In September 1978, we'd been drinking in the Mr. Pickwick pub in Milton Road and, with it pouring with rain and my Ford Consul car parked across the road, we took a Carling Black Label table umbrella to keep us dry. I was going to return it in the morning, but the pub manager phoned the police saying we had stolen it.

On the way home, we stopped off at the chippy on the corner of Gladys Avenue and bought some fish and chips, with Jimmy deciding to eat his while sitting on the car bonnet and holding the umbrella. In an effort to get him off, I started the engine and drove really slowly, just one mile an hour — only for a police car to turn up. They arrested us and, while one of them was radioing over the registration number, I asked the policewoman whether she could do me a favour and let me eat my fish and chips. They were lying on the back seat of my car and would stink it out if they remained there. She agreed and I gulped them down in the back of their Panda car.

Anyhow, we were taken to the police station, but they couldn't test me for drunk driving because I had just eaten! So I was charged with stealing the umbrella and using a car in a dangerous way for passengers — and we were put in the cells overnight. It was heard at Portsmouth Magistrates' Court the following month, with my solicitor pointing out that I couldn't have endangered a passenger as he wasn't a passenger — he was actually sitting on the bonnet outside the car. So that charge was dropped and instead we were prosecuted for stealing the umbrella and each fined £50. We had already been suspended without pay by the football club, effectively costing me my weekly wage of £100, and we missed a 3-0 victory over Crewe Alexandra. I returned for the following match, albeit as a substitute, before regaining my starting spot. It took Jimmy a month before he came back into the side.

We were eighth leading into the awful incident at Barnsley in March 1979 which saw Jimmy Dickinson suffer a heart attack in the dressing room following a 1-1 draw. He sat down and keeled over, collapsing on Peter Mellor, before being taken away by an ambulance. It was upsetting to see that happen right in front of us, especially when we all thought he would die. Horrible. Although Jimmy thankfully survived, he wouldn't manage again, with first-team coach Frank Burrows stepping up to become caretaker — before being appointed permanently in May 1979 with two matches remaining.

That was the season when Peter Mellor became my roommate and he was good fun. One time he came out of the shower and I said to him: "Did you hear that noise? Quick, have a look down the corridor, Jimmy Dickinson is listening at the door." As he went out, naked as anything, I shoved him out the room and shut the door behind. He stood there, wearing absolutely nothing, banging on the door, shouting: "That's funny, now let me in." Then Mr. Deacon and his wife appeared, walking down the corridor, so I had to let Peter in — and he gave me a blue arm!

Little did I know that our April 1979 match against Wimbledon would be my final Pompey appearance — and my last meaningful action would be damaging ligaments in my right ankle and not even finishing it. I subsequently missed the final eight fixtures of the season as we finished seventh in the Fourth Division. That summer, I went on holiday with Dave Pullar to Florida for a month, where George Best was playing for Fort Lauderdale Strikers in the North American Soccer League. We were staying at the Seagulls Hotel, when I took a call from Mr. Deacon asking me to immediately catch a flight back as Pompey had received a bid — and he wouldn't say who from. I still had another week of my holiday left, but I did as requested and later discovered the interested club was Brighton.

The Seagulls had just been promoted to the First Division as runners-up to Crystal Palace and I was instructed to travel there for talks with manager, Alan Mullery. So I went with my mum, her best friend, and my three-year-old half-sister. I was happy at Fratton Park, but every footballer wants to play at a higher level. Pompey received a club record £150,000 and the offer of a friendly against Brighton, which didn't take place until 11 months later in May 1980. Everything made sense and, at the age of 21, I was off to play in the top flight.

Going from the bottom league to the First Division never daunted me. I was confident in my ability as a centre-half and, as it turned out, I had a brilliant captain in Brian Horton, who was fantastic for me. For 90 minutes he would be on everyone's case, yet I learnt even more from him than I had from Frank Burrows. Should he make a mistake, there were 10 other people screaming and shouting at him, which is what he wanted. He desired a reaction from you, yet was also very supportive.

I loved it at Pompey, a local boy playing for his local team. It meant everything playing for my club, the club I supported, the club I cheered on from the Fratton End with my Uncle Eric. I'm still a mush, too. Once a mush, always a mush.

TEDDY SHERINGHAM

38 games, 10 goals (June 2003 — May 2004)

Pompey 4
Bolton Wanderers 0

Premier League, Fratton Park, Tuesday, August 26, 2003

Pompey: Hislop, Schemmel (81 mins, Primus), De Zeeuw, Stefanovic, Zivkovic, Stone, Quashie, Faye, Berger, Sheringham, Yakubu (84 mins, Pericard). Subs not used: Wapenaar, O'Neil, Harper.

Attendance; 20,113

One of my early visits to Fratton Park was as a Millwall player — an encounter I recall specifically because I was studded in the ankle by Noel Blake, resulting in blood pouring from my boot. "Look, I can hear your boot squelching," Pompey's centre-half told me. "Why are you doing that?" I looked at him and replied: "You did me five minutes ago, now you're making out you're my mate!" He continued: "Seriously, your boot is soaking with blood. You should go off." He told the referee Ray Lewis and he called on a physio, who advised I was substituted. My foot had been cut near a vein, which explained there being so much blood — and the bloke who caused it wanted me to leave the pitch out of concern!

That was May 1987, I had just turned 21 and was up against Blake and Billy Gilbert, a pair of big, ugly centre-halves. It's not good for a young lad cutting his way in the game to face those two! Mind you, elsewhere on the pitch, Micky Kennedy was scrapping with my teammate Les Briley in midfield, which I stayed away from. Little did I realise that, 16 years later, Fratton Park would be my home for one season under Harry Redknapp, a club sharing similarities with Millwall. Both possessed honest, working-class support whose big day was the match on a Saturday. They demand you represent their team in the manner they would play; giving your all, flying into tackles, standing up like a man, prepared to fight and battle, giving no inch. The supporters want you steaming into challenges, not pulling out. Blake, Gilbert and Kennedy epitomised that for Pompey fans.

I had become a free agent in the summer of 2003 after Tottenham Hotspur decided against offering me a new contract. Glenn Hoddle was manager and, to be honest, I didn't get any vibes there would be a new deal so it wasn't a surprise, especially at 37 years old. I totalled seven seasons at White Hart Lane, consisting of two spells, and, while I understood their reasoning, I was definitely disappointed. Regardless, I remained keen to continue my career and had been speaking to teams in Qatar. There was also interest from Portugal, yet I never really felt my game suited the continent. I liked the Premier League, where there was more hustle and bustle, with a bit of flair on top. Pompey had just won promotion as Division One champions — and were the only top-flight club to contact me. I knew it would be a good club to play for with great support so, in June 2003, I joined on a 12-month deal.

Obviously I'd met Harry Redknapp over the years, but I didn't know him that well. Nonetheless, I was aware of the way he liked his teams to play — attack-minded with a bit of flair. When Pompey approached, I was certain I'd enjoy playing for him and it was a no-brainer. Harry favoured operating with a number 10, utilising people like Eyal Berkovic at West Ham United and then Paul Merson at Pompey, with hard-working players around them to make them tick. He played the game how I wanted. This was never about trying to show Spurs I was still capable of playing in the Premier League, because I wasn't in a world where I was attempting to prove people wrong, and the move definitely wasn't motivated by finances, even though it was good money. It was simply about continuing my Premier League career.

Harry didn't do an awful lot of work on team pattern. I wouldn't say he's any major tactician, but he had an impressive way of putting teams together. He liked players who could take people on, able to see a pass, while his sides also had a bit of pace about them. In some ways, he was very like Sir Alex Ferguson, who very rarely did anything tactically during my four years at Manchester United. Instead he'd have one-on-one chats with players before matches, focusing on what was required in the game ahead. He'd ensure you understood who their good players were, relayed what you had to look out for — and that was his tactical side. Harry was the same, holding a little chat with you pre-match to stress what the opposition's weak points were and where our own strengths lay. He was also a little similar to Terry Venables, although Terry was more tactically aware.

Harry had this wonderful knack of making players feel comfortable and, without doubt, looked after me. As an experienced player, he offered me the opportunity to miss Pompey training a couple of days a week and to instead stay at home, an approach which worked extremely well with Paul Merson the previous season. It was a great gesture but I've always been of the ilk that liked to be at training, even if I didn't do a lot. I wanted to be part of the team and I wasn't going to give people the opportunity, should things begin to go wrong, to point the finger and say: "Who does he think he is? He believes he doesn't have to train." I know what footballers are like. So I thanked Harry and told him I was happy to train every day — and I did. Now that's man-management. Fantastic. It wasn't just Harry there at Pompey, and Jim Smith was his assistant and a lovely man. As I was an older player, he treated me with respect and we were actually like mates rather than working together. Jim was great, an absolute diamond, but had a fun-loving nature about him.

Swapping Spurs for a newly-promoted Premier League club didn't bother me. My career started at the bottom to get to the top, then came back down the other side — and I enjoyed that route. I was never a Paul Gascoigne or Cristiano Ronaldo, destined to play at the top your entire career — I went from nothing to reach there. I came through the ranks at Millwall, had loan spells at Aldershot and Swedish club Djurgardens IF, before ending my career at Colchester United. A lot of players cannot handle coming down. One minute you're playing in the Premier

League for a top team, then you're in the Championship representing a not-so-glamorous club and moaning about the changing rooms, the training ground and the kit. I came up the hard way at Millwall. As an apprentice, my responsibility was hanging up the muddy kit in the hole, ready to be worn the next day. They were only washed at weekends — any kit I had throughout my career was better than Millwall's between the age of 16-19!

It's an ego thing. Some players are used to having all the glamorous stuff, getting looked after, owning a lovely house — but that's not what football's about. I arrived at Fratton Park after winning the Premier League three times with Manchester United and living an England career consisting of 51 appearances and 11 goals, but it didn't bother me whatsoever. I quite liked Pompey's training ground in Eastleigh, to be fair. There was nothing wrong with it.

Pompey were among the teams expected to be relegated in that 2003/04 season and, as a new Premier League team, that was natural. However, we got off to a flying start, with nine points from our opening five fixtures — absolutely vital for any newcomer to the top flight. We won our opening game 2-1 over Aston Villa in August 2003, with myself and fellow debutant Patrik Berger the scorers — and I'd return six goals from my opening nine matches. You're always trying to prove a point in football, and anyone who says they aren't is lying. There are always question marks, whether it's coming back from injury and people asking: "Can he still do it?" or people looking at your age and thinking: "Can he still perform in this league?" If you don't keep producing the goods then you receive criticism and find yourself out of the team. That's how football works.

Fortunately I hit the ground running at Pompey, including a hat-trick in my third appearance which helped put us top of the Premier League! We beat Bolton Wanderers 4-0 at Fratton Park, with all of my goals arriving in the second half. I completed my treble with a stoppage-time penalty. That was a special moment, representing my fourth — and final — Premier League hat-trick. What's more, at the age of 37 years and 146 days, I remain the oldest player to have scored a Premier League hat-trick, which is very nice. On a Sunday, you're sitting eating your dinner with the football on the TV and every now and again that statistic suddenly pops up, which makes me laugh. That's my favourite game for the club without a doubt. Scoring a hat-trick and getting Pompey to the top of the Premier League — it doesn't get much better than that.

In our fifth match of the campaign I put us 1-0 up at Arsenal, only for Robert Pires to dive under a challenge from Dejan Stefanovic and win a penalty, which was converted by Thierry Henry in a 1-1 draw. The cheating so-and-so. It definitely wasn't a pen and everyone could see he dived — everyone but referee Alan

Wiley. Still, I enjoyed myself, meeting Steve Stone's right-wing cross with a near-post diving header in front of the North Bank and then celebrating in front of Arsenal's fans by kissing Pompey's badge. Beautiful. I wanted to annoy them, especially with my Spurs links! Later in the season, in March 2004, they came to Fratton Park in the quarter-finals of the FA Cup and I appeared as a substitute, scoring an 89th-minute consolation in a 5-1 defeat. I finished at the near post and punched the air in front of the visiting fans. I don't know how I could give them stick considering the scoreline, but it's always nice to net and wind them up!

We may have lost to Arsenal in the FA Cup that day, but we made a habit of beating big clubs at Fratton Park in the Premier League, including Manchester United, Liverpool and Spurs. We also drew 1-1 against the Gunners on the south coast in that Invincibles season. When Premier League fans get their fixture list, they look to discover when the big teams are coming to town. It gets them excited, it adds a bit of adrenaline. When those clubs visited Fratton Park, you knew the crowd would be right up for it.

There was even more of a buzz and, should you happen to score against them, there's greater celebrations. Coming to Pompey intimidated some players, especially foreign ones not used to such an atmosphere. It's one of the last grounds with a tight tunnel, it's not the plush places you normally find in the Premier League. Fratton Park can be a bit scary for some.

Understandably, our home record was the main reason why we stayed up that season, finishing 13th and comfortably above the relegation places. It took us until the end of March 2004 before claiming our first league away win, with a 2-1 victory at Blackburn Rovers when I bent a free-kick through the wall to beat Brad Friedel before Yakubu Ayegbeni got the winner.

There was a good camaraderie in that Pompey dressing room, a lot of single young lads, and we had a good time. I was friends with Matty Taylor and Richard Hughes especially and we went to Marbella one time, it was a good little group. On another occasion, we travelled to Las Vegas with Eddie Howe and Hughesie's housemate Warren Cummings. I didn't really know Eddie but he was friends with Hughesie and that's how I got pally with him. My lasting memory of Eddie is of him always in the gym or the treatment room carrying out leg strengthening following another injury. I enjoy people's company. I don't see age, and, despite being the oldest in that dressing room, fitted in fine. There was a great team spirit, which Harry wanted.

There were good characters and quality players in there. Patrik Berger came from Liverpool and I had played with Stevie Stone for England and at Nottingham Forest. Lomana LuaLua was a lovely little character, full of tricks, flicks, cartwheels and handstands. Another great guy was Yakubu. I really liked him, and he was my regular strike partner during my Fratton Park days. I liked players who were very different to me, and he possessed raw pace and was able to stretch defences. I'd want the ball within two feet of me most of the time, while the Yak needed it in behind. As a pairing, defenders had to be aware of what was going on behind them, as well as what was happening in front — and it worked.

I played with a lot of quick players along the way; Andy Cole at Manchester United, Jurgen Klinsmann at Tottenham, Jon Goodman at Millwall, Chris Armstrong and Gordon Durie, also at Spurs. They fitted the way I played, good footballers that liked to run in behind, allowing me a bit of extra space to play in. I also partnered players who weren't quick, yet clever, such as Malcolm Allen at Millwall, who was very similar to myself in terms of liking the ball to feet, as was Nigel Clough at Nottingham Forest. I established a really good partnership at Millwall with Tony Cascarino, who was not the quickest and we were both good in the air. Yet we made it work.

It was strange playing with Yakubu early on because he was that quick. I'd receive the ball, control it to where I wanted it to be, then have a quick look over my shoulder to see where the centre-forward was running. But the Yak would instead stand there looking at me, while I was thinking: "Well, make a run. Go on." I came to understand that, as he was so quick, he was waiting for the pass before running — and was looking at me thinking: "Well go on then, put it in there and I'll go and get it!" I don't know whether he changed his game as he got older or stayed like that throughout his career. He had such raw talent and maybe it worked a bit differently for him, but he was a very good player.

Yakubu bagged 19 goals in his maiden Premier League campaign after joining permanently from Maccabi Haifa following a successful loan. Of that tally, four were scored in the final match of the season against Middlesbrough — which also turned out to be my last Pompey appearance. We won 5-1 at Fratton Park, with the Yak registering a hat-trick in the opening 31 minutes, before grabbing his fourth late on. I netted our other goal, coming off the bench for a tap-in at the far post with 10 minutes remaining. I scored on my Pompey debut and also in my last outing. Having totalled 10 goals in 38 matches that season, I wasn't retained by Harry.

It had already been made public that Middlesbrough would be my final Pompey game. On a personal level, it was an okay season. I had a very good start, with the second part not so great, even though I scored four more times in that period. I can't ever remember being told I wasn't getting another contract, but I presume I was. I was disappointed at the time, but at the age of 38 you think perhaps the

Premier League might not be for you anymore. Then I moved to West Ham in the Championship in July 2004 — and a year later was back in the top flight after winning promotion through the play-offs.

I'm a Hammers supporter and grew up watching my heroes Trevor Brooking, Billy Bonds, David Cross, Paul Goddard, Graham Paddon, Alan Devonshire and Phil Parkes. I scored 21 goals to fire us back into the Premier League and stayed there for another two seasons. I remain among five players to have appeared in the Premier League aged 40 and beyond. As it turned out, my final Premier League goal was against Pompey at Upton Park on Boxing Day 2006. David James punched the ball and I took a touch before lobbing it right-footed from a tight angle back over him. Glen Johnson put it high into his own net as he tried to clear, but it was going in anyway. Ask me what my wife told me to remember this morning and I can't — but talk about my goals and I'm able to recall every small detail!

Following relegation from the Championship with Colchester in the summer of 2008, I retired from playing at the age of 42. I was lucky not to get the big injuries which many players collect, while I never carried a lot of body weight so I didn't have to fight to keep off the bulge. I had the desire to continue playing and my love of the game never diminished. Besides, being a striker is not all about pace, it's about arriving at the right time.

Pompey handed me the chance to stay in the Premier League at a club which wanted to go places — and it was fantastic playing in front of those very, very vocal supporters. When you're at bigger clubs, there's an expectation to beat teams, yet with a newly-promoted club you're fighting for everything. It's exciting, it's adventurous, it's unpredictable. That's how it was at Pompey in that one season and I really enjoyed it. Playing football for a living in the Premier League? *Wow.*

KIT SYMONS

205 games, 11 goals (July 1987 — August 1995)

Liverpool 1 (Whelan)
Pompey 1 (Anderton)

FA Cup semi-final, Highbury, Sunday, April 5, 1992

Pompey: Knight, Neill, Symons, Awford, Beresford, Anderton, Burns, Kuhl, McLoughlin (109 mins, Whittingham), Chamberlain (10 mins, Aspinall), Clarke.

Attendance; 41,869

Terry Fenwick was open to selling me, sensing the opportunity to raise funds to build his own Pompey team. After all, I was Jim Smith's boy. Not only was our new manager perfectly happy for me to go, but since Jim's sacking in February 1995, I was also reasonably willing to leave. Within six weeks of Fenwick's arrival, he arranged for me to have a chat with his agent, the late Eric Hall, which turned out to be one of the funniest conversations in the world. Following a 3-2 win over Millwall at Fratton Park, Eric asked if we could go somewhere quiet and, with me wanting to stir it up a bit, I suggested the corner of an executive lounge, knowing it would be packed, with everyone looking over.

So there he was, saying: "Kidda, kidda, I will guarantee you a monster, monster move to a monster, monster club for monster, monster money." I was like: "Yeah, yeah right." He continued: "Kidda, kidda, and I can guarantee you an England cap." I replied: "No Eric, I don't think so. You can't." When he asked why, I pointed out that I had already played 15 times for Wales! He told himself off by repeating: "Schmuck, schmuck" and I thought to myself: "Mate, you don't even know who I am. You're just here for a quick buck." Well, after that meeting he didn't become my agent, although my 13-year association with the Blues was nearing its end. The aim had been to reach the Premier League with Pompey under Jim Smith, yet, when it became apparent that would never happen, it was clear I needed to move away to achieve my ambition.

My Pompey association began as an 11-year-old, having caught the eye of a referee while turning out for The Vyne School in Basingstoke. Our opponents Harriet Costello School had supplied the match official, Mick Critchell, who, co-incidentally, also did a bit of scouting for the Blues. I actually scored a penalty that day — and 10 years later would be taking a spot-kick in an FA Cup semi-final against Liverpool! Soon I was training at Pompey's satellite centre in Basingstoke every Wednesday night, with youth-team manager Alan Ball regularly taking sessions. The likes of myself, Mark Kelly and Lee Sandford all came through that centre to play for the first-team, reflecting the talent in the area at the time. However, despite being keen to sign schoolboy forms with Pompey at the age of 14, my mum was extremely conscious about doing the right thing.

She was bringing me up on her own, after my dad passed away from kidney failure when I was seven, and believed I needed to also look at other clubs before reaching such an important decision. "How do you know Pompey's the right one if you haven't compared it to other potential destinations?" she said. She was absolutely correct, so I spent 18 months also attending schoolboy weeks at Arsenal and a few Southampton training camps.

I supported the Gunners as a kid, with Basingstoke basically a London over-flow. My heroes were Liam Brady, Frank Stapleton and David O'Leary, while I watched the 1979 FA Cup final against Manchester United on TV. Unsurprisingly, Arsenal's youth facilities were incredible, they had money to throw at it, yet I preferred Pompey — where I felt far more at home. If anything, dipping my toe in the water at Arsenal and Southampton reinforced that decision. Mind you, two years later I was a bit lucky to be taken on as a Fratton Park apprentice. If I'm being honest, I was definitely borderline.

The turning point arrived after several of the under-18s went down with injury ahead of travelling to Tottenham Hotspur, the best team in the south-east counties division, so they chucked in a few of us schoolboys. Spurs lined up with Ian Gilzean, son of Alan, and future Sunderland, Luton Town and Northern Ireland international Phil Gray, and both battered me. We were smashed six or seven nil and, in my mind, the chances of earning a YTS had been blown away — only to receive a phone call afterwards offering me terms! Apparently what clinched it was, despite getting hammered, I'd had a go and didn't give up, demonstrating the right character and mentality. Sometimes you get chucked in and need to sink or swim — and fortunately, I was wearing armbands.

Pompey was a brilliant grounding. My intake included Chris White and Chris Stanley, with Mark Kelly and Lee Darby in the year above and the group below consisting of Andy Awford, Darryl Powell and Darren Anderton. As an apprentice, my job was to clean Fratton Park's away changing room every day, which was horrific. On a normal day, us youngsters would change in there, then either jump onto the minibus taking us to training at Moneyfields or, on occasions, we'd run there. At the time, dressing rooms contained these big communal baths and the state of them was disgusting.

You'd find all sorts of horrible things in there — and I'd have to clean it! Old Gordon Neave handed you a tub of Vim and a tattered old scrubbing brush and you had to make the place spotless. My mate Chris White, who also came from Basingstoke, was assigned the responsibility of sweeping the corridor and, every time he used this old brush, the dust flew into the air and came back down again. It was a never-ending job, yet Gordon would tell him off for the floor being too dusty. Give him a hoover or something, then he might have half a chance!

I also served as Mick Quinn's boot boy and he would give me a £20 bonus at Christmas, which wasn't too bad back then. Mind you, I had to work hard for it. Quinny was sponsored by Hi-Tec, but the boots were rubbish, so he would actually wear Puma Kings to play in. Before every game, I needed to black out the Puma swoosh and paint the Hi-Tec logo over the top, which was a white line with what looked like a key coming off it. If that wasn't difficult enough, typically Gordon Neave wouldn't allow me a proper paintbrush, so I used sticks and rags to draw the logo onto the boots. It was an absolute shambles. When Quinny was banged up in Winchester prison in January 1987 for two offences of driving while disqualified, I was delighted because I didn't have to do his boots for a while! They were very different days, with apprentices expected to go through an initiation process, such as being stripped naked and covered in boot polish, then under instructions to run around Fratton Park, with the office staff coming to the window to watch. Obviously that wouldn't be allowed to happen in the current climate, and rightly so. Yet for me, it was a good grounding and I believe benefited us further down the line.

My digs were in Tamworth Road, Copnor, staying with a family who had two boys, while Peter Osgood was one of my youth-team managers, formerly a big centre-forward for England, Chelsea and Southampton. He'd join in with training, stamping on my toes and smashing me during sessions, telling me I needed to toughen up. He demanded I went around kicking strikers, but that was never my way of playing, so I wouldn't — I was quite stubborn!

In an attempt to get a reaction, Osgood would kick lumps out of me in training and tempting me to boot him back. Nonetheless I'd stay calm and refuse to retaliate. He was brilliant, though, we all loved him, as was another coach Graham Paddon, while Dave Thomas was also around. Throw in Alan Ball, who was youth-team coach when I arrived, and you realise how lucky we were to have people of that calibre working with us day in, day out. Yes, Arsenal had incredible facilities, while Pompey were training on a cabbage patch at Moneyfields, but it was real. Facilities are not what it's all about and you can have a good environment without top surroundings.

Growing up at Pompey coincided with the presence of Alan Ball's gremlins and, as an apprentice, it would scare the life out of me walking into that changing room. They were bonkers, fruit loops, characters who intimidated those at the same club — so imagine how match-day opposition felt! As I grew older and came to know them, I discovered they were top, top guys, but as a kid entering that dressing room, they would ruin you. It was a tough school, with fiery characters like Mick Kennedy, Noel Blake and Billy Gilbert — and they were ruthless. I'd watch Kennedy on the pitch and he was vicious, with a first tackle every time that was waist high; Mick Tait was a lovely guy yet made of granite. He was as hard as nails, who would normally go in fair, but still smashed people. Bally worked on shape the Friday before a match, which involved the first-team facing the youths.

I'd be up against Paul Mariner, who, on one occasion, cleaned me out with an elbow across my nose, splattering blood everywhere. Bally was screaming, having a go at Mariner for smashing me, then I realised he was actually shouting at me! "Get off the pitch, clean your face up," he was roaring. My nose was plastered across my face and the manager was moaning at me about it. Welcome to football. I soon learnt not to challenge Mariner in the air and instead I'd drop off and let him bring it down onto his chest. He was a former Ipswich and England player and getting on a bit by that stage, but looked out of this world in training on a Friday because the young centre-half wouldn't go anywhere near him!

It's a strange statistic that my opening five league games for Pompey came under four different managers — Alan Ball, John Gregory, Frank Burrows and Jim Smith. I made my debut aged 17 years, eight months and one day in the Simod Cup against Hull City in November 1988. Billy Gilbert suffered a stomach muscle injury during the match, so I replaced him as a 29th-minute substitute. Then, two months later, Bally handed me my Football League debut against Leicester City, drafting me in late following injury to our skipper Kevin Ball — and it turned out to be his last game as manager. I always thought he was a fixture at Fratton Park, there as long as he wanted, and now he was gone. It was my first experience of a manager being sacked — and three days after my Second Division bow. We lost 2-1 at Filbert Street, putting us 13th in the table, yet I had no idea he was that close to being dismissed. I first met Bally coaching 11-year-olds in Basingstoke and he loved football, with such an infectious passion and enthusiasm.

He was replaced by his coach, John Gregory, and I retained my place alongside Graeme Hogg in the centre of defence for his first match in charge, a 2-0 win over Shrewsbury Town at Fratton Park in January 1989. I had done well, but 17 is still fairly young to be making your debut as a centre-half, so subsequently I didn't get much game time over the next few years. One of Gregory's first changes was to introduce wearing a shirt and tie when turning up for training and, having recently left school, I'd use one of my old shirts!

One day Mickey Fillery came in with a short-sleeved shirt, some lairy tie and Bermuda shorts, just to make a point — and the manager's new rules were soon ripped up. Gregory wanted to make big changes too soon — let's not forget some of the gremlins were still about — and, considering that culture and that group, it was never going to be easy. Unsurprisingly, he alienated some of the older players, which is always dangerous.

Gregory's assistant, Frank Burrows, succeeded him as manager in January 1990, initially as caretaker, by which time I had totalled five first-team appearances, but he had taken a shine to Andy Awford. Awfs was a good young player, an England schoolboy receiving a lot of press who, despite being a year younger, was now in front of me, and it didn't appear as though I'd get a chance. Frank went on to manage the Blues for 14 months — and my sole appearance was a start against West Brom in November 1989 in a 1-1 draw. He was a lovely, lovely fella and football is about opinions. He preferred a centre-half to go around smashing people, something not in my nature. As a player, I would stand up for myself and compete, certainly not getting bullied, but it wasn't my style to kick people either. I'd rather outplay them and defend the right way.

My contract was coming up for renewal in the summer of 1991 and I wasn't getting anywhere near the first-team, so had decided to leave Fratton Park. I'd been given a first-team taste extremely young and loved it, I had the bug and wanted to play more, yet there were no longer any opportunities. If I hadn't sampled that aged 17, I would definitely have been more patient, but instead I was frustrated — and certain I could perform in the Football League if someone gave me the chance. I was actively looking to leave, although, perhaps crucially, I didn't have an agent. Loads of people were phoning wanting to represent me, but I wasn't really enamoured with agents, while mum considered them all dodgy. In my mind, I was pretty close to leaving, but, looking back, there were no concrete offers. Then it all changed — Frank was sacked in March 1991, with Tony Barton acting as caretaker for the remainder of the 1990/91 season. Although I never featured in his 12 games in charge, he calmed me down and was a lovely, lovely man. That summer, Barton was overlooked for the job permanently, with Jim Smith arriving — my favourite Pompey manager.

Jim's remit was to reduce the wage bill and get rid of some of the big hitters, while he was willing to chuck in loads of us kids to supplement his team. The outcome was a trip to Blackburn Rovers on the opening day of the 1991/92 season when half the Pompey fans must have been asking: "Who?" when they saw his side running out. The way pre-season had panned out, a lot of the younger players were involved in first-team friendlies, but I don't think we necessarily expected to start the campaign. It was a bit of a surprise, albeit a pleasant one, and worked out very well, backed up by brilliant senior pros like Alan Knight, Martin Kuhl, Warren Neill and Mark Chamberlain, who helped us massively. Their influence was huge.

Jim would batter me and Awfs, calling us Sloppy and Floppy, but we knew he loved us really. Awfs was Sloppy, left-footed, laid-back Larry, so casual — while I was Floppy because I was tall and skinny. That's where Neil Sillett, the physio, was really good and, being really tight with Jim, was a brilliant buffer. After being on the receiving end of the manager, Sill would reassure us: "He loves you two, he's always talking about you. He thinks you can go all the way and have great careers." Jim would be tough on us young boys — and everyone for that matter — but was superb to play for. The senior players were used to it, they could take being shouted at and screamed at, whereas if we didn't have Sill as that buffer to explain things afterwards, we might not have responded as well.

For a team to field one young centre-half at that level is quite rare, but to have two playing together is unheard of. You just don't see it. What's more, me and Awfs were best mates and already had that relationship as a central-defensive pairing, which was so important. Pompey often fielded a back three in that 1991/92 season, with Guy Butters coming into the middle, heading it away while also possessing a good range of passing, with the big left-to-right diagonal in his locker.

As a partnership, I was tall and would look to dominate the headers, with Awfs sweeping up and attempting to come out and play. You'd get dominant centre-halves who were stoppers and couldn't use the ball particularly well, yet I'd like to think I was a bit of both. Although nowhere near as good as Awfs in possession, I could still play a bit and had a spell at Pompey where I'd go on these mazy runs out from the back and have a bit of fun. Jim would go mad at times, though, insisting I gave the ball to someone who could play! People have this perception of him as this motivator with a habit of throwing tea cups — which he was more than capable of doing — but he was tactically astute too, excellent in his game knowledge and communicating it to his players. We revered him, held him in such high esteem, while the odd word of praise delivered by him was massive. If you got a "Well done" off Jim Smith, it was brilliant.

Our first season under Jim would see us reach the 1992 FA Cup semi-finals and finish ninth in the Second Division, although a fixture backlog at the end of the campaign impacted our league placing. Before our FA Cup fourth-round game against Leyton Orient in January 1992, Jim took us for a round of golf at the Meon Valley Hotel, Golf and Country Club. We subsequently won the match 2-0, so it became a tradition on the Wednesday before every round of the cup. The manager was very superstitious and liked his routines. The 1-0 FA Cup quarter-final win over Nottingham Forest coincided with my 21st birthday weekend, with my party held in a hall at the University of Portsmouth that evening and most of the boys coming along for a great night. Following the game, I was called into Fratton Park's chairman's lounge, where our shirt sponsors Goodmans presented me with one of their portable CD players as a present, all wrapped up too. I thought that was a lovely gesture. On the Monday morning, to mark reaching the semi-finals of the FA Cup, a team photo was organised on the Fratton Park pitch. Also to commemorate the feat, Goodmans handed portable CD players to all the players — apart from me because I already had one! The tight so-and-sos.

Our FA Cup semi-final at Highbury generated the best atmosphere I ever experienced as a player. Representing Wales was something I am very, very proud of, but absolutely nothing came close to walking on to Arsenal's pitch in our tracksuits before kick-off and witnessing those amazing scenes. You can talk about moments when the hairs on the back of your neck stand up and that day in April 1992 was the most incredible of atmospheres. Really special.

Liverpool were on their way down following a period of dominance in the domestic game, with Graeme Souness in charge, yet they remained a very, very good side and had players who knew precisely what they had to do to win games of football. They weren't just this silky football machine — and I'm sure they looked at us before the game and realised if they halted Mark Chamberlain then they stopped a lot of Pompey's creativity and good forward play. Chambo was a special player, laid-back and a lovely guy with a real talent that made him, on his day, virtually unplayable. Then Ronnie Whelan took him out and he had to be substituted after 10 minutes. Still, Darren Anderton's extra-time goal put us within touching distance of beating Liverpool, until Whelan — who else? — levelled four minutes from time. It was an equaliser which arrived in slow-motion, John Barnes' free-kick pushed against the inside of the post by Knightsie and they reacted quickest.

At the time I wasn't massively disappointed because we had a replay and were still in it, with another game to focus on and a second crack at Liverpool. Besides, we'd already faced them and nearly won, so maybe we could finish the job at Villa Park. Why not? The clubs still couldn't be separated, though, and, following a goalless draw after extra-time in the replay, the semi-final was to be decided by a penalty shoot-out. As a professional footballer, I had never before taken a penalty — and certainly wasn't meant to have the responsibility that evening, until a change of plan. Jim Smith came up to me and said: "You were brilliant tonight. Take a pen?" So I agreed. Perhaps someone else was down to take it and pulled out, I don't know. I didn't even practise them, of course I didn't. I was a centre-half and taking penalties was not really my thing. Probably the last time was an 11-year-old the day a Pompey scout spotted me. As I walked towards the spot, it occurred to me: "What have I done here?" I aimed to the right, Bruce Grobbelaar dived to the left, and the ball went down the middle — that's how awful I am at taking penalties! We lost 3-1 and I was the only successful taker, with Martin Kuhl, Warren Neill and John Beresford all missing. I did take one more spot kick in my career, which was against Notts County at Fratton Park in February 1994 — Steve Cherry saved it and we drew 0-0.

It was my first full season in Pompey's first-team and we had lost in the semi-finals of the FA Cup. I reasoned we'd do better next year — yet never again came that close. I was young and you don't realise, it's only now when you truly understand how near we were to a Wembley final. Still, it had been an incredible maiden season under Jim Smith. We'd reached the FA Cup semi-final, finished ninth in the Second Division, while, on a personal level, I was named *The News/ Sports Mail's* player of the season, which was an incredible honour, especially for a 21-year-old. In addition, I was an ever-present, featuring in all 59 of Pompey's fixtures and never receiving a booking, which vindicated my stubbornness not to listen to Peter Osgood about kicking people. Don't get me wrong, I picked up plenty of yellow cards later in my career as I got older and slower, but, at that stage, I was determined to make it on my terms — and I'm proud of that.

That breakthrough 1991/92 season would also mark my Wales debut, following 39 career appearances for Pompey. In February 1992, at the age of 20, I played the full 90 minutes in a 1-0 friendly victory over the Republic of Ireland in Dublin. All of my family are Welsh and my dad John worked for the AA, whose headquarters were in Cardiff, before relocating to Fanum House in Basingstoke, so my family also moved. In 1971, a year later, I was born in Basingstoke, although my older brother, like my parents, is from Cardiff, so I was the only one from England in my household. Growing up, I'd be battered by my family as the Cockney so-and-so until I started playing for Wales! I went on to make 36 appearances and scored twice for my country over 12 years, with 17 of my outings coming as a Pompey player.

We had Paul Walsh in our ranks for the 1992/93 season, having been recruited from Tottenham Hotspur, yet sold John Beresford to Newcastle United and Darren Anderton to Spurs. Walshie arrived at Fratton Park with something to prove, having obviously been a top player at White Hart Lane and Liverpool, representing England five times. This was the chance to show people he still had an awful lot to offer — and was phenomenal for us. As a strike partnership, he and Guy Whittingham were very, very different players, yet brought out the best in each other superbly. Guy couldn't stop scoring, rattling in 47 goals in all competitions, and, while Walshie didn't necessarily put them all on a plate for him, they were our driving force and, following a 2-0 win over Wolverhampton Wanderers, we topped the table in April 1993 with two games to play. However, the following match we lost 4-1 at Sunderland, having been reduced to nine men after the dismissals of Guy Butters and Walshie, with the latter smashing the mirror in the dressing room in our absence. Despite beating Grimsby Town 2-1 in our final fixture, we finished third, missing out on automatic promotion through goals scored.

As it turned out, dropping two points at Oxford United in November 1992 would prove decisive. Jim was back at his old club and swanning around the Manor Ground boardroom with a big cigar. Ahead of the match, me and Awfs had been handed permission to stay over in Lambourne afterwards as we were going racing at Newbury the next day. Well, we were 5-2 up with 13 minutes remaining and cruising — only for it to finish 5-5. Oxford actually scored twice in injury time to level, through Jim Magilton's penalty and then Chris Allen. We returned to the dressing room and Jim was incandescent, effing and jeffing and throwing tea cups about. In fact everything was flying around.

Me and Awfs kept our heads down, dodged the bullets, then sneaked out to the Lambourne home of racing journalist and Pompey fan Steve Taylor. At Newbury Races the following day, we made our way to the bar and the first people to walk into the room were none other than Jim and his wife Yvonne! To be fair, the Bald Eagle was brilliant with us. "All right boys," he said. "It was awful last night, wasn't it?" We replied: "Yes gaffer, sorry about that." Then he bought us a drink and was fine. Years later, when I was working for Fulham's academy, I mentioned that Oxford match and how we'd somehow drawn 5-5, yet justified I had played all right. Well, they managed to get footage of the game and put it up. I was at fault for at least three of the goals. I was terrible, all over the place! YouTube is a killer these days.

Now I'm not one for regrets, but I look back on that era and think what could have been. We should have gone up automatically that season. We had lost in an FA Cup semi-final and then, the following year, missed out on automatic promotion to the Premier League on goals scored, with West Ham United instead claiming second place. We had finished 12 points ahead of Leicester City, out of sight, yet were now meeting them in the semi-finals of the Division One play-offs. It was still in the early days of the play-off format and I remember thinking what a load of rubbish the idea was. Later in my career, I finished sixth with Crystal Palace and we reached the Premier League by beating West Ham in the 2004 Championship play-off final, so it evens itself out.

Our first leg of the semi-final against Leicester was held at Nottingham Forest's City Ground in May 1993, ending in a 1-0 defeat through Julian Joachim's late goal. Then, 72 hours later, we met at Fratton Park in front of 25,438, our biggest home crowd of the season, with Alan McLoughlin levelling the tie at 1-1 early in the second half. Minutes later, however, Ian Ormondroyd scored with a goal which was miles, miles offside after Knightsie had come flying out for the ball. According to the laws of the game, a player cannot be offside if there are at least two players between him and the ball, of which generally one is the goalkeeper.

That night, however, there was just me on the goal-line when Ormondroyd put it in, with the striker ahead of our 'keeper — it was clearly offside. I'm looking at the linesman and thinking: "Come on, mate," then he started running along the pitch towards the halfway line for the kick-off without waving his flag. I've since blamed the linesman more than referee Roger Milford for that mistake. The match eventually finished 2-2, yet the Foxes won 3-2 on aggregate. That was such a good Pompey side with so many really, really talented players, yet, unfortunately, it was a nearly team. We nearly got to the FA Cup final, we nearly got promoted, and that was a shame. The likes of Whittingham, Walsh and Chamberlain were incredible footballers, possessing exceptional ability, and didn't deserve to be remembered as nearly players.

After Jim's reign as Pompey manager had begun with two good opening seasons, things started to break up a little and that was a disappointment. teammates were moving on and we weren't able to replace them with the same calibre, while losing the likes of Whittingham (Aston Villa) and Walsh (Manchester City) was always going to be huge. Having finished 17th in 1993/94, the following season was even worse, as we languished in 19th at the halfway point.

Then, in January 1995, Jim Smith was sacked following a 1-0 FA Cup fourth-round defeat to Leicester, which left me questioning my own Fratton Park future. I would never have left Pompey if he was still there, certainly not for quite a while. I felt I owed him and certainly wasn't looking to quit while he remained as manager. There had previously been talk of me leaving and I remember attending my cousin's wedding in Cardiff in May 1994 and spotting the back page of *The Sun*.

According to them, Blackburn Rovers, on their way to finishing as Premier League runners-up in 1993/94 under Kenny Dalglish, had identified me as the £2m replacement for David May, who was to join Manchester United. The headline screamed: "Kenny bags Kit" with a big picture of me. Well, I didn't have an agent so it really was news to me, prompting a phone call to Neil Sillett asking him to find out from Jim what was going on. He soon rang back, saying: "Jim knows nothing about it" — and that was the end of that. We played Blackburn in the FA Cup third round later that season and, while marking Tim Sherwood at a corner, he asked me: "You coming then? Are you signing for us, or what?"

Until Terry Fenwick arrived as Jimmy's replacement in February 1995, I wasn't aware of any interest, certainly not to me directly. Then again I wasn't looking to leave and didn't have an agent to push for it, which is generally how most of these things work. Yet circumstances change and, after finishing 18th in the 1994/95 season, I spent the summer of 1995 hoping a club would call. Premier League

Sheffield Wednesday approached and I was reasonably interested, however it fell through at their end as they were expecting to sell someone and use that money to buy me, but it didn't happen. Regardless, I had to be patient. Although aged 24, I was experienced enough to realise how football worked and I needed to remain professional, keeping my head down and working hard at Pompey. It's about conducting yourself in the right manner and I was still at Fratton Park for the start of the 1995/96 season, playing in an opening day 4-2 win over Southend United. That game saw Mart Poom and Jimmy Carter make their debuts, yet for me represented a Pompey farewell, with a career-changing phone call that evening from Manchester City manager Alan Ball.

City had been beaten 5-1 by Heart of Midlothian in a pre-season friendly at Tynecastle that day — and Bally was eager to make changes. "We have Tottenham at home next Saturday in the first game of the Premier League season — and I want you in my starting line-up," he told me. I flew to Manchester on the Monday, using Awfs' agent to oversee the deal. Bally relayed how he regarded me as a future City captain and I signed in a deal valued at £1.8m, with Pompey receiving £900,000 plus Fitzroy Simpson and Carl Griffiths in part exchange. I had a big history with Bally, from coaching me as a schoolboy to signing pro forms under him and then making my first-team debut.

That and the chance to play for Manchester City was the pull, while I knew Fenwick wanted me out. I was really happy at Pompey, really, really happy. I loved the city and everything about the club, then, when Jim went, I could see things were going to change — and they did, straight away. Even in the final season under Jim, the recruitment wasn't at the same level and we had gone from challenging for promotion to hovering around the relegation zone. I'd been at Fratton Park for eight years and, coupled with Jim's departure, it made me realise this was the time to move on.

Fenwick probably wanted me out more than I wanted to go, because I loved Pompey. It's one of those cities that's brilliant if you play it right. I knew so many fans, businessmen, the CID and old Bill, the 657 lads. It's a city, but also a village, and, if you're decent with people, it's the best place to be. However, if you take liberties or don't show people the right respect then they don't suffer fools either — which Gerry Creaney found out the hard way. A goalscorer for Pompey is generally revered, but you still have to behave the right way with people and conduct yourself correctly — as Gerry discovered when he suffered a fractured cheekbone after being attacked on a night out in Southsea with Mark Chamberlain in April 1995.

These days when my path crosses with Fenwick I get on well with him. We always stop and speak and I quite like him as a fella, but at Fratton Park he was the new manager who wanted to bring in his own players. Whereas I was Jim's boy and somebody he wanted out to create money for reinvestment into the squad. I have no hard feelings, that's football. Probably the best outcome for both of us was me leaving in August 1995 after 204 games and 11 goals.

Life at Manchester City started off quite badly as we failed to win any of our opening 11 Premier League games in the 1995/96 season, while Walshie returned to Fratton Park inside my first month in a swap deal which brought Gerry Creaney to Maine Road. That was a big blow to me personally and I was devastated. Walshie was my mate from Pompey and a top player. I ended up with two relegations in two years at City, while later enjoyed two promotions in two years at Fulham. Yet Pompey was special. I had gone from a snotty-nosed 16-year-old just out of school to learning the ways of the world in a city like Portsmouth, which was a privilege. There was nowhere better.

KEVIN HARPER

128 games, nine goals (March 2000 — February 2005)

Pompey 3 (Bradbury, O'Neil, Harper)
Barnsley 0

Division One, Fratton Park, Sunday, May 6, 2001
Pompey: Flahavan, Hiley, Primus, Tiler, Vincent, Harper, Brady, O'Neil, Sharpe, Bradbury, Lovell (88 mins, Crowe).

Subs not used: Tardif, Nightingale, Wolleaston, Panopoulos.

Attendance; 13,064

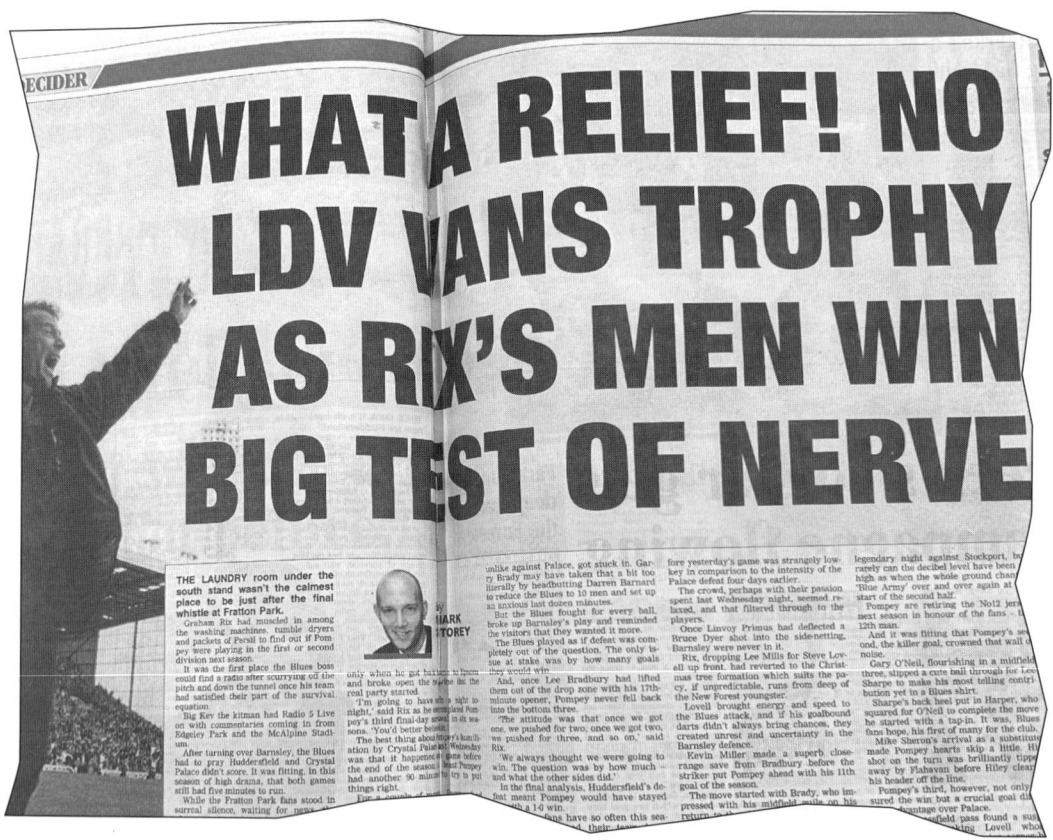

In his 2003 autobiography *Legend*, Alan Knight wrote how he had rarely seen a Pompey player turn things around after being on the receiving end of so much stick from the fans. I was the exception. It wasn't smooth sailing, but I'd like to think every supporter and each of my managers will say Kevin Harper worked his socks off, whether playing good or bad. Ultimately, some have described me as a Blues cult hero, an accolade I am immensely proud of.

It was during the 2002/03 season when the negative reaction was at its loudest. While warming up at Fratton Park before kick-off, I'd hear our team read out over the PA, then had to stomach the accompanying boos from my own supporters which greeted my name. I don't know why I warranted such treatment. I had scored against Barnsley in a final-day 3-0 win to keep us in Division One in May 2001 — now I was part of a side sitting top of the table under Harry Redknapp and eyeing the Premier League. I wasn't performing poorly, but, if you looked at that team, I was no big name, therefore probably the least of the favourites. I actually have no issue with the booing — fans have their opinion, managers have their opinion — yet it was hurtful and I didn't want to hear it. Still, I had the last laugh.

My background was bad. I was brought up in adversity, and it's all about how you deal with that adversity. I'm a pretty strong character. I grew up in Possilpark, Glasgow, an area which could be regarded as a modern-day slum in what was, at the time, the drug capital of Europe. I was a black kid in a white area and it was rough and tumble; there were drug dealers everywhere, shootings, stabbings, stolen cars. The usual things which happen in any ghetto, I guess. I would play kids' football and receive racial abuse over the entire 90 minutes from parents positioned along the edge of the pitch. Things like that can either make you or break you. Looking back, it was horrific, but, at the time, that was normal. So you'll understand why Pompey fans booing me before kick-off or while retrieving the ball for a throw-in was nothing compared to what I went through as an 11 and 12 year-old.

Did I play amazingly well all the time? No, of course I didn't, that's football, but nobody goes out to play badly. I don't know if I brushed the criticism off as such, everyone has their breaking point, I've got mine, but you get through the tough times and it drove me. I didn't want to be a failure. Yet while some were booing, teammates inside the dressing room such as Paul Merson and Steve Stone were telling me: "Kevin, the fans might not see it, but we know what you're giving the team and the important role you play." I appreciated that. I consider myself a team player, probably at the detriment of my own game, coming in at right wing-back when Stone was injured, slotting in at left wing-back when Matty Taylor was missing. Wherever it was, you'd always get 100 per cent effort and hard work from me in absolutely anything.

Then, around Christmas 2002, the booing stopped. The fans started singing: "Kevin Harper Football Genius," most likely tongue in cheek, yet, all the same, a nod of recognition for what I brought to the team. That chant will never leave me until the day I am no longer on this earth. It was wonderful to hear, especially having gone through the tough stuff. It's emotional talking about it all these years later but then again, any time I speak about Pompey is emotional because it's such a special place for me. I played 40 games and scored once in that promotion-winning season under Harry Redknapp and I believe I was an important cog in that wonderful team. Hopefully the fans agreed in the end.

I arrived at Fratton Park from Derby County in March 2000 for £300,000 — and it turned out to be the best move of my career. Manager Tony Pulis viewed me as a key member of the team, something which wasn't happening at the Premier League Rams. Pride Park had been my home since September 1998, when I left Hibernian and Scotland for the East Midlands. I scored six minutes into my full debut, heading past David James in front of the Kop at Anfield in a 2-1 win over Liverpool, but started just five more games in the top flight. I could have stayed with Jim Smith's side and sat on the bench, but a footballer wants to play, so, in December 1999, I joined Division One Walsall on loan for the remainder of the season — only to be called back after two-and-a-half months to sign for Pompey.

Dropping down from the Premier League didn't concern me, with Pulis and chairman Milan Mandaric assuring me it was the right time to come to Fratton Park. I took them on their word — and what they said was true. At first I didn't really understand Pompey — I had never particularly heard of them as a football club, if I'm being honest — but it was the best move of my career. Apart from making my debut for Hibernian at Dundee United in August 1996, they were my best times. It's a club so close to my heart. I know people often say that, but, genuinely, I love Pompey. It will always be a special, special place.

Let's not forget that the club were struggling at the time of my March 2000 arrival, just one point above the Division One relegation zone, and, following a 1-0 debut defeat at Birmingham City within 24 hours of my transfer, we had sunk into the bottom three. Initially it was about stabilising the club following Alan Ball's departure as manager, but, ultimately, Tony and Milan were determined to push on, which dovetailed my ambition of a Premier League return.

I like Pulis as a man and as a coach as well, and learnt a hell of a lot from him, as I did with all my managers. He made me more aware of positioning, taught me how to understand the game, and, being a tough taskmaster, educated me on fitness. I adapted to the defensive side of the game, playing at times as a second right-back in a 4-4-2 at Pompey because he wanted his wingers to track back. Training was tough; it was constantly shape, shape, shape, so you knew exactly where your position was. A lot of my teammates felt it was repetitive, which I can understand, but I became a better, more rounded player as a result. While in Scotland, I didn't try hard enough to be one of the best players — then, at the age of 22, I travelled to England and realised I had to up my game.

Put it this way, Pulis' football wasn't as expansive as Harry Redknapp's after him, but Tony firstly had to make sure we didn't go down, because there was a point in 1999/2000 where that was a real possibility. Regardless, I enjoyed playing for him — I was in the team week in, week out and, while I appreciate some don't like his style, as a winger it was about me getting the ball, bursting into the box and creating chances, which suited me. As a club, Tony moved us forward, but not as quickly as Milan wanted and, considering the style of play, we were probably going to be a mid-table Division One side for a while.

After steering us to 18th and avoiding relegation, Tony set about rebuilding in the summer of 2000, with Linvoy Primus among the arrivals. Having left Reading, he featured in our opening pre-season friendly, a 2-0 win at Dorchester Town, and his Pompey journey became a fantastic story. Linvoy was an old-fashioned centre-half — he headed it, he kicked it and he tackled anything that moved, although he would be the first to admit he was not the best passer of the ball. He was so raw when he joined, but could read the game beautifully and, as he developed, putting in that trademark hard work and commitment, he became better and better, to the point of being inducted into the Pompey Hall of Fame.

I was surprised at Pulis's departure in October 2000, but not shocked, if that makes sense. There were things going on behind the scenes, with a certain person reporting matters back to Milan which weren't true. That disappointed me. I don't believe any player should go running to the chairman in order to further their own ambition. This was a senior player, who I shall not name, and he delivered the message that Pulis had lost the dressing room. Coupled with results at the time, Milan reached the decision to remove him. If you don't like the manager, fair enough, but you shouldn't be running to the chairman saying things like that — especially when he actually hadn't lost the dressing room, certainly from what I was seeing. Granted, we were going through a tough spell, winning two of our opening 11 league games, while some players weren't performing as well as they could, yet Pompey were in no danger of relegation.

What that person did to Tony Pulis is not behaviour I would involve myself in. Some people look after themselves before others — I am not one of them. If I didn't like a manager, I would tell him to his face, not approach the chairman in an attempt to get him the sack. I never thought that happened in football — but clearly it did. That wasn't the sole reason why Pulis left, the team's performances were also part of the issue, yet I felt sorry for him. Tony's an honest guy and a really good coach, surely if you can stoop that low to remove the manager, what are you saying about yourself to other players?

Pulis was replaced by my teammate, Steve Claridge, whose four-and-half months in charge was the worst I had under any manager in my career. He started me just four times and clearly didn't regard me as suitable for what he wanted. He also claimed in his 2009 autobiography *Beyond The Boot Camps* that I once faked a groin strain to get three weeks off at Christmas. That was absolute rubbish — don't start telling lies about me in your book. Ask any of my managers, apart from Claridge, and they will tell you I always wanted to play and never feigned injury. I played almost the whole of our Division One title-winning season with a double hernia, which says everything.

As a player, Claridge was a colleague. I wasn't best pals with him and didn't dislike him as such — after all, I had seen the good things he did for the club, while I admired his attitude. Although, in terms of going out for a beer with him or spending any amount of time together, I wouldn't. I accept it's difficult to switch from being a player to the manager, but you just want honesty, which is why I never fell out with Jim Smith at Derby or, later in my career, at Stoke City under Pulis. You don't want somebody talking complete nonsense about you, especially putting it in a book so you can't defend yourself. If you have an issue then come and speak to me, but Claridge never did. Not that I ever read his book, I wouldn't, yet I've heard plenty about it — and what he claims is the furthest thing from the truth.

I can't actually recall Claridge as Blues boss. It made no mark on me whatsoever. From the day he came in as manager, I genuinely believed he was destined to fail because he didn't possess the respect of the changing room — and it was no surprise he lasted 137 days. It was a forgettable time in my footballing career under someone I didn't respect and didn't regard as the right person for the job. As a player, however, Claridge's record speaks for itself. He did a fantastic job for the club and his approach towards fitness and playing was great. At the age of 34, he was in top, top shape and condition. A model pro.

Graham Rix was appointed as Claridge's replacement in February 2001, with our former manager subsequently joining Millwall, initially on loan. I liked Rixy, I liked his philosophy, I liked the way he wanted to play. He possessed so many good ideas on football. The biggest compliment I can give is that some of the players he worked with during his time at Fratton Park weren't ready for his forward-thinking approach. By his side was Jim Duffy, an ex-manager of mine at Hibs, operating as the bad cop to Rix's good cop. Still, the pair took over a Pompey team positioned 17th in Division One, just three points above the relegation zone with 13 matches to play. I must admit, I never ever thought we'd be relegated, not even after a 4-2 defeat to Crystal Palace in our penultimate game. Fratton Park was a cauldron of hate that night, it was nasty, but we deserved it. We were terrible and didn't perform.

It came down to the final day of the season, with Barnsley visiting Fratton Park in May 2001. We occupied the final relegation spot and required victory, yet even that was no guarantee of staying up, with one of Palace, Huddersfield Town and Grimsby Town still needing to lose. I entered the changing room ahead of kick-off on that Sunday afternoon and the atmosphere was so different — I knew we were going to win. There was that vibe, unlike anything I'd felt before during that season; a steely focus and quiet confidence. Everybody seemed above the pressure of the situation. The only other time I felt that at Pompey was Manchester United in the FA Cup third round in January 2003, when I didn't even hear the 67,222 crowd. It was as if I was playing in silence, such was my mindset. We lost 4-1 that day, with David Beckham netting a free-kick and Ruud van Nistelrooy scoring twice, while I remember Ryan Giggs being incredibly sharp in the opening 15 minutes.

What unfolded against Barnsley would establish it as my favourite Pompey game. With hindsight, that was where our journey into the Premier League began — and I was fortunate to be one of the few who accompanied the club along that path. What really resonated with me was seeing the fans' faces after that 3-0 win kept us up, then seeing their reaction when promoted to the Premier League two years later.

Lee Bradbury handed us a 17th-minute lead over the Tykes and then, on 63 minutes, I played a one-two with Lee Sharpe before squaring from the left across the six-yard box for Gary O'Neil to tap in his first senior goal. I completed the scoring 12 minutes later, popping up at the back post to meet Steve Lovell's left-wing cross with a first-time left-footed finish from seven yards for my second of the season. Following a home defeat to Birmingham City, Huddersfield were the club relegated — we had survived by a point.

In public, it was difficult for us to celebrate staying up because, in the cold light of day, we should never have been in that position, yet there was relief among the players. Certainly relegation wouldn't have given Pompey the subsequent highs of the Premier League, winning the FA Cup and all those amazing players. You don't realise it then, but, upon reflection, it was a special, special moment.

The summer of 2001 saw Milan Mandaric splash out on a new strike force, with Mark Burchill arriving from Celtic and Peter Crouch coming from QPR, while Robert Prosinecki was also unveiled as a Pompey player. Rix was unfortunate that Burchill collected a season-ending cruciate knee ligament injury just a month into his time at Fratton Park following an innocuous moment in training when he cut across the back of Prosinecki and accidentally clipped his leg. That hit us hard, with the Scottish striker having netted four goals in his opening six Blues matches and hitting it off superbly with Crouchy. After that setback, he was never the same player.

As for Prosinecki, I couldn't believe I was on the same pitch as him. He was such a fantastic player, and a really nice guy. This was him aged 32, and I'd hate to think what he was like in his prime. He was head and shoulders the best player in the league — and playing for an average side. That drag over ... he could have said: "Listen Kevin, I'm now going to do this," and I would still fall for it. Everyone did. I recall one game running down the right flank and shouting for the ball — "Robbie, Robbie, Robbie," — but it never arrived. At half-time he approached me, pointed to his eye and said: "Kevin, I see you." Fair enough, I didn't need to call any more, he was aware, such was the quality of his footballing vision. We had a good on-pitch relationship in that 2001/02 season, the guy was a magician, yet for some reason always fluttered over to that right-hand side where I was! Paul Merson is the only person I saw take a football club to new heights, he changed the very fabric of Pompey, but the best footballer I played with was Prosinecki by a country mile.

I was mesmerised, you'd watch this guy in training and matches thinking: "How can you do that? How can you have this ball on a piece of string?" You knew if you made a run — and if it was a good run — he'd produce a perfect ball nine-and-a-half times out of 10. He certainly didn't mix with his teammates, but I found him engaging and we had good conversations in broken English. He was always welcoming and willing to answer your questions. Our training ground was at HMS Collingwood in Fareham, which wasn't the greatest and wasn't the worst, but, from where he came from, it must have been awful — along with playing alongside with probably the worst bunch of players he'd ever come across!

He did whatever he wanted during that first and only season at Fratton Park, yet let's not forget this was Prosinecki coming to help out Milan, not the other way around. Back then in football, not many smoked apart from some on a night out with the drinks flowing, but he'd walk around the training ground puffing away. He didn't care. As for that infamous February 2002 match with Barnsley when he scored a hat-trick to put us 4-2 up, only to eventually draw 4-4 in the final six minutes, afterwards was the first time I saw or heard him angry. We had thrown it away and, in the dressing room, he was saying in broken English: "How can we do this?" That just showed the level he was at — and we were nowhere near him.

That season also saw the arrival of Japanese international goalkeeper Yoshi Kawaguchi. He was a really nice kid, but it was an exercise in publicity which didn't work. He signed for a club-record £1.7m, yet couldn't dislodge Dave Beasant from the team, who was performing well for us. It came to a head at Sheffield Wednesday in November 2001 when the team were shocked to learn that Bes was being shifted out of the team for Yoshi — and everybody knew the decision had come from upstairs. Yoshi was nowhere near Bes in terms of ability. He was a good shot-stopper and had a decent leap but he was not strong enough physically, really thin up and down, and small for a goalkeeper at 5ft 11in. Compare that to the commanding 6ft 4in Beasant, with his massive shoulders and intimidating presence in the box. In fairness, it must have been really, really difficult for Yoshi coming over here, not speaking the language, and being signed to sell football shirts rather than based on his ability.

With Bes in goal, we had conceded twice in four matches heading into Hillsborough, yet there were rumblings and changing-room chat that he was being dropped on the say-so of Milan Mandaric. For any manager, when that happens you know the writing's on the wall. You either stick to your guns and go against the wishes from upstairs, therefore getting the sack — or do as instructed. I don't know what the situation was, so cannot comment, but it must have been difficult. Yoshi played that match and conceded 26 seconds into his debut through Simon Donnelly's goal, although we went on to win 3-2, with Crouch netting twice and Neil Barrett grabbing the other. Yoshi subsequently kept his place for 12 successive matches until a 4-1 defeat to Division Three side Leyton Orient in the FA Cup third round in January 2002.

It wasn't the end of the controversy, though, and, following a 5-0 defeat at West Bromwich Albion, Mandaric announced the players wouldn't be paid for February. As Pompey's PFA rep, I organised a meeting with Milan, which was also attended by my teammate Shaun Derry, chief executive Peter Storrie and the PFA. We ended up receiving our pay as normal at the end of that month. It was crazy but I loved Milan. He was such a character and you could chat to him, while you have to admire what he did for the club by eventually leading it into the Premier League.

Rix was sacked in March 2002, which wasn't a surprise to anyone. We all knew what was going to happen, despite Harry Redknapp repeatedly saying he didn't want the job. For me, it was always a case of when he became Pompey manager, not if. Harry arrived in June 2001 as director of football and you asked yourself: "Why is he coming here?" It seemed Milan was waiting for the right time — and it eventually came around. I felt sorry for Graham, yet once the Yoshi thing happened it was game over. I still speak to Rixy — he's a very, very good coach, up there with the best I came across — a good guy and, most of all, an honest man. I don't believe he was best suited as a manager, but very good coaches tend to want to be the boss at some stage.

With Harry appointed as manager on a three-year deal, I started his first match, a 2-0 defeat at Preston North End, as he began to assess which players had Fratton Park futures over the season's final five games. What followed was a huge turnaround of players. I recall being on holiday and reading how Pompey had signed this person and that person and thinking: "My word. I'm not going to get into this team. No chance." I saw the calibre of player being brought in and knew I had to do something different to ensure I wasn't left behind. I didn't even make the opening four squads in the 2002/03 promotion season and it was up to me to change that, so I did more running, worked harder in the gym. There was no way I'd be getting tossed away.

If I wanted to work on my fitness, I'd mark Steve Stone or Matt Taylor in training because I knew they would run up and down all day. If I wanted to learn defensively, I'd stand with Paul Merson or Svetoslav Todorov and try to stop them. If I wanted to learn about operating as a striker, I'd play against Linvoy and Arjan De Zeeuw. I was going to sink or swim. Sure enough, through sheer hard work and determination, I managed to become part of what Harry achieved at Pompey.

Having said that, during the summer of 2002, he never indicated he wanted me to go. Whether Harry was trying to orchestrate it in the background, I genuinely don't know, but what he probably discovered was that I'd never let him down and gave everything — the type of players you need in your side. Football is a wheel and we all add different cogs, different people do different things. I have no issue carrying out somebody else's running, there were times at Fratton Park when I was chasing up and down the pitch and not getting a touch of the ball during the opening 15 minutes, but I knew it would eventually arrive and then it was up to me to do my bit.

Redknapp's first summer would also signal a reunion with my former Derby boss Jim Smith, who had sold me to Pompey more than two years earlier. He joined as Harry's assistant yet for me it was never an issue, having departed Pride

Park with no ill feelings towards Jim. Our relationship was great at Fratton Park in a campaign which would see us reach the Premier League. Few will actually know that I played almost all that season with a double hernia, which required taking three anti-inflammatories for training and then two for a match. I don't believe it affected my performances as I featured 40 times that year, yet it came to a head against Rotherham United in our penultimate match in April 2003. We won the Division One title that day following a 3-2 success, with three first-half goals delivered by Todorov (two) and Merse, but, after trying to cross the ball down the left, my hernia went. I couldn't move and had to be substituted at half-time, ruling me out of the final fixture at Bradford City before undergoing a summer operation.

We scored an incredible 97 league goals and collected 98 points that season as we reached the Premier League as Division One champions, yet we wouldn't have achieved that without Paul Merson. As mentioned previously, Prosinecki was the best footballer I played with, yet Merse lifted an entire football club through his presence, the way he played, his hunger to be successful — he was a huge catalyst. I found him a joy to be with, funny and approachable, although Merse was the exception to the rule about training the way you play! Sometimes he'd wander about on the training pitch, sometimes he wouldn't train, sometimes he was hot, sometimes he'd swan around, yet, on the Saturday, the switch was flicked and he'd be sensational. It was a special time and, to mark the achievement, I have the Division One medal tattooed on my right arm, along with the dates of our success. Below is the title I subsequently won at Norwich City in 2003/04, having played nine times on loan in their promotion season to reach the Premier League. Both are reminders of difficult moments in my career, but it was well worth it. I achieved two promotions to the Premier League — there are footballers a lot better than me who didn't get anywhere near such success. It's a special, special achievement.

The biggest disappointment of my career was failing to receive Scotland international recognition in that 2002/03 season because I genuinely deserved it. I was playing regularly for a Pompey side top of Division One, and the following season competed in the Premier League, yet there were those in Scotland playing five games and being rewarded with a cap. In March 2003, following a 1-1 draw at Preston, Scotland manager Berti Vogts informed me I was going to be called up for my first squad, yet I was honest with him and admitted my double hernia issues, explaining I may not be able to train, although certainly could play. I added: "But if you feel it will be beneficial to instead select somebody who is 100 per cent, then I totally understand." I could have gone and bluffed it, but I was probably honest at the wrong time — and didn't get the call-up. I finally made it in September 2003, for a Euro 2004 qualification double-header against the Faroe Islands and Germany, but wasn't included in matchday squads for either. The following month, I was among the substitutes at Hampden Park for a 1-0 win over Lithuania. Manchester United's Darren Fletcher came off the bench to score the winner on his second international appearance, but I remained unused and was never again called up. I felt I warranted a cap earlier in my career, especially at Hibs when I scored four goals in five games for the under-21s, but it never arrived.

Still, the summer of 2003 saw the arrivals of the likes of Teddy Sheringham, Dejan Stefanovic, Patrik Berger and Amdy Faye ahead of our maiden Premier League season, with no room for me in Pompey's squad for our 2-1 win over Aston Villa in the August 2003 opener. The following match was at Manchester City, marking the first game at the City of Manchester Stadium, and I was introduced as an 82nd-minute substitute in a 1-1 draw. However, it became abundantly clear I would have to go elsewhere for regular first-team football so, in September 2003, I joined Division One side Norwich on loan, reuniting with my old Blues teammate Crouch. Nigel Worthington was overseeing a promotion challenge and the Canaries eventually became keen to sign me permanently, only for me to suffer a calf injury against Walsall which prematurely ended my loan — and the prospective move fell through.

Back with the Blues, I returned from injury at the turn of the year and featured eight more times in that 2003/04 season, including a 1-0 win over Liverpool in the FA Cup, with Richard Hughes scoring a second-half winner. However, it had reached the stage where I knew I wasn't going to play as much as I needed. I didn't want to leave — I was settled in Whiteley, living up the road from Guy Whittingham — but I had to be realistic. There was a month's loan at Leicester City, only to collect a calf injury on my debut at Rotherham, then, during my absence, Micky Adams resigned, with director of football Dave Bassett becoming caretaker manager and sending me back early.

I had reluctantly accepted that I didn't have a Fratton Park future, but was surprised to see Harry Redknapp quit in November 2004 and a week later his replacement, Velimir Zajec, handed me my first Blues appearance of the 2004/05 season, coming off the bench at half-time in a 3-0 Carling Cup defeat at Watford. He was my fifth Pompey boss — and that was my final outing. In February 2005, with my contract nearing its end, I signed a two-and-a-half year deal at Championship club Stoke, reuniting me with Pulis.

In terms of Pompey managers, there were three proper ones — Pulis, Rix and

Redknapp — and all were different, all teaching me different things. Under Tony I was guaranteed to play, under Rixy I was guaranteed to play because we were that rubbish, while with Harry I was never guaranteed to play, no matter how well I did. Even during that title-winning season, every time we approached a game I couldn't be sure whether I'd be playing. As ever, managers have opinions on players and I just hope that, should anybody mention me to Harry, he credits me as an important part of the side which won the Division One title in the best season of my career at a club I still love.

JOHN McLAUGHLIN

197 games, one goal (July 1979 — May 1984)

Northampton Town 0
Pompey 2 (Davey, Purdie)

Fourth Division, County Ground, Saturday, May 3, 1980

Pompey: Mellor, McLaughlin, Ellis, Davey, Bryant, Brisley, Laidlaw, Brown, Hemmerman, Perrin, Purdie. Sub Not Used: Gregory

Attendance; 10,774

Frank Burrows' words resonated with me. He was a man I trusted, a former teammate, and now he was attempting to recruit me for Fourth Division Pompey in his first managerial job. "I can see this club going places," he assured me. "I want you to be part of its success." As a footballer, that's what you want to hear. Your ambition is to win things, otherwise it's a bit of a waste of a 10 or 15 year playing career. I can never understand those happy to stay at a club which isn't going anywhere. You're in football to win trophies, it's not just about money.

I came through at Colchester United and was right-back in the England side which won the European Under-18 Championship in June 1973 in Italy. We beat East Germany 3-2 in the final after extra-time, with the likes of Tony Morley, David Price, Glenn Keeley and Barry Siddall in our team. Yet, by the age of 24, I had never won anything domestically, so a move to Pompey interested me. As it turned out, my five Fratton Park seasons saw me achieve two promotions, representing the most successful time of my entire playing career. By the summer of 1979, I had spent six years with Swindon Town and, with my contract up, I felt it was time for a change. Under manager Bobby Smith, we'd finished fifth in the Third Division and a new deal was on the table, but the circumstances weren't right and I had rejected it. A few clubs up north were interested, including Chesterfield. Then Frank Burrows phoned and asked whether I fancied coming to Fratton Park — of course I did.

We had previously played together in the same Robins defence for three seasons, me at right-back and him at centre-half. Frank was strong, tough, he didn't take any prisoners and would let you have it if he thought you weren't doing your job. He played in the 1969 League Cup final against Arsenal, partnering his future Pompey assistant Stan Harland in the centre of Swindon's defence in a 3-1 victory. It was obvious he'd become a manager from his attitude on the pitch and the way he liked to organise. After being appointed first-team coach at the County Ground following retirement, you could see his strength on the training pitch. You knew what route Frank's career was heading.

Frank had quit Swindon 18 months earlier to become Pompey's first-team coach, only for the manager Jimmy Dickinson to suffer a heart attack, with Frank appointed permanently in May 1979 following a spell as caretaker. Now he was overhauling the Blues' playing squad and wanted me as his fifth signing of a busy summer, with the chance to join him on the south coast something I couldn't turn down. We were friends and as a teammate I would go out for a drink with him now and again, but obviously when he became my manager that stopped, otherwise that respect goes — and Frank was one for drawing a line which you couldn't cross. Yet he remained a good guy and, years after he left Pompey, whenever he was passing by he'd pop into my Cowplain home to visit. One day he came around and was cut to bits on his legs, with blood pouring down them. He'd just been jogging in the woods and fallen into a ditch. That's Frank! He's the only bloke I know that, in the winter, would have his sleeves rolled up and wear his shorts as high as he could.

I signed for Pompey in July 1979, with a tribunal later setting the fee at £45,000, but I wasn't the only player recruited from Swindon that summer, with Steve Aizlewood following me to the south coast later that month. We called him "Baz" after the Sherlock Holmes actor Basil Rathbone, on account of he was always inquisitive and seemed to know everything that was going on. He was as soft as anything, but definitely not on the pitch. He'd put his head in where it hurts, regularly breaking his nose or having blood dripping down his face, requiring stitches. If there was a tackle to be made, he'd make it, while Frank often declared him the best timer of the ball in the air he'd ever seen. Certainly I never saw a better header of the ball. His neck muscles were incredible. He could hit the halfway line with a headed clearance.

Me and Baz were among five debutants for our first league match of the 1979/80 season, with Archie Styles, Terry Brisley and Alan Rogers also lining up for a team which won 3-0 over Hartlepool. It represented a great start to the campaign, especially for me as I scored along with Steve Bryant and Colin Garwood — and then never got another goal for Pompey again! It was a left-footed shot from the edge of the box which squirmed in a bit of mud, went through a ruck of players and into the bottom corner. Pompey's fans must have thought they'd signed a goalscoring full-back, but it was my only goal in 197 appearances for the club! Not that it particularly bothered me because making a goal was just as good as scoring one, and I was quite happy if I put one into the box and someone got on the end of it. I could hit a good ball and loved whipping a delivery in for Billy Rafferty and Alan Biley, and I remember Rafferty scoring with a flying header from one of my crosses in a 3-0 win at Walsall in September 1982. Having said that, full-backs were full-backs back then and my priority was defending. Aston Villa's John Gidman was the first attacking right-back I knew and he would bomb on like a right winger. I'd never seen that before. Today it has become the norm, but not back then. Full-backs played completely differently. Besides, Baz never used to like me drifting too far away. He wanted security near him!

We maintained our fantastic start to the season and entered the new year second in the Fourth Division — then it all went a bit pear-shaped. We won three out of 14 league games and, amid the poor form, sold our 17-goal leading scorer Colin Garwood to Aldershot in February 1980, which shocked us. 'Gabby' grabbed goals out of nothing and was such a good player in the box. He wasn't as lively outside it, admittedly, but if the ball was delivered into the penalty area, you expected him to get on the end of it. He was such a character as well, a bit of a comedian. He didn't care what clothes he wore and was really good in the dressing room. Losing your top striker would affect any team — and instead we were looking to David Gregory to prove that cutting edge. He had arrived from Bury two months before Gabby's departure and was a different type of player. He was lively, ran the line, a good athlete, very leggy, and had a bit more movement, so you could put it down the flanks, whereas Gabby wanted it in the box.

Despite being frustrated by our bad run, team morale and spirit at the club remained high. We knew something had to come good and we needed to keep doing what we were doing, working hard on the training ground and hope that Saturday went right. We weren't kids, we'd been through it in football and there was undoubtedly a strong mentality — and we won five and drew two our last seven matches to claim the final promotion spot in fourth place.

It was sealed at Northampton Town in May 1980, the last day of the season, with Steve Davey and Ian Purdie scoring in a 2-0 victory. It was one of the greatest games I ever played in — the circumstances, the result, the way we played. It was phenomenal. We headed into that match knowing even a win may not necessarily be enough to go up, as we also required Bradford City to lose at Peterborough United. At the final whistle, we were still awaiting the outcome from London Road, but a roar from the crowd told us what we wanted to hear — Bradford had suffered a 1-0 defeat and we'd been promoted to the Third Division. The dressing room was crazy. Mick Robertson from ITV's *Magpie* was in there to see the lads, then, when we arrived back in Portsmouth, we celebrated with a party in Joe Laidlaw's Waterlooville flat.

Joe was a class act; our skipper, a terrific midfielder, and joint-top scorer with 17 goals. He didn't always do a lot of running but he didn't need to, because he had a good brain, could pick a pass, and possessed fantastic vision. It has to be said that Joe wasn't a great pro in training, he'd turn up late or do a bit of cheating on the sprints by starting his run before the whistle had gone. However, you knew that, come Saturday, he was up for the game and would put in a superb performance. What a character. He liked a drink and a bet, like most pros in those days.

Back in the Third Division for 1980/81, we had new signing Mick Tait in the side and began the season well, winning our opening four league games to top the table, yet we would spend the majority of the campaign falling narrowly short of the three promotion spots. The highlight of the season was a League Cup fourth-round trip to Liverpool in October 1980, when we took 12,500 to Anfield for a Tuesday night game. What an experience. Our fans produced a wonderful ticker-tape reception as we came out to face the likes of Kenny Dalglish and Graeme Souness, which I'll never forget. We actually put in a really good performance, but Bob Paisley's team scored twice in the final 10 minutes to give the scoreline a harsh look at 4-1. Their third goal, scored by David Johnson, was also well offside.

Having finished an encouraging sixth, the 1981/82 season was something of a struggle and we were 15th when Frank Burrows was sacked in March 1982, although rumours that the board were thinking of a change had long reached the dressing room. Just seven weeks earlier, Bobby Campbell had been appointed first-team coach — and you could see what would happen. Maybe it was time for a change and Bobby brought with him a different footballing philosophy which involved playing it out from the back, as opposed to Frank being a bit more direct. Inevitably training also changed, with fresh ideas, which you'd expect from somebody who had previously coached Arsenal and Fulham at higher levels. Now there was more focus on ball work in training, and certainly not as much long-distance running which Frank favoured.

Bob was a decent guy, a fiery character, but honest. Frank would come into the dressing room and probably grab you by the scruff of the neck if you hadn't done something, whereas Bob dished out a rollicking, then it was an arm around you five minutes later. Sometimes, after a disappointing result, Frank would tell us there'd be no staying for a drink and we'd be going straight back on the coach. Our director Jim Sloan, who liked a drink, was known to have been left behind after not making the bus on time — Frank had a bit of a temper! One time Frank nearly got off the coach on the way back home because someone was giving us some stick from a car and he wanted to get at them.

The summer of 1982 brought the arrivals of Neil Webb and Alan Biley ahead of a season which would see us claim the Third Division title. Webb was very skilful, good with the ball at his feet and liked running at players. You could see him developing into a much better player. It was his trickery, he was quite deceptive, and could whip the ball in, later representing Nottingham Forest, Manchester United and England. Biley was special, a phenomenal player, and better than our level. I was surprised he never made it at Everton, where we had signed him from. What a player he was; strong on the ball and brave as well. The fans loved him and he loved that adulation, making him a better player. His partnership with Billy Rafferty totalled 45 goals in that 1982/83 season, with Billy good in the air and able to hold the ball up and creating a very good striking double act. It was a fantastic team.

We clinched promotion in May 1983 with a 2-0 victory over Southend United, with Kevin Dillon and Biley the scorers. I had recently returned from an Achilles problem and Bobby wanted me to play, so I had five or six cortisone injections to get me on to the pitch before I had to come off in the 60th minute because I couldn't run any more. Following that victory, there were still two more matches to clinch the title — and I was ruled out for both through my injury. The Achilles was shot to bits and also impacted upon my pre-season that summer before clearing up. Peter Ellis replaced me at right-back against Walsall and then for the title decider at Plymouth Argyle, which I watched from our bench. The Pompey fans were unbelievable that day, with 9,000 of them packed into Home Park as we won 1-0 through Biley's 26th goal of the season.

It was great to reach the Second Division as champions but, for me, promotion on the final day of the 1979/80 season was more special. With Pompey having plummeted so far down the Football League, being part of helping it rise again meant more — especially in a match we needed to win on the last day. I know we had to beat Southend three years later to secure promotion, which was a fantastic feeling, but Northampton was the start of the climb. Looking back, Campbell's team was the more talented, but then you're talking about different divisions. Each one is slightly better, so naturally you play more football in the Third Division than the Fourth Division. Of course, for the second promotion in 1982/83, we also had players of the calibre of Biley, Webb and Dillon in our side.

Bobby Campbell signed a new strike partner for Alan Biley for our return to the Second Division — with Mark Hateley arriving from Coventry City in May 1983. I hadn't heard a lot about him before he arrived at Fratton Park, but what a terrific player he turned out to be. He was quick, good with the ball at his feet and excellent in the air. Hateley also had that aura about him, like all players with that extra something, and, 12 months later, I was at home watching him on television scoring for England against Brazil.

Ahead of the final match of the 1983/84 season, Campbell was sacked, with reserve-team manager Alan Ball stepping up as caretaker for the last game against Swansea. I retained my place as we won 5-0 at Fratton Park, which included an Alan Biley hat-trick, and, unsurprisingly, Bally was appointed permanently that summer. We'd finished 16th in our first season back in the Second Division, which I didn't think was too bad. There were some good results and we were never threatened with relegation, so you would think Bobby deserved another year — so the decision to dismiss him was a bit of a shock, although the players had an idea it was going to happen. Still, he had gone — and that match would also mark the end of my own Pompey career.

Within days of the season concluding, Alan Ball told me I wasn't part of his plans. I was released along with Steve Aizlewood, Peter Ellis, Ernie Howe, Steve Berry and Trevor Inch. When you get the call to visit the manager's office at that time of year, you have a feeling of what's coming. Had they offered another season, I would have happily played on, even if I may have been regarded as a squad player at the very least, so it came as a bit of a shock. I thought I was worth an extra 12 months and I couldn't have been that bad a player to feature in 197 games over five seasons, winning two promotions. It was very disappointing that Bally didn't fancy me but it's a game of opinions and these things happen.

My family love the area and I wanted to stay here. It's fantastic being near the coast so when Bournemouth came in with a two-year deal under Harry Redknapp, that seemed ideal. I took part in pre-season, we went on a tour to Germany, and I was scheduled to play in a friendly against Fulham — but just didn't fancy it. I phoned Harry and told him: "I'm not coming, I'm going to pack up football." So I did.

I was aged 29 and could have played on for another four or five years because I was always fit — but I no longer wanted to. Being shown the door at Pompey hit me hard and instead I made a life-changing decision. It felt right to retire. Sometimes you ask yourself whether you've made the right call, especially when getting up at 5am for a job driving a lorry dropping off cavity wall insulation for Shell. I also played part-time for Fareham Town, where Richie Reynolds was manager, before getting fed up with it and leaving after a few months. I enjoyed some of it, but when you've played in the Football League for such a long time, naturally the standard's totally different.

To be fair, the decision to leave football worked out for me and I spent 25 years working as a French polisher. I enrolled on a six-week night school course in French polishing and cabinet making at Havant College and, after graduating, went through the Yellow Pages and rang five French polishers. The last — Geoff Pearce in Middleton — was interested, and that's where my second career began. We worked at the homes of Eric Clapton, Roman Abramovich, Andrew Lloyd Webber and Dire Straits' Mark Knopfler, while I was polishing in the kitchen of Elton John's Windsor home while he was practising in the lounge ahead of his Live Aid performance later that day in July 1985.

That was my second career. In my first, it was fantastic to play a role in a big club like Pompey twice achieving success, going down as part of their history. You want to win things in football — and, thanks to my time at Fratton Park, I managed to do that.

JAMAL LOWE

119 games, 29 goals (January 2017 — August 2019)

Pompey 2 (Thompson, Lowe)
Sunderland 2 (McGeady 2)
Pompey win 5-4 on penalties

Checkatrade Trophy final, Wembley, Sunday, March 31, 2019

Pompey: MacGillivray, Thompson, Burgess, Clarke, Brown, Naylor, Close (113 mins, Walkes), Lowe, Pitman, Curtis (56 mins, Evans), Bogle (69 mins, Hawkins). Subs not used: Bass, Haunstrup, May, Vaughan.

Attendance; 85,021

I was born in Harrow, just 15 minutes away from Wembley, but the 2019 Checkatrade Trophy final was my first visit to the national stadium. I have this thing where I refuse to go to any stadium unless I play there, or my career has finished. I want the first occasion to be: "Wow, I'm playing here." I don't want to see Ed Sheeran at Wembley; I'll wait until he's performing at The O2. I am not going to see Beyonce at the Tottenham Hotspur Stadium; I'll watch her somewhere else. The first visit will be through my own football experience, rather than being a spectator. Growing up, I'd visit Wembley Market all the time and from Barnet's training ground you can see the Wembley arch. It's local, but I vowed never to set foot there until I was playing. I wanted it as my football memory — and what a memory it became.

On that day against Sunderland the pitch was unreal, the stadium was unreal, the atmosphere was unreal. And what a roller-coaster of a match. I scored the best goal of my career by a country mile and, for a brief period, believed it would be the winner. Still, I'm glad the game went to penalties — it means I've now scored a penalty at Wembley too!

With the match having entered extra-time, on 114 minutes Matt Clarke produced a through-ball. I controlled it with my right foot at first, took a couple of touches and, after noticing where the goalkeeper was, it was clear just one thing was open to me — chipping him. Jon McLaughlan had come off his line, yet I couldn't dribble around him because there were defenders nearby, while there wasn't the space to curl a shot past him. So my only option was to get it over him from the edge of the box. It was like Notts County in that promotion game — I looked at the 'keeper, saw the chip was on, and hoped for the best.

At one point I thought it was going to land on the roof of the net and a millimetre higher, it would hit the crossbar and bounce out of play. Yet it dropped. Everything was in slow-motion and there wasn't a sound in the stadium as everyone held their breath. Nobody moved. Time stood still as 85,021 supporters waited to see where the shot ended up — it was incredibly dramatic and unreal. It is the best goal and the best atmosphere I have ever played in to this very day.

I had burst into Barnet's first-team six-and-a-half years earlier as an 18-year-old and I thought that was it, that I'd cracked it. Having started a few League Two games, within the club I was being talked about as the star boy, taking all the corners and free-kicks. In my mind, I was a big thing. A couple more games — or maybe waiting until the end of the season — and I could get a move. Then it all collapsed. When you're released, like I was by Barnet in January 2015, it's tough. If you aren't ready for the real world then you can be in real trouble, because football's such a bubble. Luckily for me, I was aged 20 when let go, still quite early in my life and with every chance to bounce back. Yet it was still sink or swim.

Over a four-year period I played for Barnet, Hayes & Yeading, Boreham Wood, Hitchin Town, St Albans City (twice), Farnborough and Hemel Hempstead Town (twice). However, by the 2016/17 season, my performances at Hampton & Richmond were beginning to attract interest, having struck up a really good understanding with Nicke Kabamba. It was our second campaign together, having previously won the Ryman League Premier Division title and scored 34 times between us. Nicke was up front, while I operated as the 10 or on the left wing, and steadily more and more scouts began to turn up for our National League South matches.

At the time I worked as a football coach at Coombe Hill Junior School in New Malden, taking the after-school club from 3.30-4.30pm. It was for a company called Love The Ball and, when those sessions became booked up with more kids wanting to attend, I then also set up a lunchtime class. Next I was asked to take all the school's PE sessions! More hours meant more money and I no longer had to get there at 7.30am, do nothing until the lunchtime session at 12 noon and then sit around waiting for 3pm for the after-school class. It worked well. At the same time, I coached Metropolitan Police's under-15s one evening and the under-nines on Sundays. I spent two years at Coombe Hill, then quit in June 2016 to focus on being a personal trainer. I was going full out. With the little money I'd saved, I joined a gym and still owned the coaching equipment I had bought for my school job.

My ambition was to be like Jamie 'Velocity' Reynolds, a personal trainer with Nike whose one-to-one training sessions with Marcus Rashford, Jack Grealish and Cristiano Ronaldo were well respected. The idea was to start off with non-league footballers and work my way up. I had balls, cones, hurdles and ladders and we trained at West Harrow Park, near my mum's house. There was also Greenford Recreation Ground, where we'd climb over the locked gates to train. Initially Nicke Kabamba came along with a few boys from Conference South, then more joined in and suddenly I was thinking: "Do you know what? This could actually be a thing." Then I had to pack it all in — Paul Cook and Pompey came along and saved the day!

My performances with Hampton & Richmond had prompted the likes of Stevenage, Gillingham, Barrow and Eastleigh to make approaches to sign me, yet none of those clubs were as big as Pompey. The Blues were offering the lowest wage of them all, with Eastleigh tabling the best deal — but moving to Fratton Park was a no-brainer. With the transfer window not until January 1, I signed a pre-contract agreement in October 2016 for an undisclosed fee. It meant I remained with the Beavers until the window opened, although I initially trained with the Blues for two days to meet everyone, staying at the Royal Beach Hotel. Of course, I now had a different bit of pressure to contend with, in terms of wanting to perform during my remaining time with Hampton & Richmond and not giving the impression I was sacking it off before heading back to the Football League. Thankfully I scored five goals in my final nine matches, finishing with 23 in 31 appearances by that stage of the season.

Following a three-and-a-half year absence from the Football League, a period in which I represented nine non-league clubs, I was back at the age of 22. Joining Pompey at the same time was my Hampton & Richmond teammate Nicke Kabamba, fresh from 25 goals that season. That was a big help, having someone I knew who I could chat to and, without doubt, enabled me to settle. Funnily enough, I arrived at Pompey as a left winger and then they put me on the right, despite not playing there since the age of 15! I had been practising cutting in and shooting on my right, which was my natural foot. Now I needed to figure out how to do it on the opposite flank and relying more on my left foot, which worked out.

At one point in my early Pompey days, I was in Fratton's Tesco Extra shopping with my girlfriend Holly when the back-page headline in the *Portsmouth News* caught my attention. It read 'Lowe Price' and was an interview with Hampton chairman Steve McPherson claiming I would become a million-pound player. "Oh my days," I thought, and bought four copies. We were buzzing, so happy with that story, this was crazy, as if I would ever be worth £1m. We filmed a video of me holding up the paper inside the supermarket and sent it to all my family, while keeping a copy of the newspaper for myself.

Having been handed this second Football League opportunity, there was no way on earth I was letting it go. Had I subsequently proven not to be up to scratch, people would have labelled me a non-league player not good enough to step up — a stigma I desperately didn't want. I needed to be the fittest and strongest at Pompey. With Roko at my disposal, the best gym I had ever seen, I would arrive early before training every day to work on fitness. Then after training, I focused on extra finishing on the grass before going home. Rinse and repeat. My non-league routine involved training every Tuesday and Thursday evening — and now I was a full-time professional footballer and my body was challenged with coping with much-increased demands.

As a consequence, every day me and Matt Clarke would turn up an hour before training to work in the gym. We maybe didn't carry out the exact same fitness work, but we'd be there together, before eating breakfast with the rest of the lads and taking part in training. It's a routine I've maintained to this day and I feel it makes me a better player. It's about doing things right, following the correct preparation. In my head, I'm an hour ahead of everyone else coming in for training. Whether that is true or not, I don't know, but that's how I feel.

My Pompey debut was a half-time introduction off the bench for Gaz Evans in a 2-1 win over Leyton Orient in January 2017, lifting us into fourth in League Two. However, it took until my 10th appearance to register my maiden Pompey goal — and a first in the Football League. The moment arrived in a 3-1 victory over Yeovil Town, scoring from a tight angle after cutting in from the right — and, to top it off, it arrived in front of the Fratton End.

Michael Doyle was so tough on me during those early months. I couldn't believe it. If ever I misplaced a pass, he was onto me. On one occasion, he produced a poor pass in training and blamed me for where he passed it! He was this Roy Keane figure; strong, loud, hard-tackling. Considering who he was, I never said anything back and got on with it. Off the pitch, though, he was lovely. Doyler had an aura about him and when I joined and entered the canteen in those early days, I was scared to sit near him. Gary Roberts could be at his table, Carl Baker and Gaz Evans as well, but I wouldn't. I was a little intimidated. He was okay to me in games but in training, should you miss a chance, mess about or not track your runner, he'd be straight on to you. That was his job, I guess, because he was the captain, extremely vocal and focused on upholding standards. I soon realised his approach was mainly for my own good and, even though we were together for just half a season, I learnt so much. Mind you, when I scored my second goal at Notts County to help us win promotion, during the celebrations he punched me in the stomach! Not a massive punch, just a little dig, but that's just how he was, making sure you were on your toes the whole time. You couldn't get away with being big time around Michael Doyle because he'd bring you straight back down — even while celebrating a goal which won promotion.

We headed to Meadow Lane in April 2017 knowing that victory, plus results elsewhere, could seal a return to League One with three games to spare. Christian Burgess is one of the most relaxed people ever and, while some people were in the zone ahead of the match, on the journey there he was chilling and we were joking around with him. "It's a big game for you today, Burge mate," some of us were telling him. He replied: "I've played bigger games in my back garden!" For our third successive fixture, I was named on the bench, yet, in my head, I was imagining coming on to score the winner. As it turned out, that's precisely what happened.

It was a perfect start, taking a 14th-minute lead through Gaz Evans' penalty after Kal Naismith had been fouled by Richard Duffy. Gaz struck his spot-kicks in the same place every time and no goalkeeper ever realised, it was incredible. Goalies didn't get near any of them either and it never made any sense. They were unsavable. However, early in the second half Jorge Grant equalised to make it 1-1 and, with the scores remaining level in the 69th minute, I was introduced for Gary Roberts. Cookie told me to get the winner — he always said stuff like that. This was my chance, with my mum and dad also in the crowd.

I had been on the pitch for eight minutes when Naismith slipped the ball to me from the left and, from the edge of the box, I took two touches before striking a right-footed shot which took an awkward bounce in front of the keeper and found the net to make it 2-1. I hadn't hit the ball cleanly, while Adam Collin probably should have done better, to be honest, but let's give him the benefit of the doubt because the bounce killed him. I'm certainly not complaining.

Then, in the 90th minute, Kyle Bennett won a free-kick just inside Notts County's half which Michael Doyle took quickly, putting me clean through. The routine hadn't been planned and it was completely off the cuff. I never even thought he was going to play it as we should have been wasting time. Why risk it? Yet I'd noticed their line was very high and no-one was marking me, so I made the run and Doyler played me in. There was a little glance at the linesman, I was onside, then the goalkeeper began to come out — he's getting dinked! It was the maddest commentary line ever from *Express FM's* Niall McCaughan: "Nonchalant, fantastic, brilliant. Yes, I've watched it back quite a few times on YouTube! That chip was instinctive. I would put myself in that position as many times as possible in training so, should it come to it, it was natural. Of my two goals that day, that second was my favourite as we won 3-1 to earn automatic promotion. Funnily enough, I should have been on the right wing, but both goals arrived from the left as I naturally gravitated over there.

The team coach took us back to Fratton Park that evening, where we celebrated with Pompey's supporters, before the team headed off to Drift, in Palmerston Road, to carry on the festivities. Having only been at the club four months I was a bit uncomfortable drinking in front of the manager, so I had one Malibu and Coke all night. Knowing Cookie as I do now, he wouldn't have cared how much I drank whatsoever — but if I wanted to play the following week against Cambridge United, so I felt it best not to get plastered within sight! It was a fantastic feeling walking back to my Edgeware Road home in Southsea in the early hours of the morning. I lived two minutes from Fratton Park and initially walked to matches, but in the end it became a 45-minute trip as I was stopping and chatting to everyone when they recognised me, so I drove in the end.

After also winning our next two matches, we entered the final game against

Cheltenham Town in third position, but still with a chance of taking the title. I never thought we could do it and it didn't even occur to me. These were just end-of-season happy vibes, there was no pressure. We'd done the hard bit and earned promotion — so let's go and have fun. Once again I was on the bench and replaced Carl Baker in the 60th minute as we ended up running out 6-1 winners, with my fourth Blues goal putting us 4-0 up. During the game, there were random cheers going off among the crowd when nothing was happening on the pitch, indicating results were going our way elsewhere. Sure enough, we were crowned League Two champions. Incredible.

I had no idea Cookie and Leam Richardson would be walking out on Pompey for Wigan Athletic after winning the title, yet I have nothing but good things to say about the pair of them. During the early weeks of my time at Fratton Park, Cookie called me into his office to tell me how well I was training, before adding: "If you don't play in the Championship, you've only got yourself to blame." I will never forget those words until the day I die. That's all I needed to hear, the belief he had in me. What an absolute legend. I was a 22-year-old with a bit of impostor syndrome, chucked into this well-oiled machine winning most weeks — and the manager really believed in me, which meant everything. Then, just 26 days after becoming League Two champions, the players received a text from Leam saying they were both leaving. That was it, and it was a real shock.

The new manager was Kenny Jackett who, along with his assistant Joe Gallen, made me a better player. Their constant message centred on how I may score three times a season from outside the box if I was lucky, yet the majority of goals are netted from inside the penalty area — so I had to find a way to get in there. I remember watching a YouTube video of Raheem Sterling's Manchester City clips, sprinting into the box and scoring tap-ins. The same for Leroy Sane. The ball doesn't always arrive, but you still need to make that run, as fast as you can, driving into that box so, should it drop, you'd be there. I would score 25 goals over the next two seasons, usually from the right wing and all from open play, with not a single penalty.

I actually started the opening League One match of Kenny's reign on the bench for the visit of Rochdale in August 2017, with Gareth Evans on the right wing and Carl Baker, who had previously played there under Paul Cook, asked to perform in the centre of midfield. I was introduced in the 39th minute for the injured Tareiq Holmes-Dennis, although I didn't finish the match after the only red card of my career. It was harsh, I came on eager to impress and was a little high on Jamie Allen as we both went in on a loose ball. I thought it warranted a booking, but instead I was banned for three matches.

My first league start under the new boss was a 1-1 draw at Wigan, partnering Brett Pitman up front, then the following match I found myself at right wing-back against Rotherham United in a televised game at Fratton Park. It was an awful game, we lost 1-0, and I was used in that position just once more that season, subsequently spending the remainder of the campaign on the right wing. What really annoyed me about that Rotherham defeat was missing a free header on the six-yard box, planting it over the bar with pretty much an open goal in front of me. During the next few weeks at the training ground, I had our goalkeeping coach John Keeley pinging balls hard into the box which I attempted to head into an empty net. I must have headed about 500 footballs in a week, my teeth were aching! My heading was unacceptable. I wondered how I could be so bad at it? However, all that work paid off three matches later as I scored twice in a 4-1 win against Fleetwood Town — and my first was a far-post header from Dion Donohue's right-wing corner. Mind you, I've probably scored just six headers in my whole career!

By April 2018, we were placed ninth for the Fratton Park return of Paul Cook, with his Wigan side sitting top of League One on their way to the title — and what a great night that was. The players built up that game high, so high. I don't even know why, because it wasn't like he left us on bad terms and criticised our abilities. Yet the way we approached that was as though it was the biggest game of our season, as if we were playing Southampton. Why have we a rivalry with Wigan, for starters, and why have we a rivalry with the old manager who got us promoted to this league? We won 2-1, with me scoring the second, and the atmosphere was fantastic, although I never saw my former manager after the game. The team's running stats were the highest you could get, such was the energy we put into it, but after that we didn't win for five games, losing three of them. It was like a World Cup final for us. Everybody put all their energy, heart and soul into it, then afterwards it died away. I can't actually explain why we treated that Wigan match in that manner.

We finished our first campaign back in League One with a 2-0 victory over Peterborough United, although Brett Pitman took a goal off me so he could reach his 25th for the season. I fired in an angled shot in the first half which he poked in at the far post, but it had already gone in. He'd helped it into the net once it was over the line. Pitts was trying to bully that referee all game and ended up being awarded it. Good for him, he was on a big bonus if he hit 25! I'm saying it's mine, he will say it's his. We'll let the people decide — but to this day it's my goal. I remember winning 2-0 at Shrewsbury Town in March 2019 when Ben Close's first-half shot skimmed off my toe and went in, completely accidentally, I was actually trying to get out of the way! Closey was celebrating and I was thinking: "That's actually my goal!" But I honestly didn't care too much. I didn't want to steal it like that, I'd rather score where it's clear and definitely your goal. Still, that win over Peterborough ensured we finished eighth, five points adrift of the play-offs, and, with 50 appearances and eight goals, I had been heavily involved.

Kenny's second season in charge was 2018/19 and we should have gone up automatically. Although our aim was always the play-offs, we were almost over-achieving by leading the table for so long. Before the campaign, nobody in our dressing room was expecting the top-two and it was certainly never a case of: "Let's win the league and smash everybody." The play-offs were the more realistic route. Considering we were top for so long, ultimately it seemed like a failure, but that was never the target. We raised the bar and made it feel more of a downfall — but then should have won the play-offs.

We went from six points clear with a game in hand on second-placed Luton in December to finishing fourth, yet it's hard to say whether we would have gone up should Ben Thompson have stayed. I don't want to pin it on his return to Millwall, but you cannot argue he was a really good player and had something different which we never replaced. Ben possessed a lot of energy, a lot of quality, and he could dribble through midfield, get us up the pitch and start attacks in a way no other midfielder in our squad could, so he was a big miss. I guess Andy Cannon was a replacement because he was similar to Ben and I could see how that worked, but he just wasn't fit during the second half of that season, and neither was Bryn Morris.

In March 2019, we headed to Wembley for the Checkatrade Trophy final, a fixture which would attract a crowd of 85,021 — the biggest in the competition's history. Aiden McGeady was on fire in the first half, we couldn't live with him, and he scored with a free-kick to leave us trailing 1-0 at half-time. Ronan Curtis started the match, despite having just come back from surgery to save his finger and barely training, which was a bad decision, in all honesty. After three weeks on the sidelines, his legs could never have played 90 minutes and then extra-time. It was impossible. It would have been better to instead come off the bench for 20 minutes. Gareth Evans replaced him in the second half and changed the game, providing the cross from the left which was headed home by Nathan Thompson at the far post for an 82nd-minute equaliser.

I shared a hotel room with Tom Naylor the night before the final and the conversation had turned to how each of us would celebrate should we score against Sunderland. Nayls was going to do something stupid. I'm not going to say what was planned but there's no way he would have done it, let's put it that way. As for me, my plan was to take off my shirt and run away — which he described as boring! Even if I had a dance routine planned, I wouldn't have been able to perform it after that goal in first-half stoppage time, because the emotion was too high. I wasn't thinking; all I could do was remove my shirt and run as fast as I was able. It was an entirely natural reaction. Referee Dean Whitestone booked me for the celebration, but I didn't care.

Then, with one minute remaining, McGeady grabbed his second of the game to make it 2-2 and send it into a penalty shoot-out. What followed was my first and last spot-kick for Pompey — and thankfully I scored. In that situation, they don't really ask who fancies it; you put yourself forward. It's about who's confident at that precise moment, then you decide the order. In the week leading to the final, we had a session in training practising penalties, with some people clearly nervous taking them. So imagine what they were going to be like at Wembley. The usual suspects volunteered — Gaz Evans, Brett Pitman and Lee Brown — but one or two weren't confident in that situation. Christian Burgess said he'd take one and would have been fine but Matt Clarke was a nervous wreck when taking penalties. You could see in training that he really wasn't comfortable, despite being such a good player. Nathan Thompson didn't want one, while Ben Close and Ronan Curtis had been substituted so couldn't be considered.

Craig MacGillivray was a serious goalkeeper — I was surprised Pompey let him go on a free transfer two years later — and he saved Lee Cattermole's penalty, which meant Oli Hawkins had the fifth spot-kick to win us the Checkatrade Trophy — and I fancied him to score. Some two weeks earlier, Sky Sports' *Soccer AM* had been at the training ground filming their 'You Know the Drill' segment with Jimmy Bullard, which included Oli and myself taking spot-kicks in competition with each other. He missed all four, putting them over the bar. It was hilarious but, on the day, I knew he'd score. This was his time.

I managed to hit goalscoring form during the league run-in, netting in six of our last 11 matches, including at Wembley, as we faced Peterborough in our penultimate game. Positioned third with two fixtures remaining — both at Fratton Park — and a game in hand on Luton Town and Barnsley at the top, trailing both by four points, there was still an outside chance we could win automatic promotion.

Now Brett Pitman was one of the best finishers I've ever played with. He was ruthless, selfish, and hungry, which are good characteristics for any striker. I remember against Oxford United in March 2018, Nathan Thompson put me through down the right and I could have squared it to him, but instead attempted to go around the goalkeeper to score myself. Unfortunately I was forced a bit too far from goal, so had to pass to him from the byline — and he tapped home from two yards for a 3-0 victory. He later jokingly called me greedy, but he would have done exactly the same!

So Peterborough visited the south coast in April 2019 in a must-win game and it was 2-2 heading into the 73rd minute, when Brett broke down the right and, with just their keeper Aaron Chapman to beat, he elected to square a pass to Viv Solomon-Otabor, who scored from an offside position. Ivan Toney got their winner two minutes later and that was the end of automatic promotion. Brett either had to be selfish in that position or Viv needed to hold his run and I certainly don't know why he chose that particular moment to start passing. Just finish it, that's what he does! Brett was trying to do the safe thing, yet it was no time to be safe. Take responsibility on your shoulders — and if I was him, I was definitely shooting.

I was rested for the final match against Accrington Stanley, with a 1-1 draw securing us fourth place and a League One play-off semi-final game against Sunderland. The whole winning the league thing had clouded our vision a bit and the reality was a slap in the face. It was tough to stomach, but I still felt the play-offs were our route to take — and we didn't capitalise on that.

I haven't got a bad word to say about Kenny Jackett as he always played me — apart from the second leg of that Sunderland semi-final. Trailing 1-0 for the decisive fixture at Fratton Park in May 2019, he dropped me, Ronan Curtis and Anton Walkes from the starting line-up, bringing in the fit-again pair Pitman and Lee Brown, while Solomon-Otabor was also recalled. I was our 17-goal top scorer and had started all but two of our league games that season — but I was left out of such a huge match. It didn't make sense. I don't know why I was dropped, no-one ever explained it to me. I was informed the previous day and none of my teammates could believe it. I couldn't believe it. I'd played 54 games in 2018/19 by that point and I know tiredness has been mentioned by others as a potential reason, but you can't be tired for a play-off semi-final second leg. That's not the day to be tired, and I was absolutely fine. Unless Kenny is asked, we will never get the answer because he didn't tell me. I replaced Solomon-Otabor in the 53rd minute, but the game finished goalless and we lost 1-0 on aggregate. Ronan didn't even get on, despite Kenny still having one more substitution left, and he kicked off afterwards.

It was a double whammy. Not only were our promotion hopes destroyed, it also turned out to be my final Pompey appearance — not that I knew that at the time. That summer, after 119 games and 29 goals, I moved to Wigan, although

I would have stayed at Fratton Park had we reached the Championship, 100 per cent. Pompey is one of my favourite clubs — if not the favourite — I've played for. It's all ifs and buts and never happened, of course, but had we achieved promotion I would have remained. Honestly. The idea of leaving the Blues only truly entered my head once the season had finished. That summer, Wigan put in their first offer and I decided it was time to leave. This was an opportunity to reunite with Cookie and play in the Championship. It felt right and I was ready to step up a level to test myself, although my departure became a little more difficult than it needed to have been.

Unfortunately, that Havant & Waterlooville teamsheet misunderstanding painted me as something I'm not, portraying me as the type of person I've always fought to avoid being perceived as. I am not big time, I didn't throw my toys out of the pram, I didn't sack off the game because I was sulking — yet that completely false impression was created through my absence from that Westleigh Park pre-season friendly in July 2019. The actual truth is that 24 hours earlier at the Portmarnock Hotel in Dublin, on the final day of our pre-season tour, Kenny sat me down and suggested: "Perhaps it's best you don't play. The transfer's getting close and you probably don't want to feature in case you get injured." It hadn't really crossed my mind and I would have played — this was entirely his idea. My response was: "Sure, maybe it's a good idea." I was close to Anton Walkes and Louis Dennis, we were in a WhatsApp group together, so I messaged that I'd no longer be playing and explained why, before telling them to do their best.

Instead I spent Saturday afternoon chilling out at my Clanfield home, until my phone began blowing up. It turned out my name had been accidentally included on Pompey's official teamsheet and submitted to the referee. In the fans' eyes, I hadn't turned up, and now I was receiving abusive tweets demanding to know where I was. What was going on? I'm told Joe Gallen was responsible for submitting the teamsheet at that time rather than the kitman, Kev McCormack, who previously carried out the duty. Surely people need to talk about who's actually in the team? Whatever the reason, somebody's mistake made this spiral into something it didn't need to be. I'd been made to look like the bad guy — yet wasn't even meant to be playing. When I reflect on my time at Pompey, there were plenty of good memories, memorable matches, fantastic atmospheres, brilliant teammates, promotion and two trophies. Yet, what taints all of that, for me, is a mistake over a teamsheet.

Matters escalated with our chief executive Mark Catlin getting involved. The way he treated me was awful, trying to force me into staying, slapping a £3m valuation on me and insisting Pompey would reject every bid. I was told: "I would love to watch you rot in the stands." There was another 12 months remaining on my Fratton Park deal and he was behaving like that, which was horrible. I don't know why he was behaving like that. I completely understand that he wanted the best business for the football club and the biggest transfer fee possible, but it became personal. Me sitting in the stands and rotting, and him loving to see that, has nothing to do with finances or what's best for the club.

I didn't do anything nasty, he just made it nasty for no reason. I had done nothing but work hard since the day I arrived, I was far from a bad egg, yet Catlin flipped it into something acrimonious, which was upsetting at the time. I was eyeing a move to the Championship, a level I never thought I would reach. I should have been celebrating, proud of such an achievement, but he turned it sour. As soon as I was aware of Wigan's interest, that was the club I wanted to join, but what made it drag on was the whole Paul Cook factor. Bad vibes remained following his departure as manager two years earlier and Pompey didn't want it to be a smooth transition, with me caught in the middle.

Their relationship with Cook wasn't my problem, not my issue, yet I was in the crossfire. Initially they didn't want to sell to Cookie, so made it as difficult as possible. Had it been another club they were selling me to, it would have been done for cheaper, but with it being Wigan, they decided to go as hard as possible. That's business and I have no problem with business, except it became personal. Training-wise, the ongoing situation didn't affect me because, whether staying or leaving, I needed to be fit. People were advising me to sack off training to force the move, but that's not me and I never wanted that perception. Players at the club, outside the club, agents, they were all telling me the same thing — no chance. Word gets about and I didn't want a bad reputation, so I continued to be at the front of all the running, working hard. Anyone in Pompey's squad at the time can tell you that was the truth.

There were people in the Pompey hierarchy who sucked it all out of me and I was devastated. Some nights I was receiving 10 phone calls from the club, and I sat there thinking: "Is this even worth it? Stop calling me, stop talking at me." I was inexperienced, aged 24, and these older people were shouting the odds, making me feel as if I was the bad guy — and it was hard to take. It was phone call after phone call and I'd get off them and would be upset. Holly could hear the conversations and all these awkward chats with people at the club, it wasn't really my thing. I would rather no-one talked to me, and just let me know when the transfer was completed. Every time I stepped on to the pitch, I had given absolutely everything — and now this.

I must admit, I was a shadow of myself in the pre-season friendly at Stevenage.

Normally I'm energetic, happy, smiling, just buzzing to be there, but they took it out of me. They made me question everything. Do I still want to be here? What have I done to deserve it? Matt Clarke joined Brighton & Hove Albion in June 2019, that same summer, and the transfer was smooth. It was handled well and the perception of his departure was: all the best for the future, we love you, etc, etc. Yet I was viewed as the guy who threw his toys out of the pram, behaving big time, the guy who hasn't shown up for friendlies. How had it come to this? Me and Clarkey had done exactly the same thing — we both worked hard, we both deserved the chance to step up from League One — but I was the one trying to steal a move to the Championship. Send him off with a bouquet of flowers, but make me out to be the villain.

My final Pompey outing was in a behind-closed-doors friendly at Brighton's training ground, although I was taken off by Kenny in the first half when the message came through that Wigan's bid had been accepted and the move agreed. I left Fratton Park in August 2019 for in excess of £2.5m and posted a farewell message on my Twitter account, saying that "...a lot of things happened behind closed doors which left me questioning the integrity of some of the decision makers at the club. Not only this but being able to test myself in the Championship has only ever been a dream of mine." I was responsible for writing that, nobody else did it on my behalf. I was so upset and it was a dig at Mark Catlin and the director of finance Tony Brown.

It tainted my time at Pompey for a while, but I couldn't let that dictate my whole affection for the football club. That wouldn't have been fair. Now I can look back and be proud of what I achieved there. I'm grateful to have been involved in some successful moments in the club's recent history.

I have now played internationally for Jamaica and featured in the top seven divisions in England and Wales — Ryman Premier, Conference South, Conference, League Two, League One, Championship and Premier League. Pompey has been my favourite club, it has to be. I've had some really good times at other teams, but, as a whole, those two-and-a-half years at Fratton Park make it my number one. Of my three children, two — Bonnie and Dexter — were born at Queen Alexandra Hospital, while Ziggy was born in Bournemouth. In terms of football, Pompey marked my return to the Football League. I went from playing in front of 400 fans to 17,000 — and what a wonderful place to start my journey again.

PAUL HARDYMAN

136 games, four goals (July 1981 — June 1989)

Newcastle United 1 (Mirandinha)
Pompey 1 (Hardyman)

First Division, St James' Park, Saturday, December 12, 1987

Pompey: Knight, Swain, Ball, Whitehead, Hardyman, Dillon, Horne, Connor, Hilaire, Baird, Quinn (59 mins, Gilbert). Sub Not Used: Perry.

Attendance; 20,455

HE NEWS, MONDAY, DECEMBER 14, 1987

News Sport

Sun
side
up
Cha

One touch of 'Dinha' dazzle

We
an
o it'

PEY'S walk-
unded will try
their injury
ms behind
onight when
ke on mighty
n in the Pru-
Cup final at
rt Hall.
ild-up to bas-
showpiece
been marred
ession of inju-
ey men Colin
c Glass, Rich
and Mike

ch Dan Lloyd
confident his
p outfit have
kes to topple
mpions and
nge for last
i defeat.
's morale has
ted by scor-
fortable win
London on
night while

CALVIN

NEWCASTLE 1, POMPEY 1
MIRANDINHA MANIA has gripped the North East this season — and for 75 minutes Pompey's exhultant support at St James's Park were wondering what the fuss was all about.

The stumpy, bow-legged little Brazilian whose acquisition will cost Newcastle around £1m., is the new folk hero of Tyneside.

Every time the ball reached him, a buzz of anticipation went up from the Geordie fans.

But for 75 minutes that buzz trailed away to a sad end as 'Dinha' was snuffed out by Kevin Ball or Clive Whitehead.

Twice in the first half Newcastle gained free-kicks 25 yards out — and each time to the strident delight of Pompey's supporters, Mira's shots buried themselves high on the terrace behind Alan Knight's goal.

By the 75th minute, his anonymity against the fierce but fair policing of young Ball was beginning to strain even Geordie bias.

Then a corner was partially cleared, Mirandinha gained possession — and Pompey's fans knew what all the clamour was about.

He worked himself an opening — and from 20 yards or so a shot whistled past Knight's despairing dive and Newcastle were level.

"It was a magnificent strike, absolute class — but it was just about the only kick young Ballie allowed him all afternoon," manager Alan Ball ruefully admitted.

It was desperately hard on Pompey who had generally looked the better side — but

it allowed people to talk about football as well as indiscipline when it was all over.

For again it was a match scarred by controversy with the sending off of Kevin Dillon and Newcastle's Peter Jackson after a mass punch-up in Pompey's goal mouth.

Without Mirandinha's seventh goal in 13 League appearances for his adopted club — and without Paul Hardyman's equally magnificent left-foot drive which had put Pompey deservedly ahead in the 31st minute, that double display of referee Neil Midgley's red

By MIKE NEASOM

card might have obscured much that was good about the afternoon.

Much that was best came from Pompey, particularly in the first half when, driven on by Hardyman's eager willingness to get forward on the left, they had completely dominated the home side.

Hardyman in that period produced his most mature and positive football of the season, and Pompey looked well capable of chalking up their second successive away win.

After the break though they tended to sit back and allow Newcastle to mount waves of increasingly desperate pressure.

But with Ball shackling 'Dinha', Alan Knight producing three high quality saves — and referee Midgley twice refusing to yield to crowd-demanded penalties — Pompey looked capable of defending their lead until the little 'n's block-busting shot.

The punch-up came in the 25th minute with Pompey well in charge and having gone close with a shot by Ian Baird which hit the outside of a post.

Neil McDonald floated a free-kick to the far post, the ball was nodded into the middle of the Pompey area where Knight claimed it, was challenged by Jackson, and all hell broke loose.

For a spell Mr. Midgley seemed to stand back as players brawled and punches were thrown. Eventually he stepped in and when comparative calm was restored sent off Jackson and the furiously protesting Dillon.

Then Hardyman brought sanity back to the afternoon with a goal of stunning quality — he gained possession 30 yards out and his left foot shot ripped into the far top corner of Newcastle's net.

It was the youngster's second senior goal — but he was quickly to add to his stature with a superb interception in front of his own net which denied Paul Goddard a simple equaliser.

In the second half Pompey rode wave after wave of attacks — but rode them magnificently until Mirandinha's magic moment.

NEWCASTLE: Kelly, Anderson, Wharton, McCreery, Jackson, Roeder, McDonald, Bogie, Goddard, Mirandinha, Cornwell. Subs, O'Neill and Craig.
POMPEY: Knight, Swain, Hardyman, Dillon, Ball, Whitehead, Horne, Connor, Baird, Quinn (Gilbert 59), Hilaire. Sub, Perry.
REFEREE: Neil Midgley (Kearsley).
ATTENDANCE: 20,455.
BOOKINGS: Newcastle, Jackson (sent off fighting). Pompey, Dillon sent off fighting; Baird (dissent), Whitehead (foul).
POMPEY MAN OF MATCH: KEVIN BALL.

THE
the Spa
a rapidly
for Ter
Yester
cold win
White
watched
1-0 defeat
of-the-tab
The de
the defeat
barely c
chance, h
promise o
mas bac
the form
ager.
In
manag
was at
first
what th
erable t
He sa
admit th
poor tea
of the sea
six or sev
formance
slowly in
the resul
needed b
give th
belief in

Cl
in

Aston Villa were reigning First Division title holders under Ron Saunders and in the process of being crowned champions of Europe, yet a 16-year-old from Fareham Town's youth team had caught their eye. Not that I wanted to play for them — they weren't Pompey. I love Pompey, I love the city. I was born and raised in Portsmouth, as were my sons Rob and Mark, and wife Hazel. Certainly there couldn't have been anyone more proud to play for their football club than me. It was my dream. Sorry, Villa!

At the end of the 1980/81 season, while on Fareham's books, I was asked to go into the office for contract talks. My teammate Mark Winzar went in before me and was offered £10 a week, although, unlike me, had featured for the first-team. It turned out Fareham wanted to keep me too, but, disappointingly, on non-contract forms. I told them I'd think about it — and never returned. I was well aware scouts from Villa, Brighton and, best of all, Pompey had spotted me, subsequently offering trials that summer, which would, ultimately, lead to me becoming a Football League player. It was silly from Fareham. Had they tabled £10 a week I probably would have signed, thereby entitling them to a fee. As it was, I left Cams Alders for nothing.

So, in the summer of 1981, I travelled to Birmingham for a week's trial during Villa's pre-season and sufficiently impressed to be invited back for another week and a match. Now I never wanted to be an athlete, but was eager to get fit, so regularly went to Alexandra Park and joined in with the middle-distance runners working with a coach, which meant I was as fit as a butcher's dog when it came to my Villa trial. At one stage, I was doing hill runs when midfielder Terry Bullivant turned to me and said: "Will you slow down you little pest, you're embarrassing us." I thought: "You can do one, I'm here for myself and to get a contract." I kept running and running. Eventually, I was put into a game against a men's team — at the age of 16. I did all right and Villa advised they'd be in touch one way or the other.

Brighton were also looking at me, with their manager, Alan Mullery, arranging a trial. However, he left for Charlton Athletic in June 1981 and everything got lost in the changeover, so it never happened. In the meantime, I'd also been at Pompey, representing a new era with Dave Hurst having recently been appointed youth development officer. Rob Winzar, who would later scout Mason Mount for Chelsea, was a left-back in the trials, while I was a midfielder, but, for some reason, I got put up front as a centre-forward. I told Rob to keep putting the balls over the top and I'd run onto them — and he agreed. I scored three goals and Pompey's youth-team manager Archie Styles wanted to sign me, paying £15-a-week expenses as a scholar. The problem was the club wouldn't sanction that amount, despite apprentices in those days earning £25 a week! Anyhow, eventually I had a choice between Villa and Pompey, so sat down with my mum and dad to talk things over. I was undertaking a carpentry and joinery apprenticeship at the time, which Pompey would let me continue, while training on Tuesday and Thursday evenings with the schoolboys and then playing on Saturdays for the youth team. Villa, though, wanted me to give it up to become a professional. Dad stressed the importance of finishing my apprenticeship, so I had a trade behind me should anything go wrong — and that's what I did. I joined Pompey in July 1981.

As a Pompey fan, I had grown up watching heroes like Nicky Jennings, Norman Piper, Dave Kemp, Colin Garwood, Peter Mellor, Paul Went and Mick Mellows. I'd attend matches with school friends, sometimes waiting outside the Fratton Park gates to be let in for nothing when they opened them with 20 minutes to go to allow those in attendance to leave early. I remember going on the train to watch us play at Wimbledon in the FA Cup in December 1979, wearing my Pompey silk scarf of blue, white, with red horizontal stripes, and another time I travelled to Bournemouth on a Tuesday night in October 1979, with more than 9,000 of us there to cheer Terry Brisley's winning goal in a 1-0 success.

I always think of the 1998 film *Sliding Doors* in terms of whichever way you decide, that maps your life. Would I have succeeded at Villa? I have no idea, but I didn't want to play for them. Pompey had always been my ambition. We were in the Third Division at that time, yet that move still meant more to me than playing for a Villa side which that same season would win the European Cup after beating Bayern Munich in the final, which is mad really. I never regretted it, even if my brother-in-law Eric Manca, who is from Birmingham and a massive Villa fan, was fuming!

When I eventually left my club it was June 1989, catching the train from Portsmouth Harbour, with the destination of Sunderland representing a fresh start, an improved contract and a three-year deal, yet it just didn't feel right. After eight years, I was never again going to pull on the royal blue of Pompey, which saddened me. I would later return for another 15 years as a coach, working in the academy and then serving as Andy Awford's assistant as we kept the Blues in the Football League in 2013/14. As a player, however, after 136 games, four goals and one promotion, my career was heading elsewhere due to John Gregory.

I was born in St Mary's Hospital in May 1964 and raised in Sunningdale Road, Copnor, in a household of Pompey supporters. My dad was a massive fan who stood in exactly the same position at the back of the old North Terrace with friends every game, while mum looked after the tea bar in the corner of the South

Stand and Fratton End. My first introduction was when I was four or five, going with mum, who allowed me to watch the matches, before collecting me when she closed up the tea bar and walked home.

The dream started at Langstone Junior School, when I was picked for the school team at the age of nine by a teacher, John Walters, who later became a Conservative councillor in the Milton ward and was a Fratton Park gateman. I was asked to play for the year above against Portsmouth Grammar School and that first game was like Christmas to me. I just couldn't sleep the night before. At the age of 13, as a Great Salterns School pupil, I had a careers meeting. When asked what I wanted to be, there was one answer. "Do you know how many people make it as a football player?" she replied — and told me to think of an alternative career. That night, I sat down for my evening meal with mum and dad and we talked about what the careers advisor had said. "She's probably seen you play," joked my dad.

At that stage, I represented local side Wembley FC and captained Portsmouth Schools, yet a massive setback was around the corner when I developed Osgood-Schlatter disease, which is a common pain in adolescents. It involves the tendons and bones not growing at the same speed, causing a swelling under my knee. I required complete rest for around six months and, when I returned, I had lost the captaincy, while the other boys were now bigger, stronger and quicker.

Still, since Christmas I had been training with Pompey, although you had to be aged 14 to sign as an associate schoolboy. First-team coach Stan Harland oversaw us and, with the season's end approaching, I was among 35-40 boys sitting in the away changing room at Fratton Park. Harland selected 21 players to spend the summer holiday with the club, among them Kevin Bartlett and David Leworthy, who both later played in the First Division for Notts County and Tottenham Hotspur respectively. But they needed one more player — and Harland pointed to me. I left Fratton Park that night wondering what I was doing. If I was number 22 out of all those players then something was wrong. I walked home with my dad, who could see I was upset, and told him I was going to give up. I'd been attending for about five months and never had a sniff of anyone saying they wanted to sign me. Instead I was picked up by Fareham, turning out in the Hampshire Youth League against the likes of Brighton, Southampton, Aldershot, Gosport Borough, Waterlooville and Basingstoke Town.

After leaving school, I applied for a job in the Dockyard. In those days, nearly every boy in Portsmouth would sit a Dockyard exam held at Highbury College, with about 600 competing for 200 apprenticeship offers. Thankfully, I finished around the top-100 mark, earning myself an offer. How it worked, though, is the number-one ranked lad had first choice, number two got second pick, and so on.

By the time it came to me, all the trades I wanted were unavailable — in particular a carpentry and joiner shipwright. So I turned it down and instead found work at the Department for Environment. Our offices were in Mill Lane, next to the St Vincent College in Gosport, and every day I'd ride a bike there, also catching the Gosport ferry. We looked after Haslar Hospital as well as all the naval quarters in Gosport and Portsmouth, so if doors or windows weren't fitting we'd go round and mend them.

My boss was Mr. Newman, a gentle giant with the biggest hands I had ever seen. Dave Hurst had to sit with him and go through the process of letting me come out of work to play for Pompey, and Mr. Newman was cooperative. I would use my year's holiday entitlements to work half-days on Wednesdays, allowing me to play for the reserves that afternoon. Mr. Newman often said to me: "When you make it big, when you play for England, I want a ticket. When you play in a cup final, I want a ticket." Ahead of my England Under-21 debut in March 1985, he was one of the first people I rang and, of course, I invited him. "Paul, I would love to," Mr. Newman responded, "but I'm not well enough." Unfortunately he passed away just after that — and also never saw me play in the 1992 FA Cup final for Sunderland.

As a non-contract player, I combined a carpentry apprenticeship with playing for Pompey and, in March 1982, was picked for a reserve-team debut against Northampton Town by Frank Burrows. When I turned up at Fratton Park for the game, I discovered the lads in the changing room were a bit down — when I asked why, I was told Frank had just been sacked! David Gregory joked: "He's been given the bullet because he picked you!" Still, we won 1-0, with Gregory our match winner. Bobby Campbell initially took over as caretaker boss before being appointed permanently and, the following season, I turned out for the reserves as well as Southern League Premier Division side Waterlooville. Well, the reserves went on to win the Midweek League that 1982/83 campaign, while Waterlooville were relegated on the final afternoon — the same day Campbell's first-team beat Southend United to win promotion to the Second Division. I featured on the left wing at Waterlooville, with the prolific strike pairing Colin White and Kevin Maddocks in attack for a team managed by ex-Pompey goalkeeper John Milkins.

At the season's end, John wanted me to join Waterlooville permanently and not return to Fratton Park, which would also allow me to pursue a carpentry career, having now finished my three-year City & Guilds qualification — but I wanted a crack at Pompey's first-team. I suppose it was also pivotal to my career that it was the season when I was converted to a left-back. The reserves had a match at Wimbledon and Archie Styles took us, delivering the instructions:

"You're going to play left-back tonight, son." I'd never before played there but, by all accounts, had a decent game. I slotted in and thought it was easy, playing there a few more times, but mainly featured on the left of midfield. When Alan Ball arrived as youth-team coach, also overlooking the reserves, initially he wasn't sure what my best position was. Then, following an injury at left-back, he put me there — and I remained in the role for the rest of my career.

In the summer of 1983, at the age of 19, I was summoned to see Bobby Campbell where I was offered professional terms, along with Kevin Ball, who had come through the same time as me. At that stage, we were on non-contract forms, each earning £65 a week, consisting of £35 in wages and the remaining £30 allocated for digs. Dave Hurst was also present when Bobby said: "Congratulations, we're going to offer you a pro contract. What do you think you are worth?" I looked at Bally, he looked at me and, without hesitating, I responded: "£125 a week." The manager exploded: "You what, £125 a week? Get out of here." We didn't need telling twice to leave that room! Outside in the corridor, Bally hit me around the back of the head and said: "What did you say that for?" I replied: "Well, as a carpenter and joiner that's what I would earn. I could walk out of here today and get £125 a week. So he might as well give me that." As we walked away arguing, the manager's door opened. It was Dave Hurst. "Oi, you two, get back in here."

As we walked back in, Bobby shouted: "Sit down" before asking my reasoning. I explained: "Well, that's what I'd get on the building site, gaffer." He looked at us and said: "Right, I'll give you £100. Now get out of here." As we walked away, Bally turned to me and said: "I didn't think we'd get that much. Well done." Funnily enough, a month later, I was called back into Bobby's office — and it was bumped up to £125! He told me I had done well. When we were promoted to the First Division four years later, I was earning £400 and had been given a beige Ford Fiesta, previously owned by one of the club's basketball players yet now too small for him.

Things were going well for me in the reserves, then arrived a week which would change the course of my Pompey career. It was March 1984 and Kevin Ball and myself were instructed by Bobby Campbell to play as centre-halves against the first-team in a training session at Burnaby Road. It was the pair of us, with Alan Knight behind, challenged to defend against 10 outfield players, led by Mark Hateley and Alan Biley, whose mission was to score. We knuckled down and, the longer the session went on, Bobby was getting more and more frustrated — nobody could score. We blocked, headed and cleared everything. Later that week in an 11 v 11, I played up against Dave Thomas, an eight-capped former England international and flying winger. We kicked lumps out of each other in the right way and those two sessions in that week convinced Bobby I was ready. That Saturday, Crystal Palace visited Fratton Park — and I was named on the bench.

In those days, there was just one substitute, so when Steve Aizlewood was forced off at half-time with a groin strain, I was introduced for my Pompey debut. Mick Tait switched from midfield to fill in at centre-half and I came into the centre of midfield. I can still picture Alan Biley with the ball. I was in a great position, in the centre of the goal and six yards out, with goalkeeper George Wood at his near post. It was an open goal in front of the Fratton End on my debut. What a dream scenario. Yet, rather than square it to me for a simple finish, he instead shot into the side netting! Unfortunately we lost 1-0, but it remained a special occasion, with 10,237 in attendance, including friends and relatives. I was in a daze, I'd never played in front of that many people in my life. My full Pompey debut arrived four weeks later — in April 1984 — with a visit to Charlton Athletic, when I played left wing-back in place of Colin Sullivan. We lost 2-1 and I was denied a second-half Blues equaliser by the post.

My third and final appearance of the 1983/84 season was a 2-0 defeat at Derby County — which would be Campbell's last match in charge. I was on the left-hand side of midfield and, every time Colin Sullivan threw the ball on to my head, Kenny Burns would crack his elbow against my skull! "Sully, throw it to my feet please," I pleaded. "I'm getting smashed here." We were 19th in the Second Division, prompting chairman John Deacon to make the change, with reserve-team manager Ball put in temporary charge for the final game of the season at Swansea. I didn't make the squad, but Bally afterwards reassured me: "Come back fit for pre-season, son. You'll be in the team." Sure enough, following his permanent appointment as Pompey boss in the summer of 1984, I started his first match — a 1-0 win over Middlesbrough at Fratton Park on the opening day of the 1984/85 campaign, although I was stretchered off in the first half with a hamstring injury.

Of Bally's infamous team, I was the youngest — and I also owned a Makro card. So every Thursday, ahead of an away match, it was my job to go around the players and collect £5 off each of them for our drinks kitty. Then, using this Makro card obtained through a friend who was a hairdresser, I'd buy 192 cans of lager, basically eight cases, which would keep us entertained on the coach journey back.

In July 1988, John Gregory arrived as coach under Bally, replacing Graham Paddon, who was relocated to the youth-team. Gregory's first match was the trip to Shrewsbury Town for the opening fixture of the Second Division season. In preparation for our journey to Shropshire, I had reversed my car up to the team coach and started putting the cases of lager on — when Gregory spotted me.

"What are you doing?" he asked. Well, I panicked a little: "What? All that lot? No, that's for the next few games." He seemed reassured.

We subsequently beat the Shrews 2-1, through goals from Terry Connor and substitute Mark Kelly, and, as I made my way to the coach after the game, I noticed Gregory was already on it. Now normally I'd go to the luggage hold to bring out the beers for the lads, but, on this occasion with Gregory present, I wasn't sure what to do, so boarded without them. As I sat on the coach, Bally and the director Jim Sloan entered, with the manager shouting: "Hardy, where's the beers?" I replied: "Downstairs, gaffer." He said: "Get them on, son." "How many?" I asked. Bally responded: "Bring them all on, son!" There were 14 players, plus Bally, Jim Sloan, and the physio John Dickens — and at the end of that return journey, not a can was left unopened. Bally and Sloan drank Whisky Mac, which was whisky mixed with green ginger wine. The entire way back, John Gregory, who sat at the front of the coach, was shaking his head regularly, although he might have joined us for one can of lager. I think that was him reaching an early conclusion about Pompey, later calling us a pub team! We actually had a Fratton Park match against Leicester City that following Monday and won 3-0, putting us top of the table. In the changing room afterwards, Billy Gilbert announced: "Well lads, I don't know what the hell they were drinking on Saturday night!"

My Pompey captain for a time was Mick Kennedy, who was a great to me and such a nice man off the pitch, although a massive, massive drinker. Being a young lad and, like Mick, living in Cowplain, I'd pick him up for training sometimes, or even collect his car and drive it back. You wouldn't like to play against him, though. He was an absolute lunatic, the craziest player I came across. The size of the opponent didn't matter to Mick; he would nail them. I remember him spitting at QPR's John Byrne at Loftus Road — he'd do things to rile players. He once appeared in *The Sun* describing himself as the hardest man in football, earning a subsequent FA fine. Not long afterwards, we played Millwall, whose Terry Hurlock wasn't a shrinking violet, but Mick bossed the midfield that day. He could talk the talk, but also walk the walk. What about some of those tackles? He would tell me: "If it's a 55-45 tackle in your favour, slow down and make it a 51-49 in your favour — then leave some on him." "Okay Mick, no problem." I can recall him doing it to Spurs' Paul Allen. Mick slowed down and I thought: "Ooh, I know what's coming." Sure enough, Allen ended up in a heap on the floor.

I actually won the first of my two England under-21 caps against Mick, facing the Republic of Ireland at Fratton Park in a friendly in March 1985. To play for my country in my home city was unbelievable, with all my family among the 5,480 crowd, while Pompey teammate Neil Webb was also on my side. We won

3-2, with Mark Walters, Paul Wilkinson and Tony Cottee scoring — and Mick Kennedy netting two penalties for them, which had each been conceded by myself and Webby! Playing for England, you are given two shirts — one to keep and the other to give away. A few of us knocked on Eire's changing room door afterwards keen to swap, with Mick volunteering to exchange his with me.

That Pompey team didn't just have Mick; there were Noel Blake, Billy Gilbert, Mick Quinn, and none of them were shrinking violets. All through the spine of the team were tough, mean people — and I say that in a nice way! It wasn't a bullying culture, but it was a hard environment, especially being the youngest. If you did something wrong, you'd be told and there were times when I felt low. To me it felt I was being picked on, but you must be mentally strong to make it as a footballer. Kevin O'Callaghan was a moaner, all of the time, he moaned and moaned and moaned, and didn't get on with Kevin Dillon.

One time, on the morning of playing Spurs in the Milk Cup fourth round in November 1985, I told Cally to shut up in training. He had carried on all session, and I snapped. It was a heated argument and afterwards, I apologised to Bally for my behaviour. His response was: "I can't believe it took you so long!" To him, that was what every training ground was like, but obviously I didn't know any differently. As an apprentice, you had to knock on the door before walking into that changing room. If you entered without doing so, you'd get things thrown at you — boots, kit, the ball booted in your direction — so you'd have to leave and come in properly — with a knock. They were testing to see what you're like as a person and whether you had anything to come back with.

In each of Bally's opening two seasons as manager, we were pipped to promotion to the First Division, before finally achieving it in 1986/87. Our pre-seasons involved spending two weeks at HMS Mercury, near Petersfield, on a bootcamp, consisting of plenty of running up and down hills. Real old-school stuff. You couldn't argue with the results either. In 1984/85, we were undefeated in our opening 10 league games, while the following season lost two of our first 19 matches in all competitions — although we still didn't win promotion. So, in 1986/87, Bally took us back to HMS Mercury at Christmas for a second pre-season, hopeful it would provide the push we required for the final half of the campaign. Sure enough, we were never outside the top two and went up as runners-up behind Derby.

We needed a point to secure a place in the First Division when we travelled to Crystal Palace for our penultimate game, with 10,000 Pompey fans there. With 180 seconds to go, Alan Irvine put a hopeful cross into the box and it eventually fell for Ian Wright to give the hosts a 1-0 win. We didn't have to wait long for promotion, though, with Oldham Athletic's defeat to Shrewsbury the following night enough to see us over the line without a ball being kicked. I was following the game's progress on *Ceefax* at home, constantly flicking it on. We'd not long had my youngest son Robert, so it was a quiet celebration for me, cracking open a can of beer and ringing a few people. The next day we came in for training at 10am ahead of our final match — Sheffield United at Fratton Park — and Bally announced: "We're not training today; I've got a special one for you in the pub. Let's go" and it was off to The Pompey pub. Fans began to hear about it and joined us. It was a mad day. After three years of banging on the door, on the third attempt we finally knocked it down to get into the First Division. Great times.

Bally obviously needed to strengthen the squad following promotion and, while there were good lads recruited in the summer of 1987 and not a bad egg among them, we were such a close-knit group that it was hard for others to break into. Bally recruited the likes of Clive Whitehead, Barry Horne, Mick Fillery, Ian Stewart, Terry Connor and Iain Baird, but the new-look squad didn't gel as a team. There was the odd good game, such as drawing 1-1 with Arsenal at Fratton Park on New Year's Day, when Dillon missed a late penalty to beat them. Yet it didn't click that season.

A massive highlight was playing Southampton twice and not losing to them, the first time we'd faced each other in the league for more than 11 years. We drew 2-2 at Fratton Park and then, even better, won 2-0 at The Dell. We played them on a Sunday at noon to avoid any trouble and ended up playing keep-ball with the Pompey fans giving it "*Oles.*" It was brilliant. There was also a trip to Newcastle United in December 1987, which was my favourite Pompey match. I gave us a first-half lead with my best Pompey goal — a left-footed 30-yard strike — only for Mirandinha to level in the 76th minute. Both sides finished with 10 men after a mass brawl resulted in referee Neil Midgley mistakenly sending off Dillon for punching Peter Jackson, when actually it was Kevin Ball, with Jackson also dismissed.

In the background, Deacon had bought a basketball team which needed funding. They brought over some American players who required housing and paying, and the Mountbatten Centre would host their games. It wasn't working out and Deacon had to find the money to keep bankrolling it, which is one of the reasons why Mick Kennedy had to be sold to Bradford City. Bally also wasn't happy. Coming back from a 2-1 defeat at Queen's Park Rangers in October 1987, the team coach was a bit empty, with a few of the London lads staying behind rather than journeying back to Portsmouth and some others off home to Birmingham or wherever. Bally got on the bus and told those of us left: "I've had enough, I've quit." Our response was: "Gaffer, you can't ... we've worked too hard to get here." On the Monday, he came in for training and thankfully his mind had been changed following meetings with John Deacon. Apparently, things were going to get better — yet they didn't.

It was tough, we'd worked so hard to get into the First Division and reaching it was brilliant for the city. Then we suffered relegation straightaway and, in June 1988, John Deacon had sold Pompey to Jim Gregory. The club wasn't the club anymore.

We started the 1988/89 season back in the Second Division with three straight wins and new signings Warren Neill, Graeme Hogg and Mark Chamberlain in the team, while Warren Aspinall then arrived for a club-record fee of £315,000 from Aston Villa. We were top of the league when we headed to Swindon Town in September 1988, a 1-1 draw which afterwards prompted me to put in a transfer request following an argument with Bally. Not that it got very far. Steve Foley scored an 85th-minute leveller to cancel out Chamberlain's early opener and, after the game, our manager ripped into me, blaming me for the equaliser. I defended myself, pointing out that he was wrong and that I'd actually tracked Bobby Barnes, who, as the right winger, had come across into the centre of the pitch. It was Lee Sandford who hadn't followed a marker — not that I told Bally that particular detail. We had the following day off and, upon returning to training on Tuesday morning, I was accompanied by a letter in my very best handwriting explaining how I thought it was time for a change and I wanted to go on the transfer list. At that point, I was also aware of initial Sunderland interest.

Now Bally would sometimes hold a bit of a recap of the game before a training session and he got everyone into the changing room at Moneyfields. "I've an apology to make," he announced. "Hardy, you were right son. I was wrong — and I'm man enough to stand up in front of everyone and apologise to you." Regardless, I still had this letter in my pocket and decided to hand it to him after training. I later found the manager in the Moneyfields clubhouse, sat with Dave Hurst, so handed over the envelope before saying: "This is really hard for me, but I've come to the conclusion that it's time for me to have a change. It's not something I really want to do, but there's a letter and I have one for the chairman too."

Bally answered: "Son, I'll tell you what I'm going to do with this," and ripped it up in front of me, without even opening it. "I don't care what's in the envelope," he said. "All I'm telling you is that you are my player and, all the time I'm at this football club, you will remain so. You've been brilliant for me, and I trust you like I trust no-one else, you are pivotal to us moving on at this club. You are staying."

Well, I didn't know what to say! To be honest, I never really wanted to leave Pompey, but I just felt I had to make a statement to Bally because of how he had treated me after that Swindon game. I now look back and recognise his behaviour was down to the pressure at that time. Jim Gregory was Pompey's new owner and had appointed John Gregory to the coaching staff. Bally felt the knives in his back and, four months later, lost his job. Deep down, I don't think John Gregory's a bad bloke, but he came in with the ambition of becoming manager of Portsmouth Football Club — and was probably promised the job by Jim Gregory. It was always going to happen at some stage and Bally knew that. I was sad to see him go, he had given me my chance, but his time was probably up at that stage. Little did I know that, by the end of that 1988/89 season, I would follow him.

On transfer deadline day in March 1989, Gregory reinvested some of the £700,000 transfer fee received from selling Barry Horne to Southampton to sign John Beresford and Steve Wigley. At the following day's training, the manager read out the squad for Saturday's trip to Leeds United — and I wasn't in it. I wasn't alone, there must have been 10 of us. At that point, and I can remember it to this day, the assistant manager Steve Wicks came over with this smile on his face and said: "Just letting you lads know, you've all played your last game for the club." It was a kick in the teeth. Looking around, there was myself, Billy Gilbert, Lee Sandford, Kevin Dillon, among others. We'd been part of the Gremlins, regulars under Bally, and now this; told we were no longer part of the club. It was spiteful. There were still seven weeks of the season remaining, yet the end of an era all the same.

A couple of us ended up playing for the reserves against Arsenal the following day in the Ovenden Papers Football Combination, drawing 0-0 at Highbury. Then, within a week, Beresford fractured his left ankle on his full debut, in a 2-2 draw with Watford, and suddenly Sandford and myself were back involved. We were being told: "We need you!" I played another three times in the final eight matches of the campaign as we finished 20th in the Second Division. At that point, Gregory pulled me into his office and announced I was being offered a 12-month deal to stay! I wanted a two-year contract, which would have taken me up to a testimonial, but he wasn't budging, and I left the office fuming. This was someone who had come in from out of town, didn't know me personally and had no idea about my commitment to the club.

As I walked through the door of my Cosham home, the phone started ringing. On the other end was Mike Neasom, *The News'* chief sports writer. It was almost as if he had a tracker on me! When he asked how I was, I explained the meeting I'd just had with John Gregory and he replied: "Well, I've got a bit of news for you.

Through media circles, I know there are a couple of clubs in for you. Expect calls from Dave Bassett at Sheffield United and Sunderland boss Denis Smith." Sure enough, the phone rang 10 minutes later, except it was St Mirren's Tony Fitzpatrick, who was offering a three-year deal. Later that afternoon I received a call from Gregory, asking me to come into Fratton Park the following day. It turned out he was sticking by the 12-month offer, but revealed Dave Bassett wanted to speak to me, so called him up in front of me and left the office to allow us to talk in private. Then, when I arrived home, I discovered a message on the answer machine from Denis Smith asking me to call him back. Mike Neasom was right!

In those days, clubs were entitled to a transfer fee, even if you were out of contract, with a tribunal settling it. I had already joined Sunderland ahead of the July 1989 hearing at Lancaster Gate and the outcome was £130,000. Afterwards on the train to Durham with Denis Smith, he admitted they were expecting £150,000, so were happy with the deal. As for me, deep down I was devastated. I never expected to leave Pompey — I saw myself as a one-man club, spending my entire career there — but it wasn't to be. I wasn't the only member of the Gremlins to depart Fratton Park that summer, with Mick Quinn and Kev Dillon joining Newcastle, while Billy Gilbert ended up at Colchester United. The vast majority had previously left — and were now popping up all over England causing carnage.

With Sunderland, I returned to Fratton Park in December 1989 and scored in front of the Fratton End, the same stand where I helped out at my mum's tea bar as a kid. I felt guilty for netting in that 3-3 draw, but my joy wasn't directed towards the fans, rather than the person who had let me go: John Gregory. It's sad when you leave anywhere, but I felt Pompey could have — and should have — done a bit more to keep me, particularly considering my commitment to the club. Now I was back, and I side-footed Marco Gabbiadini's pass past former teammate Alan Knight to put Sunderland into a 2-1 lead. I celebrated in front of the 7,127 crowd, not massively as Gabbiadini jumped on my back in jubilation, only for Kevin Ball to score Pompey's equaliser seven minutes from time to ensure it was spoils shared — although Gregory would be sacked three games later.

After seeing out my playing career with Sunderland, Bristol Rovers, Wycombe Wanderers, Barnet and Slough Town, Dave Hurst contacted me on behalf of Alan Ball in 1999 about returning to Fratton Park in a coaching capacity because he knew how much the club meant to me. I had scouted James Keene playing in Wells, Somerset, and passed my UEFA B licence, coaching in the Bristol area. Bally was keen for an overhaul of the Football in the Community department at the club and wanted somebody to head it who was local with good contacts. Unfortunately, Pompey were in administration and couldn't recruit any new staff, but when Milan Mandaric took over in June 1999, he eventually appointed Tony Pulis as manager and, in March 2000, I took on the role — and loved it.

From that point I worked as assistant academy manager, under-18s coach and head of Football in the Community. In addition, I was co-commentator alongside Laurence Herdman on *BBC Radio Solent* for four years, starting with the 2002/03 promotion season under Harry Redknapp. I would later become a first-team coach under Andy Awford, remaining in the role until Paul Cook's appointment in May 2015, which signalled the end of my time at Fratton Park.

I had around 25 years associated with Pompey, in numerous roles. To this day my wife calls me "Pompey Paul," although has warned she'll divorce me should I ever return, considering the way I've been treated at different times. I'd always go back though. It's my club. Sorry, Hazel!

▲ Barry Horne holds aloft *The News/Sports Mail* player
of the season trophy in 1987-88, chosen by readers

▲ Defender Tommy Youlden made 95 appearances
in a Pompey shirt after arriving from Arsenal

▼ John McLaughlin holds the distinction of winning two
promotions during five seasons on the south coast

▼ Pompey fan Paul Hardyman achieved his boyhood
dream, helping the Blues to promotion in May 1988

- ▲ North End lad Steve Foster represented his hometown club 127 times and later played for England

- ▶ Told he would struggle to play football again after serious injury, Richie Reynolds resurrected his career at Fratton Park with 160 appearances and 28 goals

- ▼ Scot John Armstrong played more than 70 times in Pompey's net after moving from Nottingham Forest

Milkins' number two

A is for Armstrong, John Armstrong, who shared the goalkeeper's jersey with John Milkins in the early 1960s after being signed by Pompey manager George Smith from Nottingham Forest reserves for £5,000 in February 1963.

He made his debut for Pompey, aged 27, against Luton at Fratton Park a few days after he signed and eventually kept 15 clean sheets in 86 league and cup games.

He once kept goal in front of 54,558 fans when Pompey lost 7-0 at Chelsea in May 1963 and played at Northampton in Jimmy Dickinson's 764th and final league game.

Born in Airdrie in 1936, he

JOHN ARMSTRONG

was released to Southport in July 1967 where he went on to make 86 appearances for The Sandgrounders.

POMPEY LEAGUE RECORD: 79 appearances, no goals.

▲ Terry Brisley scored 14 goals from midfield in the 1979/80 season as Frank Burrows' Pompey won promotion

▼ Paul Hall gallops away from Ipswich's Tony Mowbray and Claus Thomsen in a 3-2 defeat at Portman Road in 1995

▲ Former England international Mark Chamberlain was a popular Pompey performer during his six-season stay

► The big-hearted midfielder Chris Burns poses for the camera at Fratton Park, having left his bricklaying job to become a professional footballer. Just over a year later, he played against Liverpool in an FA Cup semi-final

▼ Winger Kevin Harper launches a Pompey attack in a 1-1 draw at Birmingham City in April 2002

▲ Darryl Powell, seen in action against Peterborough in January 1994, came through the Fratton Park ranks

▲ Future skipper Kit Symons played under four different managers in his first five Pompey league matches

▼ Central midfielder Danny Rose won five promotions during his playing career, including one at Pompey

▼ Gareth Evans was a highly popular figure at Fratton Park, scoring in six successive seasons for the Blues

▲ Pompey pulled off something of a coup by bringing former England international and Premier League winner Teddy Sheringham to Fratton Park for their first Premier League season in 2003/04

▼ Former school PE teacher Jamal Lowe became a £2.5m player after his route back at Pompey

▼ In April 2018 Brett Pitman became the first Pompey player in 15 years to score 25 goals in a season

▲ Despite having been transfer-listed and told he had no Pompey future, Kal Naismith was a pivotal performer in the League Two title-winning team, finishing as 15-goal top scorer

▼ Cultured central defender Adam Webster came through the Fratton Park ranks and featured in three divisions for the Blues, totalling 81 appearances and five goals

▲ Harry Redknapp is Pompey's most successful manager over the last 70 years, winning the Division One title to earn a place in the Premier League and then, in his second spell, claiming the 2008 FA Cup, European qualification and their highest top-flight finish for half a century

▶ The arrival of the Premier League winner and England international of Sol Campbell was a huge coup for Pompey and he went on to skipper the Blues to the 2008 FA Cup

DARRYL POWELL

170 games, 23 goals (July 1988 — July 1995)

Manchester United 2 (Giggs, Cantona)
Pompey 2 (Walsh 2)

Coca-Cola Cup quarter-finals, Old Trafford, Wednesday, January 12, 1994

Pompey: Knight, Durnin, Daniel, McLoughlin, Symons (24 mins, Chamberlain), Awford, Dobson, Kristensen, Stimson (85 mins, Doling), Powell, Walsh. Sub Not Used: Horne.

Attendance; 43,794

It was my best friend's Asa Owen's idea — he had heard Alan Ball was taking training for Pompey's schoolboys at Alexandra Park on that Thursday night. Asa was from my estate in Buckland and it's funny to think his suggestion would lead to a football career which saw me make 170 appearances for my hometown club, spend six-and-a-half years in the Premier League and feature in the 1998 World Cup finals in France.

I was aged 13 and barely eight months earlier had stopped training at Pompey as I wasn't enjoying it. This was Alan Ball, though. "The real Alan Ball? The World Cup one?" I replied to Asa, and we hopped on our bikes and rode down there to watch. I was a kid, I loved football, so naturally I went along wearing boots and shin pads. The pair of us stood by the side of the pitch inside the cage, watching the Blues' youth-team manager coach the kids, thinking: "I'm better than him, I'm better than him too." Noticing us, Bally called to me: "Do you want to join in?" Of course I did and responded with: "Yeah, all right."

He replied: "It's not 'Yeah all right.' This is football son. It's yes or no." "Go on then." To be honest, I did really well and afterwards he called me over: "You make sure you're back here next week — and I'm going to call you Cyrille." At the time, Cyrille Regis was the main man and it's a nickname which stuck throughout my Pompey career.

The following week I turned up once more, only this time I was invited, and everyone from the club was there, and I mean everyone, including the first-team manager Bobby Campbell. I performed again, I was in my element, and afterwards Bally turned to them and said: "I told you … I told you I've found a good one here." He wanted to meet my parents, although my dad wasn't living with us, so this England World Cup winner turned up at a Buckland house and told my mum: "Mrs. Powell, don't worry about your lad. He's going to be a football player. Any problems, just call me." And that was it. Amazing.

I've often wondered what made him ask me to train that day. I was tall, skinny and athletic, so perhaps I simply looked the part. Asa was the opposite — he was fat at the time and couldn't run but was able to pass a ball. While I joined in with training, he continued to watch. It represented my second spell with Pompey. My first time happened following a school trip to Fratton Park with St John's College, even having my photo taken with Alan Knight, a future teammate, standing next to this little kid in shorts, cap and blazer.

During the visit my teacher, Miss Pescops, collared somebody from the club and mentioned how they should have a look at me, leading to the head of youth recruitment, Dave Hurst, inviting me for training. Back then it was a Centre of Excellence, with one session a week at Alexandra Park, yet I didn't feel the love there. So, after attending for a few months, I just stopped going. I knew I was good but didn't feel I was receiving any kind of recognition or attention from the coaches, the scouts and the staff generally. At least it was never communicated, so I left and returned to playing outside mum's house.

This time it was different, Alan Ball wanted me and finally this was acceptance. He wanted me to train with his team, he wanted to meet my parents, he reassured me I was going to be a footballer. What more do you need to hear? Unlike my previous time with Pompey, suddenly I couldn't wait for Thursday evenings to come along. Bally was a brilliant coach. His technical ability, his passion, his enthusiasm, his way of working — incredible. He was a genius with youngsters. We were keen, impressionable, we wanted to play football and here was this amazing man trying to make us better. The reason why we had such a brilliant crop of young players which emerged during that era was down to him, with subsequent youth-team managers and coaches simply picking up the great work he set into motion. Micky Ross, Andy Awford and Michael Turner were in my group and invited to Lilleshall after being recognised as being among the best 16 kids in the country — and that had to be down to Bally.

I was born in Streatham, South London, and my mum was offered a job at a recruitment agency, the Brook Street Bureau, in Portsmouth. At the age of three, our family moved to the south coast into a house in Sultan Road, Buckland. Although my roots are certainly South London with the rest of the family, Portsmouth remains home. It's where I grew up, attending Charles Dickens Primary School and St John's College. As a kid, the first sport I wanted to get involved in was boxing. I was inspired by the night Marvin Hagler beat Alan Minter to claim the world middleweight title in September 1980. It was at Wembley Arena and, after winning, he sank to his knees with people throwing beer bottles and cans at him in the ring, shouting racist abuse. He was amazing, I wanted to be like Marvin Hagler. My dad, who was very briefly in the Army and had boxed there, told me: "You won't be tough enough." Still, at the age of eight, he took me to a boxing club in Stamshaw and I stood outside while he went in to enquire whether I could train there — only to return with the news I was too young and not allowed.

When we returned home, dad said: "There's something I think you can do," and handed me a football he'd retrieved from the back of the house. My brother, Richie McIntosh, was seven years older and on Pompey's books until the age of 16, yet it never really happened for him, despite being technically very, very good. Now dad was telling me: "You need to practise every day. Make it like homework … you need to fall in love with it. If you do, it will look after you." From that point, I'd spend up to an hour-and-a-half every day with a ball at the back of our house. I hadn't really played football before then — now I was obsessed. Incidentally, looking back, it was clear dad had made that up about being too young to box!

My first team was Solent United under-11s, playing a year up, while I also turned out for Fleur De Lys and Leigh Park — and I was determined to become a professional player. After my parents split up, mum went to court over something to do with dad, and, when she came home, told me: "That judge is really annoying me." When I asked what had happened, it turned out he'd asked whether she had any children, so mum mentioned her youngest was at St John's College. The judge replied: "That's really, really good, Mrs. Powell, he's being well educated. What does he want to do when he's older?" When she told him I was going to be a footballer, apparently he laughed! I was aged about 12 or 13 and reassured her: "Don't worry mum, I will be. It's going to happen." It's quite emotional thinking about little things like that.

I have no shame about my childhood. I lived on a council estate in Buckland, we never had a car, I went to school on an assisted place scheme with privileged boys and I'd go on prison visits every other weekend to see my dad, who was in and out of there. Back in the day he ran nightclubs in Portsmouth, one of them The Bistro in Southsea. Yet, in between everything going on, I had that real passion for football, playing every moment. Bally would tell me to come into Pompey first-team training whenever I wanted, so I'd be training with professional footballers from a young age.

Growing up in Portsmouth, I encountered racism. We fought every day — your dad would fight their dad, one brother would fight your brother. It was constant. Going to and from school, I'd walk through Somerstown and have a few confrontations. People threatening me so I needed to stand up for myself. I had some really good friends. Some went along the wrong path and didn't have that guidance or opportunity, while there were lads I played football with whose careers didn't blossom — yet we always had each other's backs. I once received racist abuse from my own fans in the South Stand while warming-up for Pompey during a game. I was aged 17 and being told I wasn't wanted at the club, with racist language used. I shouted back to the bloke. On another occasion, I must have been 14 and working as a ball boy against Leeds United at Fratton Park, situated in front of their supporters. A ball left the pitch, so I went to pick it up when I heard: "Zigger, zagger, zigger, shoot that nigger." I ended up swearing at them and refused to volunteer to be a ball boy ever again. It's mad, isn't it?

As a kid, I supported whichever clubs the black players were representing, although it got to the point where I really liked Arsenal. Viv Anderson was the very first player on my wall, then Garth Crooks, while I posted stuff to West Bromwich Albion for Laurie Cunningham, Cyrille Regis and Brendon Batson to sign, which they did. In later life I knew Cyrille. He was working as a football agent then and was a very, very good person. The lads from that era still call me Cyrille and it doesn't bother me. It was said with love, so it shouldn't. If you're a white kid and having a worldie, leading them calling you George Best, you're not going to cry about that either.

I was a pupil at St John's College when I made my Pompey debut for the reserves in December 1987, lining-up against Chelsea at Fratton Park, with Noel Blake designated my mentor, instructed to look after me by Bally. I was up against John Bumstead in midfield, with Roy Wegerle, Graeme Le Saux and Kevin McAllister also featuring in a strong opposition side — yet I cruised it, playing really, really well in a 2-0 victory. After the match, Blakey introduced himself to my mum and brother and said: "Your lad is going to make a living in this game. I don't know how much of a living, but he definitely will." Then someone asked for my autograph for the first time. "What do you want that for?" I questioned. "I've got school tomorrow."

At the age of 17 years, one month and seven days, I was handed my Pompey debut in a Simod Cup match at First Division side Middlesbrough in December 1988. Mick Quinn and Warren Aspinall were ruled out through illness, while Martin Kuhl was suspended and another eight players injured, so Bally was forced to turn to the kids. I partnered Micky Ross in attack against Gary Pallister and Tony Mowbray, with Kit Symons also starting, among six teenagers in the Blues squad. On the journey there, we watched a video of Liverpool smashing Fulham 10-0 in the Littlewoods Cup two years earlier, with Clive Whitehead muttering: "That will be us tonight, all these kids." It didn't quite turn out that way, instead losing 2-1 in extra-time, with Bernie Slaven grabbing a 112th-minute winner. I also marked my first appearance with a goal, picking up Colin Cooper's under-hit back pass and scoring a 16th-minute leveller. I came off in extra-time, absolutely shattered. We returned to Pompey around three or four in the morning and I couldn't sleep because my head was buzzing. My best mate called in the morning and when we went to a cafe in Commercial Road, people were coming up to me and saying: "You played for Pompey last night, didn't you? That's brilliant, mush."

Just three games later I was handed my league debut off the bench in a 2-0 defeat at Swindon Town in January 1989, which turned out to be Bally's penultimate match in charge before being replaced by John Gregory. Gregory loved himself, but handed me a full Pompey bow in a 1-0 defeat at Bournemouth, five games into his tenure, and I kept my place against Ipswich Town at Fratton Park the following match, also a 1-0 loss. However, I'd have to wait another 18 months for my next Pompey appearance — and by that time Frank Burrows was manager!

Gregory returned me to the youth-team and instead I featured in a talented side which reached the semi-finals of the FA Youth Cup in 1989/90. Malcolm Beard replaced Graham Paddon halfway through the season and, after beating Arsenal and Liverpool along the way, we lost 4-1 to Middlesbrough over two legs in April 1990, with 5,804 present at Fratton Park for the first game. We should have done better and let ourselves down because, man-for-man, Boro were not as good as us. Maybe we got a little above our station at the wrong time because we should have reached the final and faced Tottenham Hotspur. Still, we were beginning to be recognised as a team of promise, with Darren Anderton and Micky Ross our stand-out players, along with Awfs who looked so composed in defence. Normally they took 10 players on as scholars at the age of 16, but extended it by two that season so they could also include Darren, who actually became the best of the bunch. After training, rather than joining the other boys for lunch, the pair of us would grab a bag of balls and practise together, working on shooting or passing. He was the only person in the group who could outrun me, he was amazing at long-distance running, and such a sweet striker of the ball who grew and grew in confidence. What a fantastic career he'd go on to have.

Frank Burrows took over from Gregory in January 1990, yet it would be almost eight months into his reign before I featured under him, coming on as a substitute against West Bromwich Albion in the opening game of the 1990/91 season. Frank was very direct, it was basically route one, and I appeared 10 times during the opening half of the campaign before drifting away again. When Tony Barton was appointed caretaker boss in March 1991, it was on my fourth Pompey manager at the age of 19! I don't remember a lot about Tony, although he took the reserves and there was one incident at Fulham in September 1990 when the ball arrived to me on the edge of the box after the keeper saved from Darren Anderton, so I chipped him. I could hear him shouting: "What the hell are you doing … Oh, what a goal!"

I always say Alan Ball made the biggest impact on my football career. I know it's crazy because Jim Smith played me a lot at Pompey, then signed me at Derby County and made me captain. Yet while I had a really good relationship with him, Bally initially got me into the building. First and foremost, you need to have the ability and, if you've got that, you then need the pathway — and that's what Alan Ball provided me with.

The first time I came across Jim Smith was October 1991 when we won 2-1 at Newcastle United and, memorably, they had a madman as manager, screaming and screaming on the sidelines. Their captain was Roy Aitken, a massively-built

Scotland international with big tree-trunk legs, and Jim was absolutely hammering him, so he kept giving it back. Then, eight months later, he replaced Barton as manager at Fratton Park. Jim was actually really quiet and calm in that first pre-season of 1991, with us youngsters looking to impress the new boss. My usual summer routine involved having a week off before resuming training. I preferred coming back in good shape and hungry. We had a few young lads like that and Jim probably saw it and thought: "I'm having a bit of that, that's what we need." Chris Burns was another. He worked his absolute socks off. Having arrived from non-league Cheltenham Town, he hadn't made a first-team appearance before Jim's arrival.

Then, ahead of the opening match of the 1991/92 season at Blackburn Rovers, our physio Neil Sillett told me I would be starting in front of the older lads. He added: "Ours is not to reason why, ours is but to do and die. The gaffer has picked you, you're in." I remember those words, but don't ask me anything about the game itself. I haven't a clue! We drew 1-1 at Ewood Park with a young team consisting of myself, Andy Awford, Kit Symons, Darren Anderton and Burnsie. That was a brave selection from Pompey's manager, but he'd been around the game long enough. Even though Jim was old school in his ways, he was very modern and forward-thinking in terms of how he'd allow his coaches and team to work and develop. He must have viewed us as a decent group of young players who could flourish with some really good senior players around us.

I started the opening eight matches, ending the season with 45 appearances and six goals, but not being selected for the 1992 FA Cup semi-final against Liverpool was a bugbear of mine, especially having started all five previous matches on the journey there. Looking back, I wasn't mature enough for that fixture, yet it still hurt. We beat Nottingham Forest 1-0 in the quarter-finals, with Alan McLoughlin the match-winner — and their right-back Brian Laws got the hump and punched me during the game! For a young kid, I got involved in a fair few scrapes and was sent off quite a few times. I was competitive and probably annoying, although I regarded myself as an honest player, and that day I irritated Laws, who gave me a right dig in the back of the kidneys.

In April 1992 we headed to Highbury for the semi-finals and I was super, super excited. I walked on to the pitch before the game and the hairs on the back of my neck stood up, I could feel the tension. After returning to the changing room, Jim announced the team — and I wasn't in it. I was surprised, so you can imagine my reaction when I then learnt I also wasn't included on the two-man bench, with Warren Aspinall and Guy Whittingham preferred. Gutted, I went outside and sat in the stand next to Gavin Maguire, who told me: "Don't worry son, you're young. You'll have another opportunity." I broke down crying. When you don't play, it's not always the case that you're happy about the result, yet I was that day, especially for my roommate Darren Anderton, who scored in a 1-1 draw after extra-time.

The following day, Jim took me aside and said: "Don't worry son, you'll be starting the replay." Days later, I appeared as a substitute in a 2-0 defeat at Tranmere Rovers and was ready for the semi-final replay at Villa Park — yet again wasn't included in the matchday squad. That was the moment I grew up and hardened overnight. That's the harsh reality of football. A few years later, I reflected on that disappointment and realised I probably wasn't ready emotionally to deal with those two matches. As it was, the boys again did brilliantly in the replay, but unfortunately lost 3-1 on penalties. That's life and that's football, but I was still part of a fantastic experience. In my career, I never again reached that far in the FA Cup, instead getting to the quarter-finals twice with Derby. That's why, when I talk to young players, I tell them to embrace every moment because it might be the last. That's the reality of football; nothing is guaranteed. Following that defeat, I was back involved and started five of the last six fixtures as we finished ninth in the Second Division.

Despite my first-team breakthrough, I would start just four league games in the subsequent 1992/93 campaign, spending most of my time on Pompey's bench, with 19 substitute outings. I started the opening-day 3-3 draw at Bristol City at left-back, which marked Paul Walsh's debut and a Guy Whittingham hat-trick, before Ray Daniel took over that role for the majority of the season. People mature at different ages and in different ways — you can be physically strong but mentally not mature, while your game understanding may not yet be there. It seemed as though I'd been around for ages after making my debut at 17, but I was never concerned Pompey were going to release me. I was still growing up. It doesn't happen overnight, it took me until the age of 22 before it dawned on me: "That's it, you've done this. You are going to make a living out of football."

It was January 1994, Pompey had a quarter-final clash at Manchester United in the Coca-Cola Cup and I was playing up front with Paul Walsh. Travelling on the coach to the game, I saw the crowds outside Old Trafford and turned to Alan McLoughlin, who was sitting next to me, and admitted: "I'm so nervous." Macca was a lovely person who looked after the young lads, while was a former United youth-team player. He replied: "Listen, there are going to be 60,000 people here and 55,500 haven't got a clue who you are. Enjoy it." The penny dropped: they didn't know me, just play your game. We drew 2-2 against an Sir Alex Ferguson team containing Peter Schmeichel, Eric Cantona, Bryan Robson, Ryan Giggs, Denis Irwin and Mark Hughes, with Walshie getting both of our goals. For our second, Mark Stimson put me through down the left and I struck an angled shot which Schmeichel saved, with Walshie following up for a close-range header to equalise. He punched me in the stomach during the celebrations. "Oi, make sure you pass that next time."

I'd had a good game at Old Trafford and been comfortable against one of the best teams in the world. As much as there's that external bravado and belief, it took me until that point to realise what it took to make it a long career. After the game, Steve Bruce took our entire squad out to a bar in Cheshire and told me: "You ran me ragged tonight, I bet you were shattered. I've never had anyone run the legs off me like that before, you didn't stop." Funnily enough eight-and-a-half years later, as Birmingham City manager, he signed me from Derby.

I was dropped to the bench for the Manchester United replay at Fratton Park to make way for debutant Gerry Creaney, a striker signed from Celtic for a club-record fee in January 1994. He was a decent player, a good goal-scorer and technically sound, but lacked pace — and rubbed everyone up the wrong way. It was his mouth, he talked a lot of rubbish and, in the end, got himself messed up by talking nonsense to the wrong people, having his cheekbone fractured while waiting for a taxi on a night out in Southsea. I actually got on okay with him and we played up front together on some occasions. He told me Celtic were interested in signing me, a rumour I'd also heard elsewhere around that time, and I tried to look after him. I tried to explain things to him, but he was silly in his ways and got himself hurt through his stupidity.

With Portsmouth being a small place and me growing up and living there, I knew everything going on in the city. I talked to Gerry, but he didn't want to listen to anyone about anything. He was rude to the wrong people, very rude, and out of order. It was awful what happened to him, but he brought it on himself. I can't say I disliked him, we got on fine, but he was full of it, and, while he liked me as a player, I don't think he particularly liked anyone in the dressing room.

I finally established myself in Pompey's team in the 1994/95 season, which would prove to be my last at Fratton Park. As a kid I was a central midfielder, yet with the Blues I played everywhere: up front, at left-back, on the left flank. Managers couldn't find my slot in the side. Jim obviously believed I had something because he kept me around and continued to play me. I had begun life in our first-team as a striker, a position Bally had converted me to. Peter Osgood, our youth-team manager, always insisted I would never be a forward as I wasn't a goalscorer, which Bally disagreed with — but I eventually found my role. I could play most positions okay, but wanted to be involved in everything, which meant midfield was always my preference.

Jim was sacked in February 1995 following a 1-0 FA Cup fourth round defeat at Leicester City, with Terry Fenwick replacing him for his first job in football management. He was demanding and very professional, and, having played at a big club in the form of Spurs, had expectations. I got on well with him and he didn't want me to leave in the summer of 1995, but I needed to get out of Portsmouth. I'd already tried to move my mum out of the Buckland estate she lived in, but she refused. In my case, however, the best thing was for me to be somewhere else, away from my friendship group and away from people I'd grown up around. At the age of 23, I had to focus solely on my football, getting away from the noise. I knew a lot of interesting lads and we were quite cheeky boys, yet it got hard. We'd grown up together and were now on a different journey — so the easiest way to find your space was to move. I still keep in touch with my best mate, Asa, but that's about it. I genuinely cut ties, I left Portsmouth and didn't return for a year. Instead mum would come up to Derby to visit. I was focused on what I had to do to further my career.

Initially I was in talks with Port Vale, with a meeting with Sheffield United also scheduled, then I discovered Jim Smith, now Derby boss, was interested. Fenwick told me: "Listen, you have a bright future, make sure you don't sign for Derby. When you come back, I'm going to give you a new deal. Just don't sign for them." My response was: "Yeah, yeah, yeah, yeah," — and I joined the Rams! I didn't actually know Jim ever liked me as a player, despite all the games I played under him. I was shocked and never got the impression he particularly rated me at that point. In July 1995, I joined Derby in a £750,000 deal.

Leaving Pompey for Pride Park benefited my career, without a doubt. No-one knows what's going to happen, but we won promotion to the Premier League in my first season after finishing behind Sunderland. I spent the subsequent six years with Derby in the top flight, before later turning out for Birmingham, Sheffield Wednesday, Colorado Rapids and Nottingham Forest.

I loved my time at Pompey. It was at the start of my career, and it was my hometown club. As a scholar, I'd walk to Fratton Park from Buckland, meeting Lee Smith in Landport on the way. Sometimes we picked up Chrissy Male from Clive Road, before walking over Fratton Bridge and around the back for training. Pompey remains a massive part of my life and contributed to an amazing journey and wonderful memories. I always say I had two football clubs — Pompey where I grew up and Derby where I became a man. They were the only two I played for, the others were little pit stops along the way. I always enjoy coming back, revisiting memories and reminiscing about my childhood and friends growing up. And my mum is still there, living in the same Buckland house.

TOMMY YOULDEN

95 games, one goal (April 1968 — July 1972)

Pompey 2 (Hiron, Trebilcock)
Sheffield United 0

FA Cup third round, Fratton Park, Saturday, January 2, 1971
Pompey: Milkins, Smith, Hand, Blant, Youlden, Munks, Trebilcock, Piper, Hiron, Bromley, Jennings. Sub Not Used: Pointer.

Attendance; 20,556

Dynamic Pompey rekindle enthusiasm

GOAL! ABOVE: Pompey players raise their arms in delight to salute Ray Hiron's goal. BELOW: Ray Hiron shoots to give Pompey a 1—0 lead.

BY REG BETTS

Portsmouth 2, Sheffield United 0

Pompey not only hit the lucrative F.A. Cup trail on Saturday — they rekindled the enthusiasm of the Fratton Park fans with a dynamic second half revival which shattered the Yorkshire side.

Let there be no mistake, this match was a crucial test of Pompey's credibility, made tougher by having to face on Sheffield United, who had put 15 goals past them in their last three meetings.

For half an hour they were almost overwhelmed by the tenseness of the situation and Sheffield sniped away at a nerve-wracked defence which seemed certain to topple, but somehow survived.

The transformation after the break was quite remarkable. Pompey started to win the ball positively, pushing men upfield on — and Ray Hiron's goal in the 57th minute sent their stock soaring.

Mike Trebilcock raced back to halt Tony Currie with a tremendous tackle and the loose ball was picked up by right-back Fred Smith, now showing more of his attacking ability.

Tommy Youlden passed to Hiron whose shot beat Alan Hodgkinson, although the veteran goalkeeper did well to get a hand to the ball.

Crushed

Sheffield's attempts to stay in the Cup were efficiently crushed and Pompey found the space to create moves of

Hiron emerged from a tackle in possession and sent a pass to Trebilcock who set the seal on one of his best performances for the club by unleashing a shot from 23 yards which almost broke the sound barrier as it jetted past Hodgkinson.

Team manager Ron Tindall commented: "We have a great deal of respect for Sheffield United. Perhaps we showed too much respect in the first half.

"We set ourselves in a slightly defensive formation to counter their strengths, but for 25 minutes we stayed in our shell and played nervously.

"Our best chance was to chase and harry, and at half-time I told the team. "We must

Alan Woodward, who scored a hat-trick in United's 5-1 win at Fratton Park in September.

When Woodward found he could not outwit the determined young Pompey defender he adopted a roving role and still got nowhere.

Eoin Hand was allotted the specific job of shadowing John Tudor and he extracted all threat from the Sheffield striker.

The responsibility of captaining the side for the first time rested lightly on the broad shoulders of Colin Blant, and his strength in the middle of the defence was reassuring especially early on when Pompey were often reduced to a state of brittle nervousness at the sight of Sheffield aggres-

JACKPOT WINNERS

POMPEY GOLDEN GOALS:
£100. Ioone (55 min. 52 sec.);
£20 home (85 min. 50 sec.).
POMPEY GOLDEN SCOOP:
18-33-35, 18-33-38, 33-35-38
(8100). 16-21-41 (£20). Work
45, 30, 81, 30, 4, 85, 66, 15, 45,
38. Lucky Code. 32-40-43.
GOSPORT BOROUGH: LF
2552. (£5): 02-19-22.
MONEYFIELD SPORTS:
31-3 (£42 7s.).

I was a hot-headed 18-year-old who had spent six weeks at home after making the stupid decision to walk out on Arsenal, vowing never to play for them again. And then Pompey saved my playing career.

The Gunners were my club and I was convinced I'd spend my career there. I represented England under-15s five times at left-back, won the FA Youth Cup with Arsenal in 1966 — beating Sunderland 5-3 on aggregate with Pat Rice and Sammy Nelson among my teammates — and had been named on the bench against Glasgow Rangers in a pre-season friendly in August 1967. This club was for me.

Pompey manager George Smith had initially spotted me in the 1966/67 season, playing right-back for the reserves against Tottenham Hotspur at White Hart Lane. Afterwards he approached Bertie Mee about the possibility of taking me on loan — which I rejected. It was silly. With hindsight, a season of Second Division football would have benefited me tremendously and, should I produce anything reasonably good, may have even bolstered my Highbury prospects. Come the following campaign, it wasn't going too well for me at Arsenal. I was in and out of the reserve side, and, around February 1968, Mee called me into his office and announced: "Look, we've got people coming to look at you — you're playing at right-back against Cambridge University in a friendly this evening."

Then I was substituted at half-time! Already growing disillusioned, I exploded. I'd had enough of being messed around. My dad was waiting in the car outside Highbury and I told him I wouldn't be returning — and I never set foot on the football pitch for Arsenal again. Honestly, it frightens me even now when I look back on that stupid, stupid decision. Around six weeks later, with me refusing to come back, Mee invited me and my parents for a meeting at Highbury to find out what I wanted from the situation. However, it developed into an almighty row, mainly instigated by my mum, who was angry and very annoyed.

Mee handed over my PFA playing registration, allowing me to leave Arsenal and play for whoever wanted me. Great — but, in reality, I then sat at home having ludicrously taken myself out of the shop window. No one was looking at me, so I could hardly expect somebody to come in and sign me. Arsenal's first-team coach Don Howe was very good and tried to fix me up with a couple of clubs, so I went to Brighton & Hove Albion for talks and received a contract offer. However, I only met the coach — the manager was nowhere to be seen — so they couldn't have been that interested. I decided it wasn't for me.

Nothing was happening. I was struggling. No clubs were coming in for me. Then one day my dad answered the phone and it was George Smith on the end of the line. "Would you like to come down and have a talk?" he asked. It was agreed

I would catch the train to Fratton Park the following day — and this time I was very interested. I signed in April 1968 for £20 a week, plus an extra pound for every thousand the crowd reached over 20,000 at Fratton Park. I was just pleased to finally have a club.

Smith had been a sergeant major in the Army and never minced his words. Believe me, he was a very outspoken character, yet you always knew where you stood. I remember being told a famous story about the time Field Marshal Montgomery, who was Pompey's president, had come into the dressing room at half-time and was dishing out tea to the players. Now Smith had a limp caused by an arthritic hip which he was frightened to have operated on, so you could always hear the shuffle of him approaching. Those in the room that afternoon heard him getting closer and closer, before entering. Smith immediately spotted Montgomery and went crazy, knocking the teas out of his hands and shouting: "I had enough of your rubbish during the war," before telling this Second World War hero to get out. Having myself witnessed Smith exploding on a couple of other occasions, I definitely believe that story to be true.

I remember at Bolton Wanderers in December 1968, I was at right-back and meant to be marking their left-winger Gordon Taylor, yet not doing a very good job of it, collecting a booking following one foul too many. It was goalless at half-time and, just as George was about to conduct his team talk, the Tannoy in the corner of the dressing room started to play music. Well, George got up on a stool, ripped it off the wall, opened the door, and hurled it down the corridor, shouting: "Have your music back." A couple of Bolton's reserve players were standing outside, absolutely aghast. Yet it was standard stuff.

Smith's routine following a Saturday match involved the players meeting in Fratton Park's boardroom every Tuesday, having been granted the previous day off. He would sit at the head of this big oval table, with the players gathered around it, before holding an inquest into the game. It was an ageing team and I was this young upstart so, on my first day, they played a trick on me while waiting for the manager. Firstly they pointed me to a seat, then I was asked whether I wanted a drink, before kindly pouring a lager from the pump in the boardroom bar and handing it to me. When George Smith entered, I was in his seat with an alcoholic drink in front of me — and he went absolutely ballistic. I had no idea what I'd done, but managed to sit elsewhere, which was opposite to him and next to Mike Trebilcock; actually the worst place to be. From that moment onwards, it became my seat at those meetings and whenever I looked up, I was right in his eyeline. It was like I was eyeballing him.

Those meetings were never tactical, merely an opportunity for Smith to have a go at the players, having built up all this anger over the weekend and needing to get it out of his system. He would go around the table to each player in turn and ask "How do you think you played?" and if you'd had a bad game and said you'd had a good one, he'd reply: "You were rubbish. You had better sort yourself out."

He always had a go at Trebilcock, the team's scapegoat. Smith had paid Everton £40,000 for him — which was a lot of money in those days, especially for a club like Pompey — and while he was a good goalscorer, the manager expected more. Then, after ripping Mike apart, he would arrive at me: "How do you think you played, Youlden?" Even when you'd had a good game it would be: "You might have done well, but you had better do it again next time." No matter what you said, he was going to come back at you, although he was generally okay with John Milkins, who was a placid sort of guy and easy to get on with, as was Ray Hiron.

Smith operated a system which involved him, Ronnie Tindall, Bobby Camp-bell and Gordon Neave rating you out of 10 for each game, like the newspapers — and that would dictate whether you warranted a pay rise at the end of the season. It was calculated on an average score and, if your numbers were down on the previous campaign, then, in their eyes, you didn't deserve an increase. I am told Bobby Kellard wouldn't have that. He'd say "I don't give a toss about that, I want my rise," and, as a result, he left for Bristol City in July 1968, which was a bad move. He was a mainstay of the team, the captain and a good influence. One day I overheard the four of them rating the players. Smith said: "I'm going to give that player a seven." Then Gordon replied: "I'm going to give him seven as well," — they all followed what George said! Then your ratings would be pinned up in the changing room.

Although Smith was prone to manic spells when he lost his temper, he could be quite thoughtful and sometimes, should I want to stay in London following a match there, he'd hand me a train ticket to Portsmouth and give me time off until Wednesday morning. Out of all the managers I played under, I liked him the best. It was strange. He was a bully, but I didn't mind that in some ways because he was straight with you, whereas other managers would tell you one thing and do another. Pompey's training facilities at Eastney Barracks were excellent, with Mike Trebilcock riding across on his bike after catching the ferry from Hayling Island, where he lived. I particularly loved pre-season under Smith at Pompey, involving organised circuits, running along the promenade, having a swim in the indoor pool next to the marine barracks, and all to the beautiful backdrop of the Isle of Wight. It was absolutely fantastic. George was a class act when it came to coaching and organising.

I was a left-back when I arrived at Fratton Park, but George Ley was a fixture there and, while George Smith saw me as a future centre-half and long-term successor to the veteran Harry Harris, I initially competed with Roy Pack for the right-back spot. I started the opening 17 matches of the 1968/69 season, primarily at right-back. Like me, Pack had come through the ranks at Arsenal and we knew each other, but I never got on that well with him. He had a strange personality, one of those players who could really get your goat. He could have made it at Arsenal, he was a good full-back and featured in a First Division match against Leeds United, but upset a few people so he moved to Pompey.

The same thing was happening at Fratton Park; he was getting on people's nerves, and, I can well imagine, driving Smith up the pole with his attitude. Towards the end of the season, I told the manager I was getting married to Carole in June 1969 and asked whether Pompey had any club houses. As it happened, he explained, one was about to become available because its occupant was to be released, although that player had yet to be told. So I had Roy Pack's beautiful three-bedroomed semi-detached house in Corbett Road, Waterlooville!

Following 25 appearances in my first Fratton Park season, I began as a regular starter in 1969/70, only for injury to intervene against Hull City in September 1969. There had been a fair amount of rain before the start of the Second Division fixture, while our groundsman, Duggie Reid, always kept the grass a little longer at the beginning of a campaign to protect the surface. In an attempt to get a bit of grip, I put in longer studs — and ended up breaking my leg and dislocating my ankle. After 30 minutes, Hull winger Ian Butler checked back and I followed him, but my studs caught in the turf and you could see the bone sticking out. It was a bad injury.

Bobby Campbell drove me to the old Royal Portsmouth Hospital, in Commercial Road, where they put me into an A&E cubicle and I was later joined by Carole. Now Bobby had a bit of expertise, having trained in physiotherapy at the hospital, as well as being first-team coach. When they asked Carole for permission to operate that night, Bobby enquired who would be carrying it out. When he found out, he insisted I wait for the female surgeon on duty the following morning, being among the top ones at the hospital. As it was, the morning procedure took four hours and, to this day, I've never had any trouble with that leg.

It was while sidelined through my injury in that 1969/70 season that I witnessed Smith fight my teammate George Ley in a boxing match, a main event which had been brewing for quite some weeks. Now Harry Harris was a wind-up merchant and, having occupied the Pompey dressing room for 12 seasons, making more than 400 appearances, he knew which buttons to press. On one occasion, the manager walked in and Harry said: "George Ley thinks he can have you in a fight, boss." Smith, who would never back down from anything, replied: "Fine, fair enough, we'll have one." So it was organised in the little gym around the back of the old Fratton End, with all the office staff present. Being injured, I sat in Smith's corner supplying him water while serving as the timekeeper, holding the stopwatch.

George Ley was quiet and unassuming. You never got a lot of conversation out of him, even when we shared Southsea digs, but he was a terrific guy, although Smith would get on to him quite a bit. Certainly you didn't want to be on the wrong side of our left-back considering he was a decent boxer and very capable of looking after himself. Now this was his chance to get revenge on the manager, having put up with his comments for more than two years. The boxing match consisted of three three-minute rounds, with George Ley pummelling his manager in the first round, at one point knocking him over the benches and into the crowd. When Smith returned to his corner, Ronnie Tindall was fanning him with the towel, while I'm thinking: "Please don't go back out there, he's going to kill you!" Bobby Campbell, as referee, asked me to knock it down to two-minute rounds, so I did. Not that it helped. By the time of the third and final round, it was down to a minute, only for Tindall to throw in the towel halfway through. If I'm not mistaken, Smith took a couple of days off after that, claiming he had to go away somewhere, but most likely spending a bit of time at home recovering!

He'd had fights with other players too, with Gordon Neave telling me of the time Smith had come to blows with Roy Lunniss, an uncompromising defender who was at Pompey a few years before me. The story went that Lunniss was in the changing room receiving treatment for a thigh problem and Smith came in swearing, wanting to know what he was doing there as he wasn't injured, before ripping a bandage off the defender's leg. That prompted a fight between them, apparently a right free-for-all, but that was standard George. He would have a scrap with anybody.

Nonetheless, you can't have the manager of a Second Division club having a boxing match with one of his players. He was in his mid-50s, couldn't stand up properly because his leg often gave way, and walked with a limp. The whole thing was ridiculous. As a 20-year-old watching this unfold, I was thinking: "Am I really at a football club which does this? This is madness." Smith, though, would not back down. He'd argue with directors, he'd argue with anyone. That was his personality. Brian Clough had nothing on him.

That proved to be Smith's last season in charge, taking on the role of general manager in April 1970 after the final match against Hull, with the team finishing 17th. Player-coach Ronnie Tindall was his replacement, an appointment we expected. It had long been clear he was after Smith's job. When I saw George move upstairs I knew he wouldn't last long in that environment. It wasn't his forte. You've either got to be a manager in total charge, or not. Not every player got on well with George, but they trusted him. I know Mike Trebilcock wasn't keen on him because he felt he had a go at him too much, which was fair enough. But most players respected this robust, outspoken individual — and no-one trusted Tindall.

Tindall's behaviour didn't sit right with me. He was coming to the end of his playing days following a reasonable career with Chelsea and Pompey, where he went up front, played at the back, and was generally a good utility player, but I'm always suspicious when a manager is appointed from within. I quite like the idea of going away and establishing yourself somewhere else, starting with a blank slate, so it's all down to you — and in the end he didn't do a very good job at Fratton Park. Ronnie was wheedling his way in to get that job, all the players knew it. I never got on well with him, I thought he was two-faced and had numerous rows in his office, before eventually leaving. I didn't mind being dropped by George Smith, but not Tindall.

But he was now installed as Pompey's manager for the 1970/71 campaign and I immediately found myself out of the first-team picture, with Tindall recruiting Freddie Smith from Burnley to play at right-back and Eoin Hand called upon when he was unavailable. I made one appearance in the first half of the season, coming off the bench against Leyton Orient, only to suddenly find myself handed the left-back role for the visit of Sheffield United in the FA Cup third round in January 1971. I was instructed to mark their winger Alan Woodward, a good player, and I had a great match as we won 2-0 through goals from Ray Hiron and Mike Trebilcock. I was at the top of my powers, quick and getting in tight, with a crowd of 20,556 at Fratton Park to see it. Woodward never got a touch. I was really proud of that display. I'd been shoved in at the deep end after four months without a match and performed, while also setting up Hiron's opener, and it remains my favourite Blues game.

The next round of the FA Cup saw First Division Arsenal visit and, being my former club, I knew nearly all of them — Pat Rice, Frank McLintock, John Radford, George Armstrong and Bob Wilson. There were 39,659 packed into Fratton Park, although I had returned to the bench after Ley had recovered from injury — but still played my part in Trebilcock's last-minute equaliser. Occasionally I was used up front and Tindall introduced me for Ray Pointer in the second half with us trailing to Peter Storey's penalty. Then, with the game almost done, Freddie Smith intercepted a pass from John Radford, ran down the right and delivered a cross into the box. I got the slightest of touches to it, flicking it on, and Trebilcock finished at the far post to make it 1-1.

The replay was scheduled for the following Tuesday at Highbury, but was called off when we were at the stadium because of a waterlogged pitch. We lost 3-2 to a team which would eventually win the double that season, while I was again on the bench, this time not used, which was hugely disappointing. You would have expected a change when losing — and I never came close to playing at Highbury again.

Later that season, Tindall's relationship with the players was damaged irreparably over our final match against Leicester City in May 1971. Smith had brought in a system which rewarded each player with a £500 bonus should Pompey reach at least 35 points in a campaign, which, in days of two points for a win, would guarantee you stayed up. Heading into that Fratton Park fixture, we needed one point to reach that tally — and were up against a Foxes side who required victory to claim the Second Division title and contained former Pompey midfielder Bobby Kellard. Now Tindall didn't like this bonus scheme, on the grounds that it didn't give the players any incentive as it only kicked in towards the end of the season. He wanted to instead introduce a restricted bonus scheme.

In the build-up Tindall announced that, as it was Harry Harris' last season before retirement, he would be skippering the team as a fitting farewell. That was all very well, but his previous appearance that campaign was as a substitute at Birmingham City a week earlier — his first outing for more than a year. Now the manager wanted to start the Welshman in a match which had £9,000 riding on it, with 18 players each standing to earn a £500 bonus. Understandably, none of us wanted Harry to feature. I don't think even Harry did. A meeting with the manager was held two days before the match and Albie McCann, who hated Tindall, led the way. He asked: "If you were a player, what would you want? Do you want us to win the bonus?" The manager's reply was — and these are his exact words: "As a player I do, but as a manager I don't. I don't think you deserve it." Well, the players were up in arms. Absolutely fuming. It was clear he was fielding a 37-year-old to weaken the side against the league leaders.

Back then, £500 was a lot of money and the directors didn't want to pay it. Tindall didn't want to pay it. I played left-back in a 2-1 defeat, with Leicester winning the title. We had missed out on the bonus, with Harry Harris making a mistake for the first goal when John Farrington capitalised on a misplaced pass. As for chairman Dennis Collett and his directors, some of the wives saw them afterwards drinking champagne and smoking cigars in celebration, so they were happy. It was an absolute scandal. Tindall lost the players after that, they had no respect for him. Whatever you say about George Smith, the players knew he was upfront. You have to be honest with them; you can't run with the foxes and hunt with the hounds in football. He tried to be friendly with the directors and friendly with the players, but there's always going to be a conflict of interest. Smith never felt he had to be on either side, he was definitely his own boss.

I finished the 1970/71 season strongly, featuring in 22 of the last 23 matches, usually at either right-back or left-back and, on the Monday morning after that Leicester result, I was on a Boeing 747 heading to America to play in the North American Soccer League for Dallas Tornado in a summer-long arrangement. My wife quit her job at Portsmouth Central Library to go with me and we became the Posh and Becks of our day over there! We were a young English couple, a novelty, giving the club a lot of publicity, regularly interviewed by the *Dallas Morning News* newspaper and on local TV. I ended up playing up front, scoring eight goals and bagging four assists in 16 matches.

I returned to Pompey for the final week of pre-season, as fit as I had ever been and playing out of my skin, subsequently starting 19 of our opening 20 matches, all in the centre of defence. However, following a 3-2 defeat at Cardiff City in December 1971, I found myself out of the team again, and, after a flaming row in Tindall's office, I put in a transfer request. He had promised a new contract when I returned from America, but it never materialised. In fact, he denied saying it, so I confronted him. I may have swore, which I shouldn't have done, and called him a "cheat" to his face, but it was now untenable. We would never have got on, plus there was lingering animosity following that Leicester game. My transfer request wasn't accepted at first and it took two or three times until he agreed. It was a gesture from me, something to force the issue because I felt I was going nowhere under him. I didn't trust him, I didn't like him, and that was probably consistent with most of the players. Looking back, though, it was a bit hot-headed. Pompey was still the best club to belong to.

With relegation a concern, I was recalled to the squad in March 1972 and featured in seven of the last 11 matches as we stayed up with one game to spare following a 2-1 victory at Blackpool, which I started. All the time I was thinking: "Is he just using me? What's going on?" And as it turned out, that was my last Pompey appearance. After avoiding relegation, I was dropped for the final fixture. Admittedly, I wasn't the easiest guy to get on with at times, I didn't like Ronnie very much and it probably showed. Sometimes I didn't pick the fights I could win and I was never going to win this one, this was the manager. The chairman certainly wasn't going to undermine him, so my last Blues game was keeping Pompey in the Second Division.

Pompey announced their retained list days later, releasing Mike Trebilcock, Jim Storrie, Jim Standen and Mick Travers and, while taking up on their option to keep me, I remained on the transfer list. In July 1972, Fourth Division Reading signed me for £4,000, but, my god, that was a mistake. Reading had the worst set of directors in the Football League. Moving there from Pompey was a bit like being at The Ritz and leaving to go to a B&B in the Thames Valley. It was a really bad move for me.

Did I make a mistake leaving Pompey without going to a much better place? Definitely. It was a great club with wonderful, loyal supporters. I left the best club I ever played for to join the worst-run club I ever played for. Dear, oh dear.

BARRY HORNE

79 games, seven goals (May 1987 — March 1989)

Pompey 2 (Dillon 2)
West Ham United 1 (Strodder)

First Division, Fratton Park, Saturday, August 31, 1987

Pompey: Knight, Swain, Gilbert, Shotton, Kennedy, Hilaire, Horne, Dillon, Fillery, Baird, Mariner. Subs not used: Quinn, Stewart.

Attendance; 16,104

It never, ever happens nowadays. Premier League clubs don't sign League Two footballers — and they definitely wouldn't start the player regularly in his first season at that level. Not a chance. Back in the day, though, it occurred occasionally — not much, but there were instances of players joining their local club, performing well and earning a big move off the back of it. A teenage Ian Rush did it at Chester before being snapped up by Liverpool. It also happened to me.

Wrexham had finished ninth in the Fourth Division and, in May 1987, Alan Ball, the manager of a Pompey side newly-promoted to the First Division, made me his first signing of the summer, paying £60,000. I ended up totalling 45 appearances in the 1987/88 campaign, scoring three times, being handed my Wales international debut and crowned *The News/Sports Mail*'s player of the season. It was a massive, massive step, hence why Bally watched me as many times as he did before pressing ahead with a deal. I'm still not sure he was absolutely 100 per cent certain about the transfer, but I'd like to think it was a gamble he was eventually satisfied with.

Towards the end of the 1986/87 season with Wrexham, I was in discussions over a move to Third Division Gillingham, who were involved in a play-off campaign. It would have represented a step up following three years in the Fourth Division and, although there had been interest from other clubs, that remained the only firm offer on the table — except I didn't want to go there. The money wasn't right, it was hardly any more than I was earning at Wrexham, and I didn't get a good feel about the place. Certainly house prices were three times as much. It just didn't make sense. Instead I was leaning towards re-signing for Wrexham and waiting until the following summer for a move. I had agonised over a move to Gillingham for a long time — too long. For 10 or 12 days I couldn't give them an answer, but eventually rejected them. The next day I headed into Wrexham's ground to inform them of my decision — and they responded by admitting Pompey were also interested. That was the first I had heard of it. It turned out they hadn't told me because they were hoping I'd join Gillingham, whose money was actually on the table. Had I agreed to move to the Priestfield Stadium, I wouldn't have been aware of Pompey. Now I knew — and it was a different kettle of fish. Within 48 hours I was a Blues player.

Bally's mate Kevin Leahy, a scout from Basingstoke, had been up and down the country 10 times to watch me, while I twice faced Pompey in the second round of the Littlewoods Cup in the previous 1986/87 season, starting for Wrexham over both legs in our 4-1 aggregate defeat. I enjoyed decent games against them, which undoubtedly also helped my case.

I was aged 25 when I arrived at Fratton Park, having graduated from university before beginning my Football League career with Wrexham. As a kid growing up in Flint, Wales, summer holidays consisted of spending a fortnight at Manchester United and a week at Everton, as well as time at Wrexham and Chester. It reached the point where I decided Manchester United wasn't right as players far, far better than me were not being kept on further up the line. Ronnie Whelan was there as a triallist before joining Liverpool, as was Alan Davies, who later represented United's first-team as well as Newcastle United and Swansea City. That proved my point; I don't believe anybody else from that time made it. Similarly, I wasn't confident enough to sign for Everton, whose approach was to recruit loads and loads and loads of schoolboys. Instead, rather than signing schoolboy forms any-where, I decided to stay on at school and study for A-levels.

I don't know why I then went to university, I can't answer that, but I studied chemistry at the University of Liverpool, also captaining them in the National Universities Cup during my second year. After qualifying with a first-class hon-ours degree, I stayed on for a PhD, involving a research project for the company British Nuclear Fuels, while playing semi-professionally for Northern Premier League side Rhyl. Having faced Wrexham in the fourth round of the Welsh Cup, they recruited me in the summer of 1984, prompting the decision to quit my two-year course after 12 months. Having come into professional football late, I was always determined to reach the best level possible.

Then, in the summer of 1987, I was at newly-promoted First Division side Pompey and naturally backed myself to make an impact, although walking into that dressing room was quite intimidating, to be honest. There was Paul Mariner, who I remember watching on TV playing for England. Micky Quinn was obvi-ously a bit of a name. Everywhere I looked were big, big characters who were mates, having largely been together for three years. They had fought on the pitch and off it, experiencing a lot together, and were as thick as thieves — and then I arrived as an outsider, so they tested me. I had arrived from the Fourth Division, so I was required to prove myself and training sessions were intense, because there were some tough characters in there. It was a hostile environment, it was harsh, but I gave as good as I got and eventually was accepted. I earned their respect during my first pre-season and, following my maiden start against West Ham United in August 1987, Eamonn Collins told me: "That's you in the team now." From then on, I started every game.

Bally had signed seven players ahead of Pompey's return to the First Division, with Ian Stewart, Clive Whitehead, Ian Baird, John Kerr, Terry Connor and Mick Fillery joining me as summer recruits. Each were good players, the vast majority possessing top-flight experience, but they weren't the full package, if you like. Fillery was a great passer with a superb touch but not a fantastic athlete. Stewart had been to the 1986 World Cup finals with Northern Ireland but hadn't played much for Newcastle United. Bally was taking a chance with them all. They were talented footballers, but there was an element of a gamble and a reason why they were available. I'm guessing that was the nature of the budget and size of the club at the time — whereas I was the only signing coming the other way, moving up the Football League.

I loved Bally, he was very passionate and brilliant for me. I wouldn't say he was a great manager, but a fabulous coach — and fantastic to drink with, which all the lads did on a regular basis back then. As an Everton supporter, the team you forever remember is when you're aged eight or nine and I recall Bally playing for us. He had moved to Arsenal by the time I started going to Goodison Park semi-regularly, with Bob Latchford my hero in what wasn't the best Everton team. Some 15 years later at Pompey, Bally was still the best player in our five-a-sides, he prided himself on that, as were Howard Kendall and Colin Harvey when I was later with the Toffeemen. A lot of players had a love-hate relationship with Bally — he was that type of bloke, possibly too emotional to be a top manager — but he still enjoyed a good managerial career with Pompey, Manchester City and Southampton. He was no mug, but coaching was his main strength.

Bally was quite smart in how he eased me into that First Division season. I came off the bench in three of the opening four matches, before being handed a full debut against West Ham at Fratton Park. Days earlier in August 1987, we'd lost 6-0 at Arsenal, with Alan Smith scoring a hat-trick, and now I was challenged with marking the Hammers' Liam Brady. He was a fantastic midfielder and Bally sent me out with the instructions: "Just make sure he doesn't have a good game. Don't let him play." Well, we won 2-1 through Kevin Dillon's double, representing our first victory of the season. Having played in the centre of midfield alongside Dillon for that win, from that moment I started all 42 of the remaining fixtures. Adjusting to the top flight was no problem at all. I really enjoyed it. Apart from when I faced Bryan Robson at Manchester United and Newcastle's Paul Gascoigne, I cannot remember coming away from too many games thinking: "I've been completely outclassed there."

Just three weeks into the season, I was handed my Wales debut as a late substitute in a 1-0 win over Denmark at Ninian Park in September 1987, at the age of 25. I didn't represent my country at any age group — I wasn't even close, as I was too small — and my first senior involvement came at Wrexham, being named in an expanded squad against Scotland in 1985 before I was cut. Clearly I was already on the radar before arriving at Fratton Park and I went on to earn 59 caps, yet that's the one thing which nags at me about not reaching the Football League earlier. By the time I made my debut, some of my teammates around the same age had already reached 30-40 caps. Over the next 10 years, I missed just two international matches, both through injury against Holland. In fairness, I reached a good number of Wales caps bearing in mind I didn't play until my mid-20s, but I would have liked more.

I scored three First Division goals in my maiden Pompey season, all arriving away from Fratton Park — and each yielding the only three league victories we managed on our travels. My first Blues goal was at Norwich City in November 1987, with a half-volley from the edge of the box after Ian Baird's shot was pushed out. Then we won 1-0 at Tottenham Hotspur in April 1988 after Kevin Dillon put me through and I buried the rebound when my shot was initially saved by Bobby Mimms. Sandwiched in between those occasions, of course, was the 2-0 triumph at Southampton.

We were struggling in 19th place heading to The Dell in January 1988 and I really didn't appreciate the animosity between the two sets of fans before witnessing it first hand. Coming from Wales, we had the Chester-Wrexham derby and Everton versus Liverpool, so I was oblivious to the strength of feeling between Pompey and Southampton supporters. I opened the scoring on 16 minutes with a six-yard volley at the far post and Terry Connor added a second just seven minutes later — and 2-0 is how it remained for an absolutely brilliant occasion.

That proved to be Micky Kennedy's final Pompey appearance before joining Bradford City days later. We got on fine, but he was a complex character and the main one in training who I had to stand up to. He may well have harboured thoughts that I was going to take the place of him or one of his mates, so he approached things in a certain way. There were a few unspoken things, nobody said anything about it or complained, but it was there. I got on as well as anybody did with Micky, who very much kept himself to himself and loved his drink, and, irrespective of his controversies on the pitch, remained a good footballer. I realised and respected what a talented player he was. His behaviour didn't really matter to me, I didn't need to be pals with people because they were teammates and I wasn't looking to make friends with everybody. Whatever Mick wanted to do, that was fine by me. In truth, his departure wasn't a big deal. I wanted to be in the team and I didn't really care about anything else which went on. It didn't matter to me.

We ended up suffering relegation that season, finishing 19th, but we weren't a million miles away from safety. The visit of Newcastle to Fratton Park in May 1988 for our penultimate match was an important one, but we lost 2-1 and our final chance of staying up had gone. It had been a tough campaign and we were always up against it. I don't believe Bally had a massive budget and our squad wasn't strong enough for that division, that's for sure.

On a personal level, my first Pompey season was an amazing success, despite the obvious devastation at relegation. I had played a full year in the First Division and clubs were now aware of me. Having sampled the top flight, I wanted to get back there as soon as I could with Pompey, yet it quickly became apparent that it wasn't going to be happening. Bally kept promising a new deal, but it never materialised and then he was replaced by his coach John Gregory in January 1989, midway through my second year. Gregory was a nice enough bloke who didn't possess the charisma or gravitas that Bally had but, as the manager, whatever he asked us to do, I would carry it out to the absolute best of my ability. However, I was aware the likes of Manchester United, Spurs and Glasgow Rangers were monitoring me and then, in the final week of the transfer window in March 1989, Southampton stumped up a club-record transfer fee to sign me — £700,000.

In truth, I never took on board that I was crossing the south-coast divide and joining Pompey's fierce rivals. It was purely an opportunity to return to the First Division at the age of 26. I was focused on my football career. I wasn't going to stay at Pompey in the Second Division when I could more than double my wages and return to the First Division — and, should there be an adverse reaction, I'd do my best to win the fans over. As it was, initially I was hated by both sets of supporters and, when I look back, I understand.

I had scored against Southampton and it was in their supporters' minds, they remembered that, while I was also an ex-Pompey footballer now playing for them. I received hate mail from both sets of fans, addressed to me at The Dell; letters making it clear exactly what they thought of me. I just put them in the bin, not giving them any credence whatsoever. I can understand Pompey fans hating me because they had given me the opportunity and I had won all the player of the year awards going but I would argue that I repaid them by doing my best every single time I pulled on that shirt. What actually bothered me was the reaction from Southampton. "Hang on," I thought. "I'm your record signing, give me a chance." They took quite a lot of winning over. After a while, though, it became a non-thing.

When the late Chris Nicholl was manager I hardly missed a game and then when Ian Branfoot replaced him in June 1991 it all went wrong. I think I eventually became accepted and appreciated by the supporters, although not massively. I won't ever say I was a fans' favourite at Southampton because I was never going to be. Nicholl was brave, very brave, in not only paying a club-record transfer fee for me, but also overseeing the first player to move directly from Pompey to Southampton in 43 years. As for me, it didn't take long to decide. It wasn't like at Wrexham when I was prepared to wait for another transfer to come along rather than switch to Gillingham; this deal was taking me back into the First Division now. I certainly wasn't going to turn it down. As it was, I spent the next seven-and-a-half years in the top flight with Southampton and then Everton.

I look back fondly on my time at Pompey, because it established me in the top flight and I enjoyed every game with an amazing bunch of real characters. I don't think I've ever been in a dressing room like that. Noel Blake, Kevin Dillon, Vince Hilaire, Paul Mariner, Alan Knight and the rest were all a bit bonkers. It was a big drinking squad and I could do that. The social scene at Ellie Jays and Martine's was great. Alan Ball and Pompey gave me the opportunity to begin what I managed to achieve in my career, it's as simple as that — and I really, really appreciate it.

TERRY BRISLEY

69 games, 15 goals (July 1979 — May 1981)

Northampton Town 0
Pompey 2 (Davey, Purdie)

Fourth Division, County Ground, Saturday, May 3, 1980

Pompey: Mellor, McLaughlin, Davey, Ellis, Bryant, Brisley, Laidlaw, Brown, Purdie, Davey, Hemmerman. Sub Not Used: Gregory

Attendance; 10,774

We returned to the County Ground's away dressing room following a 2-0 victory, yet Frank Burrows was in no mood to crack a smile. "All sit down," he barked and, like obedient schoolboys, we dutifully settled without a murmur. I positioned myself on a seat between Steve Bryant and Jeff Hemmerman on the end of the bench. Stan Harland, Pompey's assistant manager, had gone to find out other Fourth Division results on that final day of the 1979/80 season.

"Sit down until Stan comes back," Frank continued — but we didn't have to wait for his return. There may have been deathly silence in that room, but those 8,000 travelling fans announced the news. The roar outside told us exactly what we wanted to hear — Bradford City had lost at Peterborough United. Then the door opened and Harland reappeared with a thumbs up: "Boss, done. It went our way." The Blues had been promoted. We went crazy, although the manager didn't want champagne in the dressing room. Instead, we toasted success with cans of Coca-Cola.

A few minutes earlier, we had been forced to flee the Northampton Town pitch upon the final whistle as jubilant Pompey supporters invaded. One even plonked a blue and white hat on my head as I raced by, which I kept for many years. After promotion was confirmed a short while afterwards, we climbed the grandstand's rickety steps to take the accolades from our fans still occupying the pitch below. Steve Davey and Ian Purdie netted the decisive goals, although we still had to rely on Tony Cliss' winner for Posh to secure us fourth spot and the final promotion place. Not that we didn't deserve it. It could have been three or four that day. We were absolutely fantastic when it really mattered and won with style. We started the day in fifth, knowing nothing less than victory was required, yet we expected to beat Northampton. That sounds big-headed, but it really isn't. We'd hit form at the right time, winning four and drawing two of our previous six matches heading into that last fixture in May 1980. Now Pompey had their first promotion in 18 years.

The Cobblers kindly invited the players into one of their supporter bars, where we were drinking away until Frank Burrows appeared: "We're leaving now, get on the bus." He wasn't asking — it was an ultimatum. He never showed his emotion, he was a very dour Scot. Inside, Frank was probably going absolutely crazy, but felt he couldn't show it to the players because it would represent a sign of weakness. Then, as the team coach left the ground, we noticed two Pompey fans aged 12 or 13 standing by the side of the road thumbing a lift — so we offered them one. There was champagne and bottles of lager for the players and staff, while the boys were handed cups of lemonade. They travelled with us to Frogmore Road, then somebody dropped them off at their homes.

Just 48 hours after winning promotion, we played a Bank Holiday Monday friendly against First Division Brighton & Hove Albion as part of Steve Foster's transfer a year earlier, with 14,346 at Fratton Park giving us a great reception. Then, on the Wednesday, two open-top buses containing everyone from the club were given a ticker-tape send-off from Fratton Park as we made our way to Guildhall Square, with supporters lining the streets. After meeting the Lord Mayor inside, we came out and stood on the steps, where we were introduced one-by-one to thousands of Blues supporters packed into the area, proudly singing the Pompey Chimes. It represented the second promotion of my career, having previously achieved it with Millwall, the club I supported, in 1975/76 to escape the Third Division. Many guys have played professional football for 15 years and never tasted that wonderful feeling, so I consider myself extremely fortunate to have sampled it twice.

Just 11 months earlier, I was holidaying in Son Bou, Menorca, relaxing around the pool with my first wife Jill and two-year-old daughter Gemma, when I was informed by the hotel reception that there was a phone call for me. Puzzled, I discovered Pompey chairman John Deacon on the other end of the line. "Hello Terry, are you having a nice holiday? I hear you're available for transfer at Charlton Athletic and we would be interested." My reply was a bit sharp — not rude, more flippant: "I'm on holiday at the moment with my family, this is my rest following a hard season. I hope you don't mind me saying, but I'm not doing anything until I get home." Unperturbed, Mr. Deacon responded: "I thoroughly understand, Terry. Tell me when you're coming back and the next day I'll get Frank Burrows to give you a ring."

Charlton had just avoided relegation from the Second Division by a single point. My two-year contract was up and they wanted me to sign a fresh 12-month deal, but I had no intention of staying as I couldn't get on with the manager Andy Nelson and wanted to play proper football. The pattern of play comes from the management down to the coaches and at The Valley, it was basic. Just long balls into the corner flags.

It was now June 1979 and Mr. Deacon's words had got me thinking. As agreed, Pompey's owner rang the day after we returned from holiday, so I told him: "To be perfectly honest, Mr. Deacon, I don't think you'd be able to afford what I'd probably like. I've got a bit of an upheaval to come to Pompey." Naturally, I was attempting to get a really good deal and was well aware that the club were known for paying decent money at the time, trying to recruit older, experienced players to get out of the Fourth Division. He replied: "I'll tell you what, Terry ... put the phone down, have a think and call me back in half-an-hour with your thoughts. But don't worry about the finances." When I rang him, he agreed to all my terms in about two seconds: "I don't think that would hurt us, Terry." Blast, I should have gone for more! Still, I was dropping from the Second Division to the Fourth Division to play for Pompey for a pay rise. The following day, Frank Burrows came to Brentwood and sold the club to me.

Frank had taken over as manager permanently the previous month, following a 10-game stint as caretaker after Jimmy Dickinson suffered a heart attack in Barnsley's away dressing room in March 1979. The chairman was desperate to get Pompey out of the Fourth Division and quite prepared to fund whatever was necessary to achieve that. The crowd were also getting a bit rumbustious — very much a feeling of "Get us out of this division. We don't care how, just get us out." You can't blame them; they are fantastic supporters, but, like anything else, if you do not achieve success after a certain amount of time, they won't be happy. Portsmouth is a unique city — they don't care about anyone else, they're Pompey through and through. If you're born in Portsmouth and leave, you still live in Portsmouth. It's a wonderful club.

For the opening match of the 1979/80 season against Hartlepool United, there were five debutants, with John McLaughlin, Archie Styles, Steve Aizlewood and Alan Rogers joining me in the starting line-up. It was an instant impact, with McLaughlin, Steve Bryant and Colin Garwood scoring in a 3-0 success to get the campaign up and running in positive fashion. When I arrived, I believed it would be kick and rush under Frank Burrows, but I was wrong. It didn't turn out like that. He'd try to chop it up a bit, playing it short and long, yet the finite point of success was our left-footed players. Normally you'd find one good left-footer within a squad, yet we had four or five of them, all capable of excellent crossing. Rogers' delivery was superb, Steve Bryant was good, Styles was good, Ian Purdie was okay, while Keith Viney was also there — and the left was where we created the chances.

You knew Alan Rogers would go on the outside of full-backs and he was exceptional; never the quickest but capable of going either way and armed with that step-over. His superb crossing ability was tailor-made for someone like me and the primary reason I scored 14 goals in that promotion season, earning the nickname "Far Post Brisley." I had played most of my career in the centre of midfield for Leyton Orient, Millwall and Charlton, where I'd be the stopper. A good tackler, getting the ball and knocking it. Now Frank was asking me to do a specific job on the right-hand side of a midfield three, despite having no pace whatsoever. In those days, Fourth Division defenders weren't the brightest, so I'd break late into the box when I could see where the ball would arrive — and knew exactly what I was going to do with it. I was decent in the air for my size, and I wanted to get into that penalty area. What was the point of being on the edge? Most goals are scored from eight yards out, so it made no sense being positioned 25 yards away.

My maiden Pompey goal arrived in my fifth outing, netting in the pouring rain in a 6-1 victory over Scunthorpe United at Fratton Park in August 1979. It began a period of seven goals in eight matches for me and the wins kept on coming for the Blues, triumphing in 12 of our opening 14 Fourth Division fixtures during a racing start. I wasn't the only one among the goals either, with Colin Garwood and our skipper Joe Laidlaw also regulars on the scoresheet — and, incidentally, also our worst trainers.

Joe was exceptional for that team, a very good reader of the game, and we had a real rapport in midfield. Should I already be in the box for a Pompey attack, he would instead find other space, often taking up a position to tap in from four or five yards. We had this great understanding, He was a lovable rogue, but a really, really poor trainer, which you'd never realise on a Saturday because he'd run his socks off. In a match you wanted him alongside you because he never shirked, always providing 100 per cent. As captain, if things weren't going right, his style was never to have a go at people or dishing out a rollicking. Instead he'd attempt to gee us up by saying: "Come on, let's get a bit sharper." Regardless, he was a dreadful trainer, very lazy, as was Garwood. It irritated Frank Burrows but in the end, he could no longer be bothered trying to change them.

Frank had not long retired from playing for Swindon, so joined in with fitness training, with his assistant Stan Harland overseeing it. He was as mad as a March hare, taking part in cross-country runs, trying to beat us. He usually finished ahead of goalkeeper Peter Mellor, who wasn't physically fit, Joe Laidlaw and "Gabby" Garwood. Frank loved it, constantly telling them: "You two should be beating me," but they didn't give a toss. They were what they were. Their philosophy was: "Don't worry, we'll do it on the pitch on a Saturday." Gabby was a poacher, he never wanted the ball outside the penalty area, but if you got down the line and delivered a cross into the six-yard box, there would be a clever side foot or little flick and it would be in the back of the net. The real problem for Gabby, though, was that his laziness in training gave Frank a quick excuse to drop him as soon as he stopped scoring.

In September 1979, we beat Bournemouth 4-0 at Fratton Park and the two goals I scored included the best one of my career. Jeff Hemmerman, who also netted twice in that match, laid it off and, from around 23 yards, I struck a right-footed volley which flew over their 6ft 4in keeper Kenny Allen and into the top corner. I couldn't believe it. The second arrived from a typical Archie Styles run down the left, knocking a big, long cross towards the far post which hung there. I'm watching the ball, not the goalkeeper, and thinking: "I know he's going to clobber me, but I've got to go for this." From around five yards out, I closed my eyes and glanced it into the net — it was the keeper's ball, but he was still on his line! Just two weeks later, we travelled to Dean Court for the corresponding fixture, roared on by 9,000 Pompey fans, and I scored the winner in a 1-0 victory, side-footing home Gabby's corner after nobody picked me up.

That first part of the season was so good, everything seemed quite easy, while off the pitch we lived in Westbourne, a beautiful little area classed as a village, with a cricket club, a bakery I visited every morning to get fresh bread, and Emsworth up the road. As for my teammates, John McLaughlin was at right-back offering the real width. He could see acres ahead of him and was the life and soul of the party, the comedian of the squad. Peter Ellis was a very quiet individual. He wouldn't be the one bringing up conversation, instead listening to what others said and on the pitch, I don't think I ever heard him call for a ball. He was a great athlete, probably the best in the squad. Steve Aizlewood was also very quiet but talented boy, a centre-half who was extremely brave in the air, but could also play and knock short balls

We had Peter Mellor in goal, who we nicknamed "Splat" on account of how he struggled to hold the ball, particularly in training. It's like the *Beano* comic, where they are messing about playing football in a puddle and it would slip out of the fingers with the caption: Splat! In fairness, when training at Eastney Barracks, especially on the wet grass, it was difficult for goalkeepers, but he took it in good spirits. Everybody called it him and he laughed at it. Peter loved people talking about him because he felt important. You can only judge a person's football career when you're with them and, despite having previously represented Burnley and Fulham, you realised he had come to the end of his career. Still, he got on fantastically well with the crowd, they loved this blonde character with a fantastic physique — even though he wasn't the greatest in regards to protecting the goal.

Peter's goalkeeping rival, Alan Knight, was getting annoyed at playing second fiddle to him, especially being a miles better player. In training, you can properly judge a 'keeper when dealing with shots and while Peter had enjoyed a fantastic career, we all knew Knightsie was actually ahead of him. Peter was such a nice person, though; he could have been a bank manager or selling insurance because he was always smiling. When he left for Canadian club Edmonton Drillers in the North American Soccer League (NASL), I'm sure he got all the pelicans lined up looking at him and going: "Isn't he a nice man."

We marked the end of 1979 with the 6-1 thumping of Northampton at Fratton Park to enter the new year in second spot, strongly placed for promotion at the halfway stage. However, a 3-1 New Year's Day defeat to Aldershot Town sparked a run of four wins in 14 Fourth Division fixtures as everything unravelled alarmingly. Yet, amid that disappointing period, we should have inflicted an FA Cup third-round upset over First Division Middlesbrough. Our biggest crowd for three years — 31,743 — packed into Fratton Park and, after the final whistle, their midfielder David Armstrong, a lovely bloke, shook my hand and asked: "How the hell are you in the Fourth Division?" I had finished off Steve Aizlewood's right-wing delivery to cancel out Terry Cochrane's opener to make it 1-1 and then, in the final minute, Alan Rogers crossed for Jeff Hemmerman to side-foot past keeper Jim Platt. Goal. Actually, no goal — the linesman's flag was raised for offside. It was a 50/50 call; sometimes decisions go your way and sometimes they don't. Middlesbrough got away with it but they were a different team at Ayresome Park for the replay, John Neal's side winning 3-0.

It was back to the league and while I don't like being too critical of Frank Burrows, who was a fantastic motivator, he panicked a little about our declining form and was suddenly changing things around. At our best we had a settled side — nobody was injured, the team picked itself — and then when it started hiccupping, he began doing things a little too rashly. Knightsie made way for Mellor, Steve Davey missed 13 games with a calf injury, John McLaughlin was dropped, injured, dropped again and injured once more, he kept swapping between Keith Viney and Styles at left-back, while I was dropped to the reserves for three matches before returning to score on my recall against Huddersfield Town in a 4-1 victory in February 1980. In addition, we signed David Gregory and Alan Garner and, much to the real annoyance of supporters, sold our 17-goal leading scorer to Aldershot for £54,000.

Colin Garwood's February 1980 departure wasn't a surprise, I knew it was coming. The crowd loved Gabby, Frank liked Gabby because he scored goals — and that's where it ended. He didn't like him as a mate or a person he could get on with down the pub. Gabby didn't need to be fit — he scored goals from six-yards out, he didn't want to run here and there — yet Jeff Hemmerman did, David Gregory did and Derek Showers did. Frank wasn't bothered about losing him. What he really wanted was a player he could work with — and that wasn't Gabby. I know he was popular with the supporters but Frank could turn point to promotion as justification for his sale. Had he remained, Gabby may have kept on scoring, we'll never know, but he was never going to change his ways for Frank.

David Gregory had arrived from Bury two months before Gabby's departure, immediately replacing him in the starting XI, and was a different player. Underrated even. Brought in to score goals, he netted three times in his opening four appearances, but it didn't quite happen for him that season and he finished as an unused substitute in the promotion game at Northampton. What Gregory offered was pace. He liked the ball in front of him and would beat the central defender to it, with Frank preferring to play him off the centre-forward collecting flick-ons. Gregory wasn't the only new face in the side from December onwards, with Steve Perrin having also arrived while, during our bad run, Burrows recruited Alan Garner and Jimmy Brown, desperately trying to reignite our season. We had a massive squad, using 26 players in total, but chopping and changing didn't improve the results. In fact, they got worse. Then he finally discovered the winning formula once more — by returning to 10 of the players who had performed so consistently during that excellent first half of the campaign.

A 3-2 victory at Port Vale in April 1980 would herald a strong end to the season, with five wins and two draws ensuring we won promotion in fourth place — on goal difference ahead of Bradford. We scored 91 league goals that year, a club record at the time, with four players reaching double figures — myself, Laidlaw, Hemmerman and the departed Garwood.

In his first full season as Pompey manager, Frank Burrows had led us back to the Third Division after a two-year absence. He was as hard as nails, very strict, yet one of the most honest people I have ever known. When he wanted to try something new, he'd get you in the office and explain how he was changing things — and I would respond with: "Okay, boss." There was no point in arguing, I knew he was probably right, but, most of all, I didn't mind as long as the manager was being honest — and boy was Frank honest. He liked training, taking it every single day. Rather than sitting in an office, he was out with the players working on crosses, dead balls, heading. He was an exceptional professional.

Although Frank kept his distance, he was never one of the boys and wouldn't join us for a drink. It was always a case of: "Not for me, you go and enjoy yourselves." Yet he was never in it for himself, always doing things for other people, and you definitely wouldn't want to get into a fight with him because you'd lose! He was quiet, though, never a ranter and raver; instead, a gruff, hard person who'd look you in the eye and tell you the truth. I loved him as a manager, even though I didn't think he was the greatest coach in the world. He worked hard, loved his job and, as somebody who had your respect, you gave a bit extra as a result.

Now in the Third Division for the 1980/81 season, I kept my place in midfield, yet was beginning to experience problems with my right knee. I couldn't drive forward or chip a ball without it twinging, but the worst part was trying to twist and turn. It was so painful, and I became fearful of attempting certain things. The knee could collapse in matches, unable to hold my leg's weight. Gordon Neave would enter the pitch with his magic sponge, and then two or three minutes later I'd get up and it was okay. But it kept happening, and people thought I was diving! I was never a pacy player, yet now I didn't want to overstretch on a run, bracing myself for the pain once again. I couldn't continue to perform. I started the opening 20 games of the season, but no longer at the levels I wanted to.

The injury sidelined me for the League Cup fourth-round trip to Liverpool in October 1980, but Frank still took me along, which I appreciated. He could see I was peed off and struggling, so I travelled with the lads, even sitting on the bench at Anfield, albeit not being on the teamsheet. We lost 4-1 that night, but I felt so sorry for the boys because we should have won, without a doubt. There were 12,500 Pompey fans inside Anfield, it was all blue, with Liverpool fielding the likes of Ray Clemence, Alan Hanson, Kenny Dalglish, Graeme Souness, Phil Neal, Alan Kennedy, Terry McDermott, Sammy Lee and Ray Kennedy. It was an incredibly strong side. They went on to win the competition, beating West Ham United 2-1 in the final in a replay — with 10 of the side which faced Pompey lining up at Wembley. After our defeat, Liverpool's manager Bob Paisley entered our dressing room with Stan Harland and stood in the middle of the room. "Hey lads," he said. "You lost the war, but you won the battle." He was right; the boys had played fantastically well. Liverpool scored twice in the final 10 minutes to create a scoreline which didn't accurately reflect the game, but those present knew the truth.

With my knee still troubling me, Pompey's club doctor suggested going under the knife and I was operated on at Queen Alexandra Hospital. I'm sure I was told it would be keyhole surgery, but the next day there was a massive scar on the back of the knee. I was informed the problem was caused by nerves sticking to the muscles inside my knee and not releasing — yet that was a huge misdiagnosis which ended my career prematurely. I kept making comebacks in the reserves, but it wasn't right. The operation wasn't any good, it proved unsuccessful and I never returned to Pompey's first-team. I told Frank: "This is no good, mate. I'm not enjoying it and obviously you aren't getting the best out of me." With my two-year contract up in May 1981, I was released, along with fellow promotion winners Steve Davey and Steve Perrin, while Ken Todd, Steve Bryant and Alan Garner were transfer-listed.

My Football League career was over at the age of 30, but I went on to play for Maidstone United in the Alliance Premier League and then Chelmsford City, before retiring in the summer of 1982. In football, you have to be confident in your body and being able to cope through 90 minutes, but injury finished me early because of a misdiagnosis and I would require two further operations in retirement before it was put right.

When you come to places like Pompey, you don't realise how the lives of those people standing on the terraces revolve around the football club and its fortunes. You possess the power to make these people smile, laugh and be happy, and I still think of those wonderful scenes at Northampton and around the city following promotion. That, as a footballer, is so, so humbling.

BRETT PITMAN

99 games, 42 goals (July 2017 — July 2020)

Pompey 3 (Hawkins, Pitman 2)
Bristol Rovers 0

League One, Fratton Park, Tuesday, September 26, 2017

Pompey: McGee, Thompson, Burgess, Clarke, Donohue, Lowe, O'Keefe, Close, Kennedy (87 mins, Bennett), Lowe, Pitman, Hawkins (82 mins, Evans). Subs not used: Bass, Talbot, Haunstrup, Naismith, Main.

Attendance; 17,716

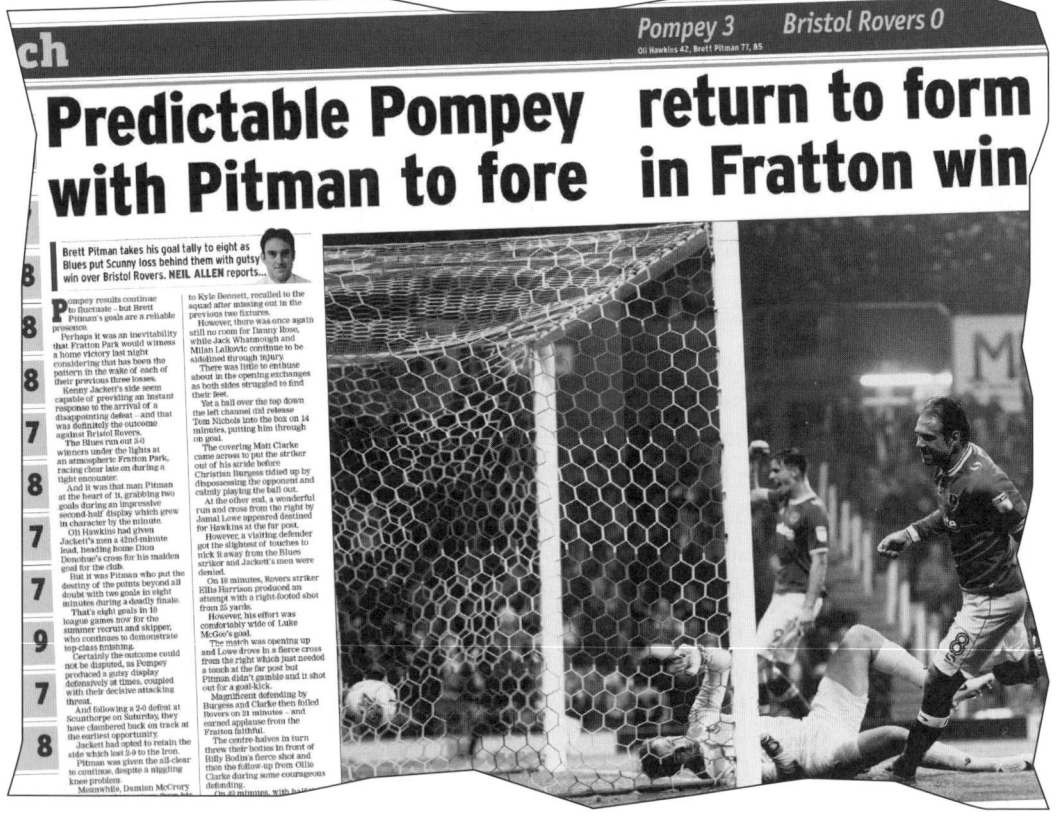

From the cinema room in our Poole home, me and my eldest son Harlow watched the second leg of Pompey's League One play-off semi-final against Oxford United. When it headed to spot-kicks after finishing 2-2 on aggregate, the camera showed Kenny Jackett looking around for penalty takers and I laughed at the ridiculousness of it all. I'd done all I could to make that squad for those July 2020 matches, yet a manager lives and dies by his decisions and, ultimately, that result probably marked the beginning of the end for him at Fratton Park.

I was desperate to feature in the play-offs and, with the Covid-19 pandemic delaying the season's end, I happily agreed to extend my expiring Blues contract for an extra few months to cover them. With the Football League calendar having been postponed for three-and-a-half months, nobody was match-fit, yet I was as fit as anybody else, having worked hard during that period. Nonetheless, I was left out of the first leg, which finished 1-1 at Fratton Park, despite clubs temporarily being granted permission to name nine players on their bench.

In the build-up, Kenny had called to inform me that I wasn't going to be involved in the 20-man squad, before adding: "But keep your phone on because I may include you in the second leg." That was fine. Following that draw, I rang Kenny to clarify whether I would now be involved for the deciding match — and the answer remained: "No." So I called his assistant, Joe Gallen, and asked whether he could change the manager's mind. "If it was up to me," he said, "I would have you." I believed Joe because he didn't need to say that and it would have been easier to agree with Kenny. Then I contacted our chief executive Mark Catlin and said: "Look, come on, this is just stupid." He told me: "I would have you, but it's up to Kenny."

That was it. It made no sense. Even if he put me on the bench and didn't use me, at least the option was there, particularly should he require a penalty taker — which, as it turned out, actually was the case. Pompey were able to name nine substitutes for those play-offs, yet couldn't find a place for somebody with 42 goals in 99 appearances for the club.

Frustratingly, I had become used to a substitute role under Kenny Jackett. Despite being the first Pompey player in 15 years to register 25 goals in a season, over the following two years I would be named on the bench a total of 55 times. It got to the point where, during the game, I'd run up and down the touchline of my own accord, just so the fans would sing my name to annoy Jackett! As soon as we went 1-0 down, I'd be out there warming-up — not because I was expecting to come on, more to wind up the manager. Now it was the semi-finals of the League One play-offs and they couldn't even find room for me among the substitutes. I watched at home as Cameron McGeehan missed his spot-kick as Pompey went out 5-4 on penalties — and I never played for them again.

My time at Fratton Park began three years earlier in July 2017. Jackett may have signed me from Ipswich Town, but there had previously been talk of Paul Cook showing interest before he quit to become Wigan Athletic boss after leading Pompey to promotion into League One. I hadn't played as many Championship games as I would have liked with the Tractor Boys in 2016/17, with 23 appearances, and had now entered the final 12 months of my deal. Besides, my eldest son was just about to start school and, with the family living on the outskirts of Ipswich, it seemed the ideal time to move back south, where we had kept our Poole home.

Dropping into League One never bothered me, I was signing for the Blues because of the club's size and fanbase, while the team were expected to push on again having claimed the League Two title months earlier. Certainly the chance to replace Michael Doyle as captain was never a deal breaker. During discussions with Kenny, he raised the subject of me becoming skipper and, while it wasn't something I had done before, I definitely wouldn't be rejecting the chance. I've always been a talker on the pitch and a voice in the dressing room, while attempting to lead by example, so wearing the armband did not change me in any way.

Other than scoring goals, I'm not entirely sure what I was expecting from my first Pompey season in 2017/18. I wasn't overly familiar with the team and I didn't know loads about the players, other than they'd just been promoted and changed managers, with something of an overhaul underway and the likes of Gary Roberts, Michael Smith, and later Carl Baker moving on. With the Blues back in League One there was a general consensus this would be a campaign of consolidation — although if a player scores 25 goals in a season, you should really finish in the play-offs at a minimum. Our next highest scorer posted eight — jointly shared by Oli Hawkins and Jamal Lowe — while all but one of my 25 goals arrived in League One, despite missing eight league matches through injury. Disappointingly, though, we finished eighth, five points adrift of the play-offs.

Still, on a personal level, 2017/18 proved to be the best season of my career. I scored more goals with Bournemouth in 2009/10, netting 28 times in 50 games in League Two, while 2012/13 I managed 19 in 28 matches after rejoining the Cherries in November 2012, helping them reach the Championship under Eddie Howe. Yet they were stronger teams than the one I played in with Pompey, with 11 players from that second Bournemouth promotion side going on to feature in the Premier League. In that respect, scoring 25 goals in Kenny Jackett's League One team, which didn't even finish in the play-offs was, in my mind, a greater achievement. For me, the common denominator with scoring goals was simply being picked every week, although, at that time with Pompey, I wasn't a League One player. I could have still been playing in the Championship had I wanted, but circumstances dictated otherwise. Mind you, I wouldn't have joined any League One club other than the Blues — and they got somebody aged 29 and still in his prime.

My time at Fratton Park began with two goals on my debut in the opening game against Rochdale in August 2017. Then, a month into the season, Oli Hawkins arrived from Dagenham & Redbridge on deadline day and, while initially we were matched up front, it didn't overly work as a strike partnership. Apart from big Steve Fletcher at the start of my Bournemouth career, I've always performed better with somebody quick, who can stretch the game and create space for me to exploit, such as Callum Wilson and Lewis Grabban. Oli actually impacted where I moved and he wasn't running to make the pitch bigger, instead coming short or standing there to receive the ball. He wasn't stopping me from performing, I was still scoring goals, but operating up front as the main man is completely different. You're the focal point, in and around the box a lot more, and the pair of us together just didn't work. That was absolutely no fault of Oli's, because some players you combine well with, others you don't, but it was a partnership which never really clicked. When Hawks did play under Kenny, it was actually a cop out for a lot of the players, who would hit the long ball to give themselves an easy way out. He had a lot of bad service kicked at him, rather than to him.

As a forward, you're not going to score on your own, you need people to provide service. It's a team game and as long as you win, that's the main thing. We had Jamal Lowe on the right wing and either Matty Kennedy or Kal Naismith on the left, so I was definitely well served. Matty was on loan from Cardiff City and I loved playing with him in particular. He was my favourite winger during those three years at Fratton Park. All he wanted to do was get the ball and cross it, which was perfect for me. I knew what he was going to do, either a stepover before crossing it with his left foot or checking back on to his right and delivering it. When you know the ball's coming in then it makes it easier, because you can time your movement, whereas someone unpredictable means you keep checking and checking, before left standing there as you have absolutely no idea when the ball's arriving. From January onwards Matty didn't play much, for some reason. He just went off it, I don't know why, and he didn't start any of the final 11 matches.

Still, life began well for me at Pompey, scoring 10 goals in my opening 12 appearances, including registering a double against Bristol Rovers in September 2017 which ranks as my favourite game. Played on a Tuesday night under the

Fratton Park lights, which is always special, we won 3-0. Both of my goals arrived in the final 13 minutes — the first a header from Matty Kennedy's left-wing cross and the second involving nutmegging Tom Lockyer before finishing into the far bottom corner. However, I ended up missing four matches the following month after undergoing an operation to remove two pieces of floating bone in my left knee, which I could sometimes feel moving about during games. It was carried out at Spire Portsmouth Hospital in Havant and, while I was there, I also decided to sort out the nose I broke while scoring my second goal against Fleetwood Town two weeks earlier. So I stayed overnight in hospital and had two operations in two days to save time!

We entered 2018 positioned sixth in League One with barely a central midfielder available after Danny Rose broke his leg during a drop ball against Northampton Town, having been consistently playing well at the time. However, despite the transfer window now open, we didn't recruit anyone to replace him, which was obviously disappointing as it was clear we needed help. If you push on and make two or three January signings, you'll finish in the play-offs, minimum — maybe even beyond that. You just don't know. Instead we brought in two kids from Wolverhampton Wanderers. Sylvain Deslandes, a left-back, was dreadful, dreadful. You could see how poor he was in training, players aren't stupid, and he played just twice for us. The other was Connor Ronan, an attacking midfielder and a good player, but aged 19 when we needed a bit more experience, someone around 26-28 who had played quite a few games and could handle being at Pompey. With Rose injured for the rest of the season, our midfield was Stuart O'Keefe, on loan from Cardiff, and two young, homegrown lads in Ben Close and Adam May. You're asking kids to do things they shouldn't do week in, week out — and they weren't ready. The players often talked about the midfield situation, discussing how we desperately needed help there. It was obvious.

I entered April 2018 requiring one goal to become the first Pompey player since Svetoslav Todorov to break the 20 barrier, a feat he achieved in 2003 — 15 years earlier. The scenario had been well documented in the media, but I wasn't overly thinking about it and, considering I had seven games remaining, I expected to reach it. That was achieved with a first-half penalty after Ben Close had been fouled in a 2-1 victory over Wigan at Fratton Park. Registering 20 goals in a season always means something for a striker, but it never played on my mind. I've never been one to set targets.

The final match of the campaign was against Peterborough United, with two needed to bring up 25 goals for the season. I broke the deadlock on 13 minutes after heading home Gaz Evans' left-wing corner, then, 12 minutes later, Jamal fired in an angled right-footed shot which I finished at the back post to give us a 2-0 lead and enabled me to reach that goal landmark. However, whoever was on the PA system announced it was Jamal's goal. I know full well when that happens it sticks and becomes fact, especially in the lower leagues. His shot was going about three yards wide — it was my goal, everyone could see that. I went mad and shouted at the South Stand where I thought the PA man was. If you score a goal and know it's yours, you want to make sure you're credited. I have a passion for scoring, that never changes as you get older. As it turned out, to this day the website *Soccerbase* has it down incorrectly as Jamal's goal — and me scoring 24 that season!

As a club, we should have done better in that first season back in League One, without a doubt. If you possess a player who scored 24 league goals in the season — and 25 overall — you should finish in the top six, that's the long and short of it. Nobody else at the club reached double figures, but I'm not blaming the lads for that. The style of football didn't suit what we had. We worked hard as a team, weren't bad at set-pieces, and had somebody who scored goals, but were set up to be negative through the playing style Kenny Jackett preferred.

At the start of the following season in 2018/19, I got the feeling Jackett no longer wanted me at Pompey. For whatever reason, he'd made up his mind, and suddenly I found myself on the bench. I started against Luton Town on the opening day, yet was dragged off at half-time in a 1-0 victory. It would be another nine games before I started another League One match, with Oli Hawkins preferred. Admittedly, I didn't do amazingly well in pre-season — I scored once in five friendlies, against Brighton in a behind-closed-doors fixture at their training ground — but for me the summer schedule is all about getting fit. I was also getting the impression the manager wasn't overly keen on having me around so, when I was taken off at the interval in the opening game, I wasn't even surprised.

In my previous league match, I'd scored my 25th goal of the campaign and finished as League One's second-highest scorer behind Peterborough's Jack Marriott — and just 45 minutes into the new season I was being substituted and then remained on the bench for weeks after. Jackett never explained why I would suddenly be out of the team on a regular basis, so I couldn't tell you the reason. He didn't say anything. It's hard to understand and difficult to comprehend, all those goals the season before and now I was a regular substitute. It was strange — and I was his captain! Mentally that rejection is tough, your pride takes a hit. I felt I should have been playing, but there's nothing you can do about it.

By the time the January 2019 transfer window opened, I'd had five league starts and scored six goals in 22 appearances overall. I was named in Pompey's line-up for the trip to Luton at the end of the month, with the Hatters now topping the league after we had led the table for three-and-a-half months. Luton were 1-0 up at the break, prompting Gaz Evans and myself to be replaced by Omar Bogle and Dion Donohue. No-one had played well in the first half but the pair of us were made the scapegoats, not for the first time either, as we went on to lose 3-2. The following night, I was at Bournemouth watching them beat Chelsea 4-0 in the Premier League, when I received a phone call from Kenny. With 24 hours remaining of the window, he told me he was bringing in two forwards — and I could leave. I was shocked.

I'd signed a three-year deal with Pompey and scored 25 goals in the previous season, so had absolutely no interest in leaving. My blunt response was: "I'm not going anywhere." The next day, three clubs contacted me asking whether I would join them on loan, yet it wasn't my agent putting my name out. It must have been Kenny. It turned out the Blues had sent a circular to the bottom of League One and the whole of League Two, making sure none of their promotion rivals were informed of my availability. Bristol Rovers manager Graham Coughlan rang while our chief executive Mark Catlin told me of Bradford City's interest, with Charlton Athletic being the other club.

Having stood my ground and refused to move, the day after the window shut I came into training and was told there were too many players to train, instead being instructed to run on my own by the side of the pitch. Well, wasn't doing that. They weren't going to embarrass me — so I asked for a heart-rate monitor and GPS performance tracker and told them I'd instead go home and do some running at Whitecliff Rec, in Poole. That went on for a few days. Kenny would ring and say: "We have too many numbers today, run at home." Then he granted my request to train with Bournemouth's under-21s to keep myself fit, which I was able to do because my friends Shaun Cooper and Alan Connell worked there.

The signings Kenny made that January were terrible. He brought in Bogle and James Vaughan when, in my eyes, you had someone better who was now training at a different club. It made absolutely no sense. Me and Gaz Evans felt we got a raw deal under the manager. Regardless of whether we had good, bad or indifferent games, you could count on us giving 100 per cent, yet I don't think we were treated particularly well. We were also popular with the fans, which may have been another reason. Ben Thompson left, I was basically gone, and the facts speak for themselves over the quality of those brought in during that window. Ben was a good player, although the feeling I got was Millwall wouldn't have let him join permanently anyway, even though Pompey had put in a big bid. Still, in any transfer window you should aim to come out the other side with an improved squad — yet we finished up worse.

Then, having been overlooked for five matches, Kenny suddenly called to say I'd be on the bench at Bury in the semi-finals of the Checkatrade Trophy! Tellingly, results had been poor and he was now under pressure from supporters, who were asking where I was because we'd started losing. It's stupid, there was no proper conversation with the manager, no clear-the-air talks, I was simply asked to come back, so got on with it. A lot of other people might have gone the other way considering what had occurred, but I'm a professional and was focused on playing for Pompey once more.

Having been unused off the bench for my opening two matches back, I was finally given a run out at Charlton in March 2019, featuring for the final 15 minutes, and did quite well despite a 2-1 defeat. From that moment I started 10 of the final 11 matches of the League One campaign, even having the captaincy restored as if nothing had happened, with no explanation from the manager. Nothing. My role had changed, though, playing as a number 10 off Oli Hawkins, Bogle or Vaughan during that period, which I was happy with. It was always my favourite position and I had played there for a lot of my career at Bournemouth, so I knew what it involved; just try to get the ball or arrive late in the box. Not that it mattered to me what position I was selected for — I just wanted to play.

Things can change quickly in football and, following two goals in three matches upon my return to Pompey's starting XI, I was skippering us at Wembley in the Checkatrade Trophy final against Sunderland. It was the only time I played at the home of football in my career, with 85,021 supporters inside the stadium, ensuring it was a special occasion for so many reasons. We were battered in the first half, but that changed from the moment Gaz Evans came off the bench in the 56th minute. He should have started instead of Ronan Curtis, who hadn't featured for two-and-half weeks after losing the top of a finger when he caught it in his front door. Obviously that wasn't Ronan's fault, yet he had trained once before the final and wasn't ready.

Fans still mention my sprint down the right wing in the second half... not bad for somebody who supposedly couldn't run! However, I covered almost 15km at Wembley that day, I could run if I needed to, even if it wasn't the main part of my game. Still, Gaz had changed the momentum, while Oli Hawkins later came on for Bogle and, even though we remained 1-0 down, we were all over Sunderland, before eventually levelling in the 82nd minute through Nathan Thompson's far-post header. With the match ending 1-1, it entered extra-time, and Jamal gave us the lead for the first time in the game, only for Aiden McGeady to grab his second and make it 2-2 in the 119th minute. Maybe subsequently claiming a 5-4 victory through penalties made it a little more special, but this was a Wembley final and the occasion of winning there made it special anyway. As captain, I walked up those steps and picked up a trophy — not many players in the history of football have enjoyed that moment. Nobody had done it for Pompey since the 2008 FA Cup final — and who knows how long someone else will do it again?

In terms of a must-win game, the visit of Peterborough to Fratton Park the following month, in April 2019, was exactly that as we attempted to break back into the two automatic promotion slots with two matches remaining. The fixture was poised at 2-2 in the 73rd minute when I broke through down the right and, with the keeper to beat, squared a pass to my left for substitute Viv Solomon-Otabor, who finished past Aaron Chapman — only for the linesman to flag offside. Just two minutes later, Ivan Toney scored his second of the game as Posh won 3-2 to condemn us to the play-offs.

Football's all about decision-making and passing to Solomon-Otabor to present him with a tap-in into an empty net was the right call. I had a one-on-one from a tight angle and on the run, I couldn't tell if he was onside or not; he had to make sure he was behind me to receive the pass. Obviously if I was aware he was offside, I would have taken the shot myself. You make the right decision based on the information at the time — and I stand by that decision; it was the correct one. It was just the fact Viv wasn't onside. This was a big game, I had the chance to shoot from a tight angle, and there was never a guarantee I would score. So the right decision was to square it and give a teammate an open goal. Maybe he got excited and ran too quickly, it can happen, and it was a shame it occurred in that particular match. I can't remember if I said anything to Viv afterwards, but I probably did!

We had to make do with the play-offs rather than automatic promotion, but firstly there was a final league match against Accrington Stanley to negotiate — and we made such a mess of it that we ended up with Sunderland rather than Doncaster Rovers in the semi-finals. Kenny Jackett rested five players for that game, including myself, Jamal Lowe, Ronan Curtis and Nathan Thompson, and we drew 1-1 when a victory would have given us third spot, putting us up against sixth-placed Rovers. We should have been avoiding Sunderland at all costs, so why we made so many changes I have no idea. The players definitely wanted to steer clear of the Black Cats, but the management felt differently, I guess. Perhaps he was resting people for the play-offs, but surely you must aim to finish as high as you can? It meant Charlton ended up third with a one-better goal difference, so missed Sunderland — and we instead faced them in the two-legged semi-finals after coming fourth.

In truth, the reason why we didn't go up in 2018/19 was actually because of our January transfer window. When you're five points clear on New Year's Day, you should be winning promotion. Tiredness could be a reason, but we lost so much momentum after mid-January when going eight league games without a win that it left far too much ground to make up. We later equalled the club record for eight consecutive victories in all competitions, including the Checkatrade Trophy final, but that still wasn't enough to return to the automatic promotion spots.

Having been dropped to the bench against Accrington, a hamstring injury sustained in training two days before the semi-finals sidelined me for the first leg against Sunderland, which we lost 1-0 at the Stadium of Light. I subsequently underwent blood-spinning injections and other mad stuff and, despite returning to start the second leg, with hindsight I shouldn't have played. I was probably 70 per cent fit and couldn't do myself justice. Had it been a regular league game, I wouldn't have featured, but, considering this was a semi-final second leg with us trailing 1-0, I desperately wanted to contribute. I knew I couldn't do everything I wanted, certainly I was unable to overextend myself or sprint full on, but, should the ball fall inside the box, I was capable of kicking it and taking the chance.

Whereas I returned to the side for the Fratton Park second leg, Jamal Lowe and Ronan Curtis were dropped, two of our best players that season who had scored 29 goals between them — and we had no idea why. Not starting them was madness, while Ronan didn't even come off the bench, despite Jackett having one more substitution available. Mind you, he played Bryn Morris over Tom Naylor in the play-offs the following season, so who knows why he made these decisions. What I cannot comprehend is considering we entered that second leg trailing 1-0, why didn't we throw caution to the wind and get beaten three or four nil? Going down fighting rather than being eliminated with a whimper like we actually were. Give it everything and, if you can't score, hold your hands up and say: "Fair enough." It just seemed odd that you don't start your 17-goal leading scorer and refuse to even play the left winger with 12 goals who had done well throughout the season.

We ended up drawing 0-0 to lose 1-0 on aggregate and that turned out to be Jamal's final Pompey match before being sold to Wigan that summer. The previous campaign he was probably too unselfish, but, in a good way, he became more single-minded in front of goal in 2018/19 and went on to do well, which he deserved because he worked hard. As for Ronan, there's a lot of bravado with him, a lot of baggage around, but at heart he's a good kid who worked hard for the team and wanted to do well. I just think all the other stuff around him probably holds him back a little.

Having failed to win promotion, we returned for pre-season training in the summer of 2019 and I was aware I needed to hit the ground running. The previous campaign I had come off the bench 19 times, while the expensive signings of John Marquis and Ellis Harrison now provided striking competition. I recognised I didn't have a great pre-season the previous summer, which meant Jackett didn't play me at the start of that campaign, so I had to ensure I was properly fit and, encouragingly, struck seven goals in six friendly outings. Regardless, it wouldn't be until 10 matches into the new season before I was handed my first start, which was in September at Burton Albion for a 2-2 draw, when I scored from the spot.

Being honest, it wasn't the greatest of shocks to find myself on the bench at that point, particularly as Harrison and Marquis had been recruited for big money. It didn't seem to matter that I was better than both of them and, while I understand that when a manager spends a transfer fee on a striker they must back them, surely it shouldn't be at the detriment of the team? That's entirely what happened. Me and Gaz Evans worked it out after their first training session. It's not hard, footballers aren't stupid and we'd been around a long time, but I was better than them by far. It wasn't even a competition. They were both good lads, I got on with them but, in terms of football intelligence and technique, they were not at my level. Then, three weeks into the season, Conor Chaplin left for Coventry City, which was a shame because none of us wanted him to go. He was forced to leave to get regular football. He was such a great lad who loved Pompey and he didn't want to go anywhere, but never had a choice. Absolutely I could have worked with him up front, but now he had gone and I was on the bench once more.

I did not give up trying to force my way back into the first-team again. It's personal pride and you always hope there'll be an opportunity — then you can prove people wrong for leaving you out. What helped was I knew I had the fans' backing, while the club hadn't managed to replace me with a striker capable of scoring 20 goals in a season, even though they had desperately tried. Still, I was named as a substitute in each of the opening seven matches in 2019/20, including two Carabao Cup matches, before everything came to a head at Blackpool in August 2019.

I was an unused substitute in a 1-1 draw, somebody with almost 200 career goals not required to come on and grab you one, which I found baffling. Gaz Evans was introduced off the bench and then, 25 minutes later, was himself substituted, which shouldn't happen to any footballer — and normally doesn't. The following Monday morning, Kenny pulled me into his office and, in a 30-second conversation, informed me I was no longer Pompey captain, with Tom Naylor replacing me. Then he did the same with Gaz, with Lee Brown taking over the vice-captaincy. He wasn't done, though, because 15 minutes later everybody was called into the centre circle of one of the training pitches, with the captaincy changes publicly announced. There are ways to handle things — and this was designed to publicly embarrass the pair of us. All the club staff were called to be present; the physios, sports science staff, office workers, whoever was around the training ground at that time. It didn't need that. The physio doesn't have to be told. In all my years of playing football, I had never seen anything like that.

I wasn't playing and wasn't featuring that much either, so it wasn't the biggest surprise, but leave me as club captain and give the armband to Tom Naylor when he's playing and I'm not. As for the vice-captain, I've absolutely no idea why you would want to change that — everything was designed to embarrass us. Not that I ever had a relationship with Kenny; he didn't really have one with any of the players. That incident didn't end our relationship — it had never started. I know I've been criticising him, but he's not a bad person, he's an all right bloke, yet he was detached from everyone. Aloof is a good way of describing him; he doesn't want to get himself into awkward conversations, so simply wouldn't have them. When Pompey sacked him in March 2021, he had a win percentage of 51.66, but the reason why he won those games was because we had good players for the level. Considering the quality we possessed and the supporters' fantastic backing, we underachieved during my three years at Fratton Park.

With the captaincy now removed, I was named on the bench for the following match, which was the first defence of our Checkatrade Trophy title. Crawley Town visited Fratton Park and I came on at half-time for the concussed Gaz Evans, scoring the winner in a 1-0 victory. It signalled a spell of three goals in six games as I found myself back in the starting XI, including facing Southampton in the Carabao Cup in an unbelievable atmosphere. We may have lost 4-0 but credit to the Pompey fans. We were getting beaten at home by our biggest rivals, yet they all stayed until the final whistle, continuing to sing and getting louder and louder. It was an occasion which really sticks in my mind.

However, I suffered a setback in October 2019 after straining my adductor in the warm-up against Gillingham and lasted 54 minutes, with the injury subsequently keeping me out of action for three weeks. That was pretty much it for me at Pompey, making just one more start during the remainder of that season — a 2-1 win over Northampton in the Checkatrade Trophy. My final Blues goal was a last-gasp winner coming off the bench against non-league Altrincham in the FA Cup second round in November 2019, and I didn't realise at the time that 18 minutes as a substitute at MK Dons at the end of December would represent my last Pompey outing. I had two more unused substitute appearances, then was dropped from the squad, and, just after the January 2020 transfer window had shut, Kenny called to inform me I no longer had to come in for training. Here we go again.

I didn't have the opportunity to leave Pompey in that window. If Kenny did try to get rid of me, I was unaware of it, and now, once it had closed, he didn't want me around. My response was: "Well, I can't not train for six months. I want it in writing and I want permission to train with Bournemouth," which I received. Kenny never told me to keep myself fit, the club didn't even give me a GPS performance tracker this time, but I was aware I'd be out of contract in six months and needed to train in the meantime, so I called the Cherries' manager, Eddie Howe, and he agreed. I trained with my good mate Shaun Cooper's under-21s or, when they had a game, joined in with the under-18s. It made sense.

During that period, I didn't hear from anybody at Pompey. No-one. No phone call or even a text. I could have played golf every day and still got paid for all they cared. Then, more than three weeks later, I received a phone call at 10.30pm on a Monday night from Kenny: "I'm going to put you on the bench tomorrow against MK Dons. Are you okay with that?" He hadn't even got anybody to ring Bournemouth to check I'd been doing what I should have — yet now wanted me back at Pompey! Before the game, he pulled me into his office and explained I wasn't his number one striker: "You might not even be my number two because we have Ellis and John, but you'll be my third choice. So, when we need a goal, you'll come on. I know that's not what you want to hear, you want to be first choice, but can you accept that?" I told him that was fine.

We beat MK Dons comfortably 3-1, so I wasn't needed off the bench, and it was the same in the next match, a 3-0 win over Rochdale. He then left me out of the squad for the fifth-round visit of Arsenal in the FA Cup: "We're probably going to go behind, it might be damage limitation," he said. "I can't see you coming on, so I'm leaving you out of that game." I totally understood where he was coming from and was fine with that. I was back on the bench for the trip to Peterborough in March 2020 and we were 1-0 down with 21 minutes remaining — so he put Oli Hawkins up front and I wasn't called upon. A few weeks earlier, I was told I was miles ahead of him in the pecking order — now I'm sitting there thinking: "What's the point?" Sure enough, the next match was a midweek fixture against Fleetwood at Fratton Park and, ahead of it, Kenny pulled me into the office and informed me I wouldn't be in the squad. Since coming back, I had trained well, not made a fuss, not said a word, just put my head down and got on with it — yet I still hadn't kicked a ball.

By the end of the week, the Premier League and Football League programmes were suspended following the outbreak of Covid-19, sparking uncertainty over whether the season would restart. The players trained separately during that period, putting whatever we did, such as a bike ride or a run, on the Strava app, so everybody was aware of what the others were doing, while Kenny rang each of us every now and then to check on our wellbeing. Yet while my teammates were needed following the resumption of the play-off campaign, with a semi-final against Oxford, I wasn't. My final conversation with Kenny was a 20-second phone call — not that I wanted to talk to him any longer than that — telling me that Pompey wouldn't be offering a new contract. There was rubbish going around that there was a contract clause for an additional 12 months if I reached 100 games, but it was nonsense. It didn't take a rocket scientist to work out exactly why I left — and it was down to one man.

I don't have overly ill feelings towards Kenny Jackett but, had another manager come in during my time at Pompey, I'd like to think he would have understood and seen what I could have done for the team. Me and Gaz Evans got on well, we were roommates and ended up in similar situations with the manager. It got to the point where we would pretty much laugh about it. You can only go around in circles so many times before you either drive yourself insane or you have to smile. Players get mistreated but normally it's down to not playing well or having off-field problems, such as ill-discipline. That wasn't the case with me. Usually there's a reason, but there wasn't. He never explained it. To this day, I don't know.

I loved my time at Fratton Park. I thrived playing in front of those Pompey fans. I loved it. It was brilliant. For me, the ideal would have been ending my career there. I scored 42 goals in 99 appearances, only to get released on a free transfer. With a record like that, I should have departed on my terms, rather than how I did leave.

CHRIS BURNS

116 games, 12 goals (March 1991 — November 1994)

Liverpool 1 (Whelan)
Pompey 1 (Anderton)

FA Cup semi-final, Highbury, Sunday, April 5, 1992

Pompey: Knight, Neill, Symons, Awford, Beresford, Anderton, Burns, Kuhl, McLoughlin (109 mins, Whittingham), Chamberlain (10 mins, Aspinall), Clarke.

Attendance; 41,869

n, SO FAR!

Seconds and inches halt Wembley march

Pompey 1 Liverpool 1 (aet)
Mike Neasom at Highbury

HIGHBURY'S giant electronic scoreboard etched the misery into Royal Blue hearts as Ronnie Whelan wrecked Pompey's 94th birthday party yesterday.

It showed there were 3 minutes and 42seconds remaining of an FA Cup semi-final of enormous passion, high skill and throbbing atmosphere.

So Pompey were a miserable 222 seconds away from Wembley when the Irishman, who has spent most of the past year battling against a catalogue of injuries, saved Liverpool's season from oblivion. Just a handful of seconds – and an inch or two of woodwork.

The ball that landed at Whelan's unchallenged feet almost on the goal-line did so after Alan Knight had turned John Barnes's viciously bent free-kick against the inside of his left-hand post.

Knight said: "Another inch or two and it would

● DUG-OUT DRAMA – both camps look on

much-criticised Colonial boy.

Grobbelaar's instinctive resue act came five minutes before the interval. Warren Neill unleashed Darren Anderton, his pass was laid off by substitute Warren Aspinall and Alan McLoughlin fired towards the top corner.

Grobbelaar was now

through Pompey's superb backline.

It was not until the 85th minute when Michael Thomas skipped a shot across Knight and just wide of the far post that there was genuine alarm.

That was matched immediately at the other end as leashed Anderton newest full

EMI-FINAL FACTS

FIRST HALF
POMPEY
target: 3 Shots off target: 5

I t was fate. If Alan Gough hadn't made that phone call to Frank Burrows, we probably wouldn't be having this conversation. People say I was lucky to be a professional footballer yet, while it was good fortune getting to Fratton Park, someone playing 116 games for such a fantastic club isn't luck. As my Uncle Colin would often tell me: "You were meant to be there. Don't let anyone ever take that away from you."

As a brickie, I was a young apprentice working in Alan's gang, subcontracted by Bryant Homes to build houses in Gloucester. I also played part-time football with Cheltenham Town in the GM Vauxhall Conference, largely as a left wing-back on account of being so fit. We'd line up with three centre-halves and myself as one of the flying wing-backs basically playing like a winger, running after balls put in the channel. My desire was to play in the centre of midfield, yet we had Steve Brooks and Mark Buckland already well established in there, with the former having represented England's semi-professional team.

Then, ahead of a Midland Floodlit Cup match against Alvechurch in December 1989, injuries to the pair prompted the manager, Jim Barron, to instead play me there. We won 6-0 in front of 246 supporters and I scored five of our goals, although actually missed the two easiest chances. Every time I hit the ball that day it went in, I couldn't do anything wrong. I had never previously scored during 18 months at Cheltenham, now I had five in one game! Not that it won me a regular spot in midfield, as I was named as a substitute for the next three matches and spent the rest of the season in and out of the side. I started the following 1990/91 season at left-back, yet, from October, was beginning to establish myself as a midfielder, playing there in an FA Cup first-round defeat at Birmingham City in November 1990. However, by March 1991, we were in the lower half of the table and Alan Gough had an idea: "I'm going to give Pompey boss Frank Burrows a ring to see if you can go there for a week." As a kid, Alan started his career as a centre-half at Swindon Town and, although he didn't make the first-team, had played with Frank at the County Ground and they'd kept in touch. Incredibly, it was fixed up — I was to go to Fratton Park on Monday for a trial, staying with my wife's Aunty Ann at her Strawberry Fields home in Hedge End.

Pompey's training ground was at Moneyfields and Warren Aspinall and Mark Chamberlain immediately took me under their wing, which I really appreciated. As part of my first session, there was crossing and shooting, and, of the 50 shots I struck, 48 must have beaten Andy Gosney in goal. He must have thought: "Where has this kid come from?" He wasn't the only one surprised — I was also thinking: "How the hell is this happening?" The following day, we were on the Mountbatten Centre astroturf ahead of that evening's visit of Millwall in the Second Division, working on shape. There was a quick match and I was in the first-team, playing in the middle of the park alongside Martin Kuhl and Gavin Maguire, doing all right. On my third day at Pompey, I was signed on a two-year deal for £25,000.

Following Wednesday's training session, Frank Burrows and reserve-team manager Tony Barton asked me: "Fancy becoming a professional player?" The money wasn't as much as being a bricklayer, but of course I wanted to be a footballer. I was given the remainder of the week off and told to return with my gear the following Monday. My Pompey wage was £300 a week — representing a drop in earnings. Previously I'd receive £300 a week for bricklaying and £70 playing for Cheltenham, meaning I was £70 down every week after joining a Second Division football club. However, I received a £10,000 signing-on fee, while my agreement stated that, after 10 first-team games, my wage would double — which I achieved in September 1991, some six months later.

Mind you, I had only been a Pompey player for a few hours before Burrows left as manager by mutual consent later that same day. As Alan Knight often said to me: "You got Frank the sack. It's your fault." Barton stepped up as caretaker for the remainder of the season and was really good to me. He was such a lovely guy, probably too nice with some of the senior lads, who realised they could push their luck a bit. We could have had Ronald McDonald as manager and I would have said yes to everything asked of me. I just wanted to be a pro footballer! Like me, Tony lived in Hedge End and sometimes I'd bump into him and we'd chat about what he needed me to work on, which you took in because he was such a lovely guy.

Still, after 125 games and 13 goals for Cheltenham, I was now a Pompey player. At the age of 23, it represented my second chance in the Football League, having been on the books of Bristol City but released at 16 on account of being too small. Two years later I'd shot up to 6ft 2in! Pompey had 12 matches remaining, but I wasn't involved in first-team fixtures for the rest of the season, instead featuring for the reserves in the Ovenden Combination. In May 1991, kitman Gordon Neave, who was overseeing reserve matches following Barton's promotion, handed me the captaincy for a game at Watford, telling the team: "I'll tell you now, this boy is going to be a great player for this club. He has heart and he's captain." I was still new to the club, but the lads clapped the decision and I skippered a side containing Kit Symons, Andy Awford, Mark Chamberlain and Darryl Powell in a 2-0 defeat.

I had been accepted straight away. Everyone was so down to earth; even former England internationals like Chamberlain, who was lovely. Most clubs have one player who thinks he's better than everyone else, but that dressing room didn't contain a single bad egg. It was a great environment. Meanwhile, having initially stayed with Aunty Ann until the end of that season, we bought a little place on the corner of Malvern Gardens in Hedge End, with my teammates Micky Ross, Shaun Murray and Andy McFarlane living on the same road. Warren Aspinall was also around that area and showed me the rights and wrongs of Hedge End, while Darren Anderton, who lived in Bitterne, would pick me up for training on the way through.

In June 1991, Jim Smith was appointed boss, representing the third manager in my opening 81 days at Fratton Park. I had been at Pompey since March, without making the first-team, and now Jim had arrived it was suddenly a clean slate. I returned for my first pre-season determined to be at the front of all the running in a bid to get noticed, thinking that maybe, just maybe, he would think: "This kid's fit, let's give him a go." You were weighed before leaving for the summer holidays and then when you returned, with Warren Aspinall usually a couple of pounds over and earning a fine. I trained all the time anyway, even during the close season, making sure I was ready for the campaign ahead. Every summer, I'd holiday with my family and then get bored waiting for the football season to start. I couldn't sit around the house doing nothing! So I'd return to the building site for five weeks to work with my mates. It kept me in touch with reality and also helped with fitness, as bricklaying is quite strenuous.

I knew I didn't have as much natural ability as some of the lads but I could get by with other assets of my game, which was breaking up play, while I could score a few goals. I knew if I was as big, strong and powerful as my opponent then I'd get the better of them. There weren't many midfielders I played against who were as fit as me at that time. They may have been better, but, if I could get around the pitch, I had a chance. The likes of Darren Anderton, Martin Kuhl and Alan McLoughlin were good on the ball, better than I was, but I'd bring the other side of the game, which they didn't have — running around and making a nuisance of myself. Don't get me wrong, I could pass, but Jim just wanted me to win my headers, win my tackles, win the second ball, get it wide, and then break into the box to see if I could score. I netted nine goals in 58 appearances in my first full season at Pompey, with only Guy Whittingham and Anderton getting more, both finishing on 13. I scored the winner against Sunderland in my sixth appearance in September 1991, but my best goal for the Blues was a left-footed 20-yard shot against Tranmere Rovers in February 1992.

It soon became clear during that 1991 pre-season that the seniors weren't doing it, which is why Jim put us young lads in, beginning with the opening game of the 1991/92 campaign at Blackburn Rovers. That summer we were based at HMS

Dryad, with myself and Darren Anderton leading the runs up and down Ports-
down Hill. Darren was a very, very good runner with his long, gangly legs and,
while I wasn't the quickest, I worked more on stamina rather than sprinting, with
the pair of us at the front. However, it was clear that some senior players weren't
putting it in for the running and would be at the back, miles behind. Professional
footballers have to be fit and that shouldn't be happening. When they were left
out, they were probably the first ones knocking on Jim's door, wanting to know
why all the kids were playing and they weren't. Jim most likely told them we were
more hungry to be in the first-team.

Still, it was a shock to be handed my debut at Ewood Park — and I'm sure Awfs,
Darren Anderton, Darryl Powell and Kit Symons were just as surprised to also
see themselves on that teamsheet. We had an inkling in the build-up, suddenly
being involved in shape work on the training ground, as well as corners and free-
kicks, yet there was always the nagging doubt that, come Saturday morning, he
might have changed his mind and put a senior pro in. Thankfully, that wasn't
the case — and we were starting against Blackburn. The other four had all played
for the first-team before, so I was the only debutant. We nearly won too, leading through Darren's second-half goal only for Kevin Moran to score a last-gasp
equaliser in a 1-1 draw — but Jim got the gamble right and was rewarded as the
season progressed.

Jim was brilliant company, you were honoured to play under him, but if you'd
had a bad game, there was no beating around the bush. Even if I had played well,
the gaffer would give me a rollocking, irrespective of whether we had won 5-0 or
lost 5-0. At half-time, he'd come in looking for someone to shout at and I would
nudge Awfs and say: "Here it comes" — then Jim would roar: "And you…" before
coming over to me. After the final whistle, he'd tell me: "I only do it to keep you
on your toes. I love you so much, I want to keep you playing well — and you are."
After Fratton Park games, we'd go to the players' lounge and you'd often bump
into Jim after he had left the boardroom and clearly drunk a couple of whiskies.
He would come over and start cuddling me, planting kisses on my cheek and saying: "He's my favourite." I'd reply: "Gaffer, get off." He was always grabbing me
like that and the players soon joked I was actually his son, giving me the nickname
"Chrissy Smith." I was also his errand boy and whenever we went out for training
and he'd forgotten something, like a whistle or stopwatch, I'd be the one asked
to get it. Darryl Powell thankfully replaced me for those duties during my second
season.

In my first full Football League campaign, we faced Brian Clough's Nottingham
Forest in the FA Cup quarter-finals in March 1992 and I was tasked with marking

their young midfielder Roy Keane. He was a little arrogant on the day, yet ended up becoming one of the greatest midfielders the Premier League has ever seen. I remember him being so quick over five yards, but I was as strong, powerful and fit as he was, so he wasn't going to get the better of me. At one point he chirped: "How much are you on a week?" and I replied: "Not as much as you!" But I wasn't bothered. In the build-up everyone was talking about Darren Anderton versus Stuart Pearce and, after two minutes, Forest's left-back chopped him down. From the resulting free-kick, Mark Crossley dropped the ball and Alan McLoughlin tapped it in. Having come to prominence in the FA Cup that year, there were rumours of clubs eyeing Darren, but he always favoured Tottenham Hotspur. We shared rooms on away trips and were big mates — we still are. In terms of his passing, technique, raw ability and the talent to bend a shot into the top corner, he was a lot like David Beckham. Darren remains one of the best footballers I played alongside, although Paul Walsh wasn't far behind, while Mark Chamberlain was another talent, albeit getting on a bit by the time I played with him at Pompey and he seemed to glide with the ball.

Our league home form was excellent, but we weren't so good on the road. If that team had been a couple of years older, we would have reached the newly-formed Premier League that season. When you look at the FA Cup semi-final first game against Liverpool, Awfs' tackle on Steve Nicol for that late free-kick was rash and he admits that, had he been a little older, he would have instead shepherded the Scot away from goal rather than lunging in. There's a theory that the Highbury goalposts at the time were square and not rounded so, when John Barnes' free-kick was pushed on to it, the ball would have gone the other way rather than shooting across the line for Ronnie Whelan to tap in. He was my man too, I was marking him, and maybe if I had reacted quicker I could have cleared it. I still think about it. It was slow-motion; perhaps I should have just dived on the ball, obstructed it even, so he kicked me instead and we'd have won the free-kick. It's hindsight, I've had more than 30 years to think about this, but, at the time, it happened in a flash.

Jim didn't say anything afterwards. No-one blames you, it's just one of those things. While I was marking Mark Wright from a few corners, Kit took over in the second half, which left me with Whelan. He was my man. Mind you, he should have been sent off for that 10th-minute challenge on Mark Chamberlain, which meant he couldn't have scored that equaliser in a 1-1 draw. It was high and over the ball, Liverpool would have been down to 10 men and we'd have probably beaten them. I was right by it and it was a bad tackle on one of our most effective players, which meant he had to be replaced by Warren Aspinall. In terms of

Warren's own career, he will probably kick himself because he should have done better. He had talent but liked everything else which didn't come with football.

It was devastating, having come so close to beating Liverpool and, to this day, when I'm on the running machine at the gym and it gets to three minutes and 53 seconds, it reminds me how close we were to an FA Cup final. That's what was left on the clock when they scored — if only we could have held on a little longer. Still, we were back in Second Division action 48 hours later with a trip to Tranmere, but the performance was dire. Their fans actually gave us a standing ovation before kick-off in recognition of the draw against their Merseyside rivals, but we were so poor and lost 2-0 to leave us in ninth. Afterwards, Jim shouted: "If some of you think you're going to be playing in that FA Cup replay you have another thing coming." I don't think I did too badly, yet, as it turned out, there was just one change from Tranmere for the Villa Park replay, with Guy Butters replaced by Ray Daniel. We actually should have won in normal time, Macca hit the bar late in the second half when it was harder to miss than score, and, with the game finishing goalless, it was on to penalties.

I was never down to take a spot-kick, although I could have taken one and it wouldn't have bothered me, yet five of my teammates had already volunteered. Unfortunately, only Kit scored, with Martin Kuhl, John Beresford and Warren Neill all missing in a 3-1 defeat. Liverpool knew they'd been in a fight and afterwards they were extremely gracious and very polite, with their players inviting some of us into their dressing room for some champagne. I sat chatting with Jan Molby and John Barnes, who were lovely guys and admitted we should have won at Highbury — and would have deserved it.

Reflecting on that cup run, not beating Liverpool in that first match was more upsetting than losing to them in the replay on penalties. We played in the division below and had gone toe-to-toe with one of the best teams in Europe, with nothing separating us over 240 minutes of football. That would have surprised a lot of people. Yet we should have beaten them at Highbury and that always nags away. It's every kid's dream to play at Wembley in an FA Cup final, so to be that close and not getting there with such a great bunch of lads was heartbreaking. It was an honour playing with those boys and we were a very close-knit group who came within three minutes and 53 seconds of beating Liverpool. Still, that Highbury match remains my favourite Pompey game. What an occasion!

Ahead of the 1992/93 season, we lost Darren Anderton and John Beresford, who had moved to Tottenham and Newcastle United respectively, although Paul Walsh arrived from Spurs. The playing system would also change as the season wore on, with Jim using Awfs as a sweeper in a back three, meaning I couldn't get forward into the opposition's box as much and became more of a holding mid-fielder. Having scored nine times in my first full season in the Football League, the following campaign I would net once in 40 outings.

We no longer had Bez and Darren, our two best players, while the skipper, Martin Kuhl, left a month into the season for Derby County. In my mind, this team was not as strong as the FA Cup side, yet Walshie was an unreal signing — and somebody who made Guy Whittingham. Guy scored 47 goals that year, earning him a move to Aston Villa, but he wouldn't have reached that incredible tally without his strike partner. Walshie was strong for a little guy and, when the ball went into him, the big centre-halves couldn't get him off it. You'd never expect a lad that size to be able to do that, but he was such a great footballer. Guy was a goalscorer, but a basic goalscorer. He wasn't a Paul Walsh, nowhere near — and Paul improved him.

On the league front, we were challenging for promotion, yet I slipped out of the first-team picture from March 1993 when Jim recruited Bjorn Kristensen from Newcastle. We eventually finished third, missing out on the Premier League courtesy of goals scored, with West Ham United joining Division One champions Newcastle — and instead we had to focus on the play-offs. Following our Division One play-off semi-final defeat to Leicester City in May 1993, Jim lost the changing room a little. Having appeared as a substitute in a first leg 1-0 defeat at the City Ground, I found myself out of the squad for the second leg, watching from the South Stand as Ian Ormondroyd scored with an offside goal as we lost 3-2 on aggregate. His team selection that day was rightly questioned — in particular George Lawrence, who, no disrespect, shouldn't have been in and around that squad as he wasn't good enough. He was meant to be a quick winger, but never seemed to go past anyone — and now was starting against Leicester.

Darryl Powell had been dropped and I was left out completely without any explanation, when normally Jim would pull the lads in beforehand and explain. When you look at that side against Leicester at Fratton Park, Jim had weakened it — and it wasn't just the fans quizzing his choices. The players were as well. This wasn't the Jim Smith of 18 months earlier. Whether it was pressure, whether the chairman really wanted the team to go up, I don't know, but he picked that side for that play-off second leg and you were thinking: "Really?" There will be other players who'll probably say exactly the same. As it turned out, the second leg finished 2-2 — and we were stuck in Division One for another season.

Early in the following season, in 1993/94, I realised it was probably time to move on. To be fair, my attitude had changed a little and I was losing a bit of faith in Jim. On top of that, a few lads started to arrive who were big-time Charlies, with a clique developing in the changing room — and I was never one for that. As part of Guy Whittingham's transfer to Villa in August 1993, Mark Blake arrived in a £400,000 deal but was always injured and believed he was better than he actually was. Gerry Creaney was definitely another, and, while I now get on really well with John Durnin, he was also like that at first, with Robbie Pethick following them like a sheep. There were five or six of this clique, most of which were the new lads, and it began to divide the dressing room. I didn't want to get involved in their banter, so I wouldn't join in with what they did. I like lots of people, but if I don't like someone then I tend not to bother — and I really didn't like them.

Durnin and Creaney were as thick as thieves and went out in Pompey together. Yet Creaney wasn't my cup of tea. He was arrogant, thought he was better than everybody else and sometimes had too much to say. Don't get me wrong, he had good ability, but was a selfish player. It had to be about him and nobody else; if he played well and we lost, he didn't care. This was no team player. Contrast that with the side in my first year at Fratton Park, I was spoiled with those boys. We were a little family, all good together. Now some of my mates had gone and we had Gerry Creaney, who wasn't popular among many in the dressing room, and his clique. That's when I knew I had to get out of the club.

I don't know why Jim's attitude towards me changed. Granted, I was no longer scoring the goals following the system change and my bit of non-league had also come out of me. I was now more like a pro footballer rather than a rare gem from Cheltenham. That edge had gone from my game — and Jim wanted that edge. Having played in those big games previously, I believed I had the right to be in the team when, in truth, Jim was correct not to select me because I wasn't performing and my desire had gone a little. In the meantime, it was in my head that I didn't want to be around those guys, so you may as well move on and play with another bunch of lads who might be like me again. In non-league, you all stick together because you only see each other on a Tuesday, Thursday and Saturday. You're a little family. Then you go to Pompey and, after two great years, you're suddenly with these lads and thinking: "I don't want this … I don't need this in the changing room."

After being involved in eight of the opening 11 league games of the 1993/94 season, I fell away from the squad and, in December 1993, was transfer-listed along with Warren Aspinall, Chris Price, Shaun Gale and Roy Young. The following week I joined Division Two side Swansea on a month's loan, managed by my old Pompey boss Frank Burrows, with ex-playing colleague Andy McFarlane also there. I made six appearances and they wanted to sign me, with Frank given the go-ahead from the chairman to meet Pompey's £60,000 asking price. It was January 1994 and I was in Frank's office when he called to complete the deal — only to be told by Jim that the price had now doubled to £120,000. The move fell through.

I found myself back in Pompey's first-team within a week of returning from south Wales, coming on as a substitute in a 2-0 defeat at home to Peterborough United. However, after starting a 1-0 loss at Crystal Palace in March 1994, I was loaned to Bournemouth for the remainder of the season. Managed by Tony Pulis, they were strapped for cash and there was never a chance of a permanent deal, rather the opportunity for me to get regular first-team football and then assess my situation in the summer. I got on really well with Tony and made 14 appearances, missing just one match, as we finished 17th in Division Two, with the likes of Steve Cotterill and Aspinall in the side.

Out of contract that summer, a letter landed on the doormat of my Hedge End home and, much to my surprise, it was a two-year deal at Pompey. Nobody had mentioned a new one, we never talked about it, yet suddenly there it was — albeit on less money. As I told my wife Bev, I'd played more than 100 games for the Blues and they were reducing my weekly wage by £200 or £300 when I knew damn well that others were on double. Not that this was about money — it was about pride and the belief I had played my part in Pompey's success over that period. I wasn't being greedy, yet why should I accept a pay cut? It was degrading. I also felt insulted that they would post a contract without speaking to me and negotiating terms.

I had no agent — Paul Walsh had always been on at me to get one, but I didn't consider myself a big enough star, so never bothered. Quite a few of the lads were worried about going into Jim Smith's office, but, on that occasion, it didn't bother me. Things had to be said and I went in there alone. I told him I wasn't signing and the manager's response was: "Well, we haven't any more money. Take it or leave it." I told him I'd leave it.

Having been out of favour for the majority of the previous season, including two loan spells away from Fratton Park, I had no idea why they suddenly offered me a new contract. After Alan Knight's testimonial in May 1994, we headed to Xanthi, Greece, for a four-team tournament called the Thrace Trophy, in which we beat Coventry City in the final to win it. I played in that match and, upon returning to England, found myself being offered this new contract. Perhaps Jim wanted me as a squad player because he could always rely on me, I don't know. What I do know, though, is he was getting hammered with Howard Kendall all the time on the whisky while over in Greece!

Although I was now out of contract, Pompey retained my registration, as it worked in those days, and in August 1994, I travelled to Port Vale on a week's trial, with their former Middlesbrough and Villa striker Paul Kerr coming the other way for Jim to have a look at. In my mind, I was moving to Vale Park; personal terms were agreed, a signing-on fee was decided with a two-year contract on offer and my wife had travelled with me to Staffordshire to look at houses. I couldn't wait. Vale manager John Rudge had agreed with Pompey to pay £120,000, with Kerr coming in part-exchange — then it collapsed. Jim no longer wanted Kerr on the grounds that he was no better than me, so instead doubled the asking price again!

I was gutted — and days later was in the Fratton Park crowd when Port Vale beat us 2-0. I knew I'd be moving somewhere, it was just a matter of when. I was never getting back into the Blues team, my attitude had changed. Even though I continued to be at the front of the running, my spark and passion for it had dimmed; probably due to the people Jim had recruited. Unlike my previous teammates, I wasn't going to break my neck for those guys. Creaney wouldn't do it for me, so why was I going to do it for him? My wife says I'm a stubborn old so-and-so and that's what it was. Feeling homesick, we ended up selling our Hedge End home and moving back to Brockworth. From then on, I commuted to Pompey training every day.

Pompey handed me a free transfer in November 1994, so Jim now had my £700 a week to give to some other kid. Despite my desire to leave, it surprised me they had turned down six-figure bids from firstly Swansea and then Port Vale. Still, I shook his hand and there were no hard feelings and no arguments. We both thanked each other for everything we had done and, if anything, he was quite emotional when I walked out the door and left for good. I probably didn't kick on in the way he wanted and some of that was down to me not willing to be around a number of those lads, but I'd lost that bit of spark. Despite being a player who always gave everything in a Blues shirt, my heart had gone out of it. From when I arrived at Fratton Park in March 1991, it would have been terrific to have kept that team for a few more years, adding a couple of quality performers and seeing how far we could have gone — which I believe would have been the Premier League.

I later played for Swansea and Northampton Town, before deciding to return to non-league in September 1996 as I was falling out of love with football and wanted my kids to have a normal life rather than moving to three or four schools by the age of six. Aged 28, I joined Gloucester City — and was back working on the building site.

I was sad how it ended with Jim. In my eyes he betrayed me a little, but he was one of the best managers I ever played under, despite his man-management skills not being that good. We subsequently bumped into each other a few times over the years and when he was Derby manager and I was at Gloucester and would always say: "Hello." With some former managers you'd stop and chat about football, but not really with Jim. Our relationship was a bit sour in the end at Pompey, but I have no regrets and bear no grudges. With hindsight, I wish I had signed that two-year Pompey deal in the summer of 1994 and stuck in there, outlasting those players I didn't like in that changing room. Spending another four or five years at Fratton Park would have been great, but, as a young lad at the time, I just wanted to play.

Hanging on the wall along the stairs at my Brockworth home is my Pompey FA Cup semi-final shirt and also the one Michael Thomas wore for Liverpool, while I have Bruce Grobbelaar's green cap somewhere in my attic. They remind me of the best time of my career by an absolute country mile. I was an up-and-down footballer who wanted to score a few goals and enjoy himself, playing with a smile on his face. For me it was never about money, not at all. If it was I wouldn't have signed for Pompey in the first place. I would have stayed on a Gloucestershire building site.

RICHIE REYNOLDS

160 games, 28 goals (June 1971 — February 1976)

Fulham 2 (Mitchell 2)
Pompey 2 (Reynolds 2)

Second Division, Craven Cottage, Saturday, April 19, 1975

Pompey: Figgins, Piper, Went, Reynolds, Hand, Cahill, Marinello, Foggo, Graham, Stewart (60 mins, Kane), Mellows.

Attendance; 17,580

Goal: Richard Reynolds goes down and Pompey go level . . . Reynolds beat Fulham goalkeeper Peter Mellor with this diving header to make the score 1—1 at Craven Cottage on Saturday. Q752-3

Two-goal fling by Reynolds

POINT SAVED — THEN IT'S OFF TO DALLAS

Fulham 2
Pompey 2

By MIKE NEASOM

As farewells go, Richard Reynolds's final fling before disappearing to Dallas would take a lot of beating.

The man who came back from the scrapheap, departed temporarily at least, on a note of near m...

HAMPSHIRE LEAGUE

Winning finale by Fareham

Pele's New York Cosmos debut was a global phenomenon, broadcast to 13 different countries and covered by more than 300 journalists — and the owner of a Hilsea chip shop was challenged with shackling him.

It was June 1975, the Brazilian superstar had signed for the North American Soccer League club for a salary of $1.4m a year and, with Dallas Tornado being the oldest team in the division, we were chosen as the opposition for an exhibition game to mark the occasion. Having represented the Tornado two years earlier, this was my second spell in America, returning that summer off the back of finishing 17th in the Second Division, having re-established myself in Pompey's team under Ian St John.

By that time, I had spent four seasons at Fratton Park, combining life as a professional footballer with running my Copnor Road business, Richie's Ocean Swell, to help pay the mortgage. It was failing when I took over in 1973 and, over the next seven years, became probably the best chip shop in town. They would queue for miles. Having taken evening classes in catering while a Plymouth Argyle apprentice as a bit of a back-up plan, I knew how to cook. Years later, I'd attend Pompey training in the mornings before heading to the shop to carry out afternoon food preparation, such as battering cod. My wife, her mother and a couple of staff ran it. Even the wife of my teammate John Collins would help, while I'd also pitch in and serve customers when I could. It was good fun, the best business I ever had, but football came first, of course.

I eventually sold it as the unsociable hours became too much, while the smell of the fat and the fish really got into your clothes, but catering and football is all I know. After my playing days ended, I ran Jerones American Diner in Chichester, Rascals restaurant in Albert Road, Crusties sandwich shops in Havant, Chichester, North End and Edinburgh Road, a coffee shop called Rich Aroma in North End, and, finally, Flutes cafe in Cosham.

Anyhow, in 1975 I was facing Pele at the Downing Stadium in New York City, a ground equipped with just three sides. A capacity crowd of 21,278 were present as I attempted to mark the best player on the planet — while the world also watched. We had played a league fixture the previous evening at San Antonio, Texas, around 150 miles from the Mexican border, before flying back the following morning to Dallas to grab fresh kit and a date with Pele in New York. Committed to two games and two plane trips within 24 hours, no wonder fatigue subsequently set in as we raced into a 2-0 lead after 39 minutes against the Cosmos. Sure enough, the 34-year-old Pele would inspire their comeback, setting up one before grabbing a headed equaliser in a 2-2 draw. I'd been trying to keep him quiet but was switched from a midfield marking role to up front for the final 15 minutes — and subsequently had his shirt stolen from me. The toerag of a guy who took my place in midfield, Wigan Athletic's Tommy Gore, instead thieved Pele's shirt at the final whistle. I did get the Brazilian to sign a postcard, however, which I still have, reminding me of the best player I came up against.

My football career began at Plymouth, where I became their youngest-ever player at the time after Malcolm Allison handed me a debut at the age of 16 years and 329 days against Derby County in the FA Cup in January 1965, starting alongside future Pompey teammates Nick Jennings and Mike Trebilcock in a 4-2 win. Just three days earlier, my first-team involvement was secured having scored nine times in our youth-team's 13-0 victory over Bugle, a Cornish village team, in the South Western League in front of 92 supporters. I developed very young and, as a 15-year-old, was as big as I am now, six foot tall and at the time weighing 12st.

At the age of 21, the moment arrived which almost destroyed my career. During an FA Cup match at Brentford in November 1969, their number six took me out just underneath the knee after I had just crossed the ball. After trying to carry on for a few months, I underwent an operation to remove the meniscus, with the surgeon warning I'd struggle to play football again. Although I managed to come back, I've never got over that injury and, to this day, remain troubled by my knee. I can hardly walk. I was sidelined for 11 months, returning for the Pilgrims in January 1971, but would feature just four more times before being released at the end of the season following 140 appearances and 25 goals.

For the final month of that campaign, they sent me on loan to non-league Yeovil Town, where I scored four goals in five games to help them win the Southern League Premier Division in 1970/71, so I knew there wasn't a lot wrong with me. However, with Plymouth advised by the surgeon that I would never recover, coupled with my contract coming to an end, they let me go, which hurt. I found myself without a club in the summer of 1971, yet determined not to let it end there — I wanted to prove people wrong. Fortunately, I had offers from Pompey and Manchester City. City wanted me to prove my fitness before deciding whether I warranted a contract, whereas Pompey, who had scouted me through Tony Barton, tabled a two-year deal, which provided the security I desired.

Ron Tindall was my first Fratton Park manager and, having not long retired from playing, took training himself. Having been on £25 a week at Plymouth, I was handed £32 a week by Pompey — with the proviso that if I proved my fitness they would be fair and increase it to a decent wage. Unfortunately, during almost five years at Fratton Park, that never happened. Admittedly, I was handed a new two-year deal and put up to £55 a week at the end of my first season when I finished as top scorer and player of the year, yet I later discovered I remained the lowest earner in the squad. I never discussed money with anyone, but one day, while talking with a teammate, I can't recall who, my eyes were opened to learn he was on £70 a week. My wife Gill's dad followed us to the south coast to live, working in the Dockyard doing lagging as he neared retirement, and he was earning more than me! Back then, signing a contract as a footballer meant they controlled you — now it's the other way around. Yet, in those days, once your deal ran out there was no free transfer; the club continued to hold your registration and, while still paying you, could demand a fee if you desired a move. It became an ongoing dispute at Pompey which, ultimately, led to my departure in February 1976 after I had brought the PFA and Football Association into the argument.

Regardless, I felt I had proved a point in my maiden Blues season in 1971/72, missing just one of our 46 matches in all competitions, while my 11 goals meant I was leading scorer, emphatically proving my knee could stand up to it. Thanks should go to Gordon Neave, our physio and kitman, who knew nothing about football injuries, but came up with a routine where I'd go in on the Sunday morning after a game and receive hot and cold water treatment, along with Vaseline and bandages. He'd use a solution of lead and opium — it's illegal now — and soak cotton wool in it. Keeping it on my knee for 48 hours removed the swelling. It was brilliant and credit to Gordon, the only Scotsman I've ever got on with!

I also received the player of the year from *The News* that first season, voted for by the fans, which I appreciated. I would bustle, didn't lose many tackles, was good in the air, and able to switch play from one side of the pitch to the other. As a striker, I was a goal maker rather than goal scorer, that was my main strength. In reality, I was a midfielder. I didn't score enough up front and I don't even know why I was selected there so much for Pompey. I was more effective in midfield, either centrally or on the left-hand side.

I was playing for Dallas Tornado during Pompey's off-season in May 1973 when, unbeknown to me, Tindall had left as boss, having been moved upstairs as general manager. I'd been recruited by Dallas' head coach Ron Newman, a former Blues player, who had already signed my Fratton Park teammates Nick Jennings and John Collins. We had a good time there too, winning the Southern Division to reach the semi-finals against New York Cosmos in August 1973, but Nick, John and myself were unable to participate any further as we were required to return to Fratton Park for pre-season ahead of the 1973/74 campaign. Unfortunately, my daughter Caryn then picked up an ear infection, so me and my family had to wait for that to clear up before coming back to England, although I still couldn't play for Dallas.

When I finally reported to Pompey on the Monday morning, I stripped and started training, only to realise someone else was taking us — John Mortimore. "Who's this fella with the tin whistle?" I thought and, after asking around, discovered he was our new manager! Nobody at the club had officially told me. At the end of the week I smelt a rat at the annual team photo session, having not been asked to appear in any of the pictures. So, following training at Eastney, I went back to Fratton Park and knocked on Mortimore's office door. "I've been training all week," I said. "Do you know who I am?" — and he didn't! I introduced myself, before explaining I had an agreement that my contract needed reassessing and I was due a pay rise. "Oh yes," he responded. "While you've been away, we've had a look at your contract and feel it's fair." So I walked out of the office and immediately phoned the PFA.

Mortimore was strange. Certainly his record doesn't say he was a good manager and I didn't have any time for him because of the way he treated me — you would expect the boss of a football team to know which players he had to select from. He couldn't actually communicate with people without blowing a whistle, very school teacher-ish. The whistle would signal the warm-up, we then finished on the whistle. Everything had to be done to the sound of it. Mortimore was part of John Deacon's Pompey overhaul after buying the club from Dennis Collett in May 1973. The new owner appointed him and set about paying obscene wages and recruiting players who didn't perform, with some already at the club pushed aside until we were required to improve poor results. Peter Marinello arrived from Arsenal, but wasn't the new George Best they hyped him up to be and didn't perform for Pompey, which was a shame. He was quick, but that's about it, and I would never have picked him. Paul Went was a good signing, a bit of a character; Malcolm Manley collected a serious injury early on; Phil Roberts was honest but not the best defender in the world; Ron Davies was past his best, but stick the ball on his head and he was all right; while George Graham couldn't run, although didn't have to with his ability on the ball. Then there were the wages, with Ron Davies the highest on £250 a week and Marinello on £200, compared to those already on the club's books on £70-plus — and my £55 a week. So you can see the pay disparity.

I took my wife to her first football match in May 1965, which was the FA Cup final between Liverpool and Leeds United, with Ian St John grabbing an extra-time winner in a 2-1 success for Bill Shankly's side. From that moment, Gill has been mad about Liverpool — not just the football club, but the humour of the people from up there — and I also came to support them. So when St John was appointed as my next Pompey manager in September 1974 to replace Mortimore, I was excited. Here was one of the best players I had seen — yet I soon discovered he's the worst manager I ever came across.

As a Scotland international striker, he was a hard worker blessed with a wonderful first touch. On the pitch he saw things other players just couldn't. However, after around three or four weeks, Pompey's players were looking at each other in bewilderment over his performance as our boss. Tactically he was really poor. In the middle of a match, with the opposition posing a particular threat, naturally the first thing you'd attempt is to stop the danger, yet St John could never spot it, not even the most obvious things, while his team talks weren't very inspiring. He also brought in his mate Chris Lawler, who played right-back in that Liverpool FA Cup win which myself and Gill had watched. What a complete waste of time he was. He couldn't run and ended up making 40 appearances — you can't be a successful football manager if you've got bias. As for St John's assistant, Billy Hunter, he was an embarrassment. A complete joke who didn't know football and had been a teammate of St John's at Motherwell. The employment criteria was: 'You're my friend, here's the job.' There's a saying that great footballers don't always make great managers, as proven by Bobby Charlton and also St John.

Ahead of his September 1974 appointment, St John had watched us lose 2-1 at The Dell, with Peter Osgood netting twice for Southampton, while I split my left eye. I went up for a far-post header in their penalty area when the half-time whistle sounded and, while everyone turned away, he got me. *Bang*. I spent the interval in the medical room getting it stitched up and was unable to play in the following match at Nottingham Forest, which represented St John's first in charge. From that point, I found it very difficult to get a game under the new manager, starting just seven of his opening 28 fixtures at the Fratton Park helm.

We had a trip to Hull City in February 1975 and St John was struggling for midfielders until Norman Piper told him that it was actually my position. Can you believe it, the manager of a Second Division side discussing with his players who he should pick? You shouldn't be doing that. Anyhow, I was switched from attack to midfield and we drew 0-0. Afterwards, St John said to me: "Cor, we found something there, didn't we," in reference to my midfield performance — and I became a regular for the remainder of the campaign. A month later we travelled to West Bromwich Albion and I mentioned to St John: "Len Cantello's playing, he'll rip us apart. Do you want me to take him?" You have all week before a game to sort out tactics and it took me to suggest what to do about Cantello, who was a hell of a player! Even then he didn't give me any instructions, there was nothing pre-game. Very rarely were there tactics delivered by St John to anybody. As it turned out, we lost 2-1 after their Scottish full-back Ray Wilson's 88th-minute winner from 25-yards, with me getting our goal from George Graham's pull-back.

That period included my favourite Pompey game at Fulham in April 1975, when I scored twice in a 2-2 draw in my final match before returning to Dallas that summer. The Cottagers had booked a place in the 1975 FA Cup final against West Ham United and lined-up against us with Bobby Moore and Alan Mullery in their side. I initially started in midfield, but was later moved into attack in the search for goals, grabbing two when up against Moore, including a last-minute equaliser, and we finished 17th in the Second Division.

Following my summer in the North American Soccer League and facing Pele, I returned for the 1975/76 season, which would prove to be my last at Pompey. I never had a lot to do with John Deacon, I always thought our owner was all right, but, at the end of the day, he was the reason why I never earned a decent wage. Ironic really as, apparently, I was his wife's favourite player! After three years at Fratton Park, I was offered a new deal of £70 a week. They had been signing all these big-name stars on £200-250 a week, yet wanted to pay me £70. No, I wouldn't sign for that. So, for my final two years, I was out of contract and they retained my registration, therefore not earning a penny more than the £55 a week I'd been on.

Through the PFA, I took Pompey to an FA tribunal, held at Lancaster Gate, which was chaired by Football League secretary Alan Hardaker, who passed judgement that the club had "cheated" me and were required to pay compensation of £3,000 per year in recognition of the poor wage I'd been paid. What's more, Pompey were instructed to negotiate a new contract. We did, with £70 the maximum they would offer, while they kept insisting the £3,000 would be built into the new contract, when they knew full well it was backdated and needed to be settled before any new deal. So it was back to the tribunal, who next ruled that, if Pompey couldn't settle what I was owed, I had to be sold. The club's response? A ridiculous fee of £250,000 on the head of an out-of-contract player — and they still wouldn't give me the wages. I attended seven of these hearings over a three-year period and every one involved reduced the transfer fee the club wanted, until it reached £60,000. As for Deacon, he kept claiming the club were financially struggling and he didn't have the money to meet the £3,000 per year compensation. I never received a penny of it.

It came to a head in the Stamford Bridge away dressing room in February 1976, one hour before I was scheduled to face Chelsea. Just as I was about to get stripped, St John pulled me aside and announced I could no longer be involved. My Pompey contract had been torn up with immediate effect after the Football League had requested my release. "You are free to go," he told me. That was it, my Blues career had ended. I remained to watch a 2-0 defeat which left us eight points adrift of safety. After all, I needed to catch the team coach to get home.

It hurt more than being told I would never play again through injury while at Plymouth. I didn't seek to leave Pompey, I just wanted to be treated fairly. It was another five weeks before I received an official letter from the Football League explaining that an independent tribunal had instructed the termination of my employment, with four weeks' notice, signed by league secretary Hardaker. Not that I ever trained with Pompey again after the Chelsea match; instead, living in Godwit Road, Milton, I'd work on my fitness running around Langstone every morning. But my Blues career was gone.

I never fell out with St John, but his inability to run a football club irritated me and, while some good kids came through during his time, he was very, very lucky as that was purely down to the excellent work Ray Crawford was doing with the youth system. Among them was Chris Kamara, who was very good at cleaning boots — he and Steve Foster did mine — although you would never have thought Chris would make it. Not in a million years! This big gangly thing didn't look like a footballer, he didn't train like a footballer, but obviously matured after I left Fratton Park and had a very good playing career and everything else which went with it.

After departing Pompey, I didn't have many options. Gillingham offered me a contract, but I didn't want to go there, so I hung it out hoping for something which appealed — and Dutch side HFC Haarlem came in. They were managed by Welshman Barry Hughes and clinched promotion to the Dutch Eredivisie on the day I was over there having a look. My debut was a 2-0 home win against Ajax as I featured in four of our opening eight matches in the 1976/77 season. However, after playing 90 minutes in a 1-0 win at Telstar in September 1976, I felt pain in my left knee, which previously had never troubled me. I required an operation at a Haarlem hospital and, despite being assured I would make a full recovery, afterwards it still felt very, very painful and I couldn't jump. I'd lost my spring. My comeback was against Feyenoord in March 1977, but I was struggling and came off 75 minutes into a 3-0 defeat. That was my fifth and final appearance for Haarlem — and my last in professional football. As I was insured, Haarlem offered £2,000 to retire, albeit with the clause that I couldn't play professionally for two years. With Gill having already returned to Portsmouth expecting our second daughter Michelle, it seemed the right time. At the age of 29, I hung up my boots.

I kept active, even training at Pompey for three or four weeks under Jimmy Dickinson, with Frank Burrows his coach. Then Ron Newman, my former Dallas manager, brought his Fort Lauderdale Strikers team across to England for a six-game tour, with a friendly scheduled against Pompey at Fratton Park in February 1978. The American team had to call upon a few guests, such as England World

Cup-winning duo Bobby Charlton and Gordon Banks, while I was also asked. I subsequently appeared as a second-half substitute and surprised myself how well I did in a 2-2 draw, setting up David Irving for our equaliser. Afterwards, Ron asked whether I would be interested in returning to America with Fort Lauderdale, but firstly wanted me to guest in another game, this time at Swindon Town. Following an hour on a snowy pitch, I attempted a crossfield pass and something snapped in my left thigh, forcing me off. There was to be no move to Fort Lauderdale.

In August 1978, while playing for Carshalton Athletic, I was offered my first management job by Southern Premier League side Yeovil, yet I turned it down as they wanted me to relocate. Instead, over the next 20 years, I worked in local non-league, firstly becoming player-manager at Chichester City in February 1979. They were second bottom of the Sussex County League Division One, on a long losing streak, and I had 10 matches to save them from relegation. We finished 12th. The following season, I recruited two new players and we won the title, losing just four games in the process, while I scored 13 goals in 31 appearances from the centre of midfield. I later managed Fareham Town, Petersfield Town, Pagham, Wick (twice), Newport (Isle of Wight), Selsey, and totalled three spells at Chichester.

I've never been a greedy person. As a Pompey player all I ever wanted was what I was entitled to — and never received it. That soured my time there. I love the club. There's no better feeling than playing at Fratton Park, Mike Neasom labelled me "Cornish granite" and, to this day, I live in Milton. Money doesn't motivate me and my contract situation never affected my commitment. I continued giving that club everything during those three years without a deal. I wouldn't think about knocking on the manager's door and asking: "Oi, where's my money?" I was still selected by various bosses because they knew I gave my all.

I sometimes feel I let my wife down. Maybe I should have kicked up a fuss and we got by, we had some great times, but how I was treated still nags away, even all these years later. Jim Sloan was a director at the club and after every game he'd come up and say: "Not bad for nothing, are you?" He was a lovely man — and never was a truer word spoken in jest.

KAL NAISMITH

94 games, 21 goals (May 2015 — June 2018)

Pompey 6 (O'Shaughnessy OG, Bennett, Naismith 2, Lowe, Evans)
Cheltenham 1 (Dayton)

League Two, Fratton Park, Saturday, May 6, 2017

Pompey: Forde, Evans, Burgess, Clarke, Stevens, Doyle, Rose (71 mins, Aborah), Baker (60 mins, Lowe), Naismith, Bennett, Chaplin (61 mins, Roberts). Subs not used: O'Brien, Whatmough, Linganzi, Kabamba.

Attendance; 17,956

Football was a disaster during my early Fratton Park days. Paul Cook got the wrong impression of me, and I think some Pompey fans had too. Granted, I'm laid back and relaxed, yet there was this wrong perception that I didn't care about the game. The manager saw me as this single lad living in Portsmouth but I wasn't even speaking to another human being, let alone going out and enjoying myself at night. Amid it all, I was still mourning my girlfriend Ashley, who passed away following an epileptic seizure in October 2014. Just seven months after her death, I was now living the furthest point away from my Glasgow home and family. Pompey was a move from Accrington Stanley which I couldn't possibly turn down — what an amazing club — yet I was in a one-bedroom Gunwharf flat on my own, isolated, and unable to afford to fly my mum down for a visit. The truth is, it impacted on my performances in that first south-coast season.

Ashley had suffered from epilepsy since the age of 11 or 12, yet back then our understanding of her condition was not as detailed as these days. We just assumed she was fine. She suffered seizures a lot, every few weeks, although differing in severity, and dealing with it became a standard procedure. Whenever it occurred you stayed with her, making sure she couldn't hurt herself. Then she'd come around after an hour, initially unsure of where she was, before becoming emotional having realised the situation. She never complained and just soldiered on. Then one day Ashley went into a seizure and never came out of it.

She was at her parents' home in Summerston, Glasgow, when it happened, while I was back in Manchester after spending the previous two days with her. I rang her before bedtime, we chatted, then the next day I went to training with Accrington. When I returned to the changing room and checked my phone, I discovered the news. Ashley was in bed when she passed at the age of 22. Nobody was there to look after her. It was never mentioned that epilepsy could kill her. You visited the doctor, were given tablets and managed it. That was it. I always made sure she slept as much as she could, as when she was tired it could trigger an attack. Knowing what I do now, we would have done things differently. I would have been a lot stricter with her diet in addition to sleep times, but I didn't know at the time. I don't even know if that definitely would have helped.

I returned to Glasgow for a month to grieve. I didn't play football, didn't do any fitness. I wasn't living well, stuck in bed and not eating as well as I should. Accrington's manager John Coleman was amazing. He let me be, although he was always on the end of the phone whenever I wanted a chat. When I eventually came back, I trained for a week and appeared as a substitute in an FA Cup game at Notts County in November 2014, before being restored to the starting line-up at Carlisle United. I had a nightmare match, I couldn't get at the full-back and was substituted after 60 minutes. I should have trained for four weeks before playing a game. My body was broken and I was mentally drained. I was tired and unfit — still in my grieving period. I don't know if Cookie ever knew what had happened with Ashley. It was never spoken about at Pompey, he never asked. But, to my surprise, as Chesterfield manager he came in for me some six weeks later in January 2015.

Having entered the final six months of my contract and with the Spireites being a League One club, this was the opportunity to step up a level. Accrington wanted me to stay, but I also wasn't too sure whether to return to Glasgow and potentially play for a team there. I decided to run down my contract and see what emerged, with Chesterfield remaining an option. However, at the season's end, everything went a bit quiet. When Cook finally contacted my agent, he wanted to take me to Pompey instead.

In May 2015, I caught the train from Glasgow to Portsmouth to discuss terms. What I now know is when Paul Cook gets you into a room, you are done. You're signing that deal! He showed me around Fratton Park, detailed plans to take the club into League One and then the Championship, then sat me in a room — and 10 minutes later I had agreed a three-year contract. I was his second signing, following Kyle Bennett, and, over the next few weeks, we were joined by Enda Stevens, Gary Roberts, Christian Burgess and Michael Doyle.

Funnily enough, my Accrington debut — and maiden Football League appearance — came against Pompey during a *Sky Sports*-televised League Two game in August 2013. Having arrived at the Crown Ground from Glasgow Rangers on a two-year deal the previous day, I started on the right wing and it finished 2-2. Now, almost two years later, I was a Pompey player.

We soon learnt how ruthless the manager was during that first pre-season in 2015. Kitman Kev McCormack or one of the coaches would tell a player: "The gaffer wants you," and they'd head to his office, before returning later and saying: "He's told me I won't play one single minute, I'm done." I remember that happening to James Dunne, one of the better players, and also Johnny Ertl. He got rid of almost every senior player who wasn't his and cleared out everyone. Even the skipper Paul Robinson, who was a lovely guy who was trying to help everyone settle, was out.

I hurt my left quad ahead of our final friendly at Gillingham but still took part in an afternoon running session, making it worse and ruling me out for five weeks. By the time I returned at the start of September, making my debut as a substitute against Exeter City in the Johnstone's Paint Trophy, the team was settled. From a seat on the bench, over the next month I watched us establish ourselves in League Two's top two — although I was barely used, so I approached the manager enquiring whether I would get an opportunity. Then, one day, he pulled me in and said: "Listen Kal, you need to play games to get up to speed. Would you consider going out on loan?" Of course I would, I was having a hard time. Perhaps a short-term loan up north could bring me closer to my family and enable me to reset — just for a month, mind.

At the time, I was closest to Christian Burgess who, like me, lived on his own around the Gunwharf Quays area, so most days we'd meet at a coffee shop and chill. It was November 2015 and we were at the Garage Lounge in Southsea when I told him how Paul Cook wanted me to go out on loan and I was keen to get as far up north as possible. Burge had spent a season on loan at Hartlepool United two years earlier and his central defensive partner, Sam Collins, was now their assistant manager so, in front of me, he texted him asking if they would be interested. The response was definite, so Burge rang him and passed the phone to me. Within days I'd signed on loan until January and they'd put me in a flat on the marina.

Cook had promised that, upon my return, I'd get the opportunity to start games. By that stage all the new lads had been given a run, except me, so now I was heading to Hartlepool with one goal in mind — to build up my fitness and return to play for Pompey. I made four appearances at Victoria Park and did really well. My confidence was back, my swagger had returned and, with the loan expiring in January 2016, their manager Ronnie Moore wanted it extended. When I explained my situation with Pompey, he replied: "Are you sure that's still the plan? We've spoken to them and they're willing to let you stay longer." I was confused, but determined to come back now my loan was over. During the long drive back to the south coast on the Sunday, I had stopped off at the services for a coffee when I received a call from Cook. He asked how I was and, when I informed him I was returning, he responded: "Coming back down where? Hartlepool or Pompey?" Then he added: "Look Kal, I'll be honest with you … since you've been away a lot of lads have gone ahead of you." He topped it off by including Ben Tollitt, a youngster in his first Football League season.

In those days I was scared of Paul Cook, terrified of him, but at that moment I needed to stand up for myself. I had signed for a great club and wanted a chance — so I insisted I'd be returning to train hard and force my way into his team. The reply was: "Right, okay. Fine." The following morning I turned up for training and he called me into his office: "Listen Kal, Crawley Town want you on loan. It's around the corner, so we can keep an eye on you and watch your games." Again

I said no, which he wasn't happy with, accusing me of turning my nose up at Hartlepool and now Crawley. I left his office believing I was done at Pompey. I had stuck up for myself and lost my temper and, if he didn't like that, then I was finished. Knowing Cook the way I do these days, with the relationship we later forged, I think he actually respected my stance and, from that moment, I was involved in all but two squads for the remainder of the season. Although I still found myself transfer-listed!

Looking back, he was harsh on me from day one and anything I did, he would scream at me. I was terrified to be late and, considering I lived on my own, I'd set seven alarms and wake up early in case there was traffic or a crash on the way into training. His unfavourable opinion of me can be tracked to July 2015, for our first pre-season friendly at Havant & Waterlooville, which I started. The previous day, Big Kev had given the lads new team tracksuits, which we tried on for size in the changing rooms and discovered the bottoms were flared. Initially I was quite a shy person, so I was listening to the likes of Gary Roberts and Kyle Bennett talking about how awful these trousers were and saying they'd be wearing their training bottoms, which were exactly the same but tight around the ankles. So I turned up for Westleigh Park for our match wearing my training bottoms — only for everyone else to have on their flared trousers. We walked on to the pitch before the game and Cook, who was in the away dugout, shouted at me to come over: "Don't ever do anything differently to your teammates again or you'll be out the door." It was a genuine mistake. I was a young kid, aged 23, and I should have messaged our captain Michael Doyle for clarity or taken both pairs. It was stupid and naive. Talk about life at Pompey starting on the wrong foot!

I ended the 2015/16 season having started the final four league games and scoring twice as we finished sixth, ensuring we were paired with Plymouth Argyle in the League Two play-off semi-finals. This was my opportunity; in my mind I was going to keep my place against the Pilgrims. Instead, with Kyle Bennett returning from injury, I was on the bench for the first leg, which was a 2-2 draw at Fratton Park, coming on in the second half. I remained substitute for the second leg, although the same couldn't be said for Conor Wilkinson, a striker on loan from Bolton Wanderers who Cook had taken a dislike to. Matchday squads may consist of 18 footballers, but it's standard to have additional players in case of an emergency. Now Cook didn't like the players knowing too much about the team, so sometimes wouldn't name the substitutes. Often we'd be warming up before a game and discovered who was on the bench by listening to the PA announcer — we were too scared to ask the manager! During the warm-up at Plymouth for the second leg, we counted one extra player and then, about 10 minutes into the game, Wilkinson mentioned how we had too many substitutes. One of the lads replied: "We know, you're not on the bench!" So he returned to the dressing room, got showered and came back to watch the remainder of the match. That happened a good few times while I was at Pompey.

I wasn't used as a substitute as we lost that Home Park leg 1-0, sealing an aggregate 3-2 defeat to knock us out of the play-offs. A few days later, we headed in for our end-of-season individual meetings with the manager, which were standard procedure. I was anticipating a pretty positive chat, considering the way my season had picked up. Instead I was told: "Right, as you know, it has probably not gone as well as you and I would have wanted. So speak to your agent — find another club." There were two years remaining on my contract and I had been transfer-listed, along with Matt Tubbs and Adam McGurk. I will never give up, I'll try to prove someone wrong to the death, yet it almost came as a relief. I had tried everything and at least I could tell myself I'd done my best. It just hadn't worked.

There was nothing in the pipeline when I returned for the first day of Pompey pre-season training in June 2016. I had no idea what to expect, but was determined to show Cook he'd made a mistake. I was living with McGurk that summer but I'm quite a messy guy, never hanging my clothes up and living out of a suitcase. This time it would be different. I hung up my stuff and neatly folded other clothes in drawers. It took me two hours, but I was doing it right. The next day I walked into the changing room at the training ground and discovered I didn't have a kit. Big Kev said: "I'm sorry Naisy, it's not my decision. I just get told." I told him not to be daft, reassured him it wasn't his fault. Then I went to see Cook, who handed me a bit of paper which contained the number of Mark Kelly, the head of Pompey's academy. "Give him a call, the under-18s begin training in two weeks. See you later." So I got in my car, drove to McGurk's house, packed up all my stuff and moved back to Glasgow for a fortnight!

When I returned, I trained with the academy under Mark Kelly and Mikey Harris and they were superb with me. Absolutely top guys. A new signing now had my place in the dressing room, while I couldn't eat with the first-team, I had to wait outside the canteen with the academy lads for Cook's squad to finish lunch before going in. None of the first-team were allowed to speak to me around the training ground, although I can recall Milan Lalkovic, a summer signing from Walsall, once coming over to my table and sitting with me and asking about my situation. At that point, the gaffer came in and said: "What are you doing here? You shouldn't be speaking to him." I responded: "Milan, sorry mate, just don't bother talking to me," before getting up, putting my plate away and leaving the room. A manager prefers to work with the players he wants, I understand that, but for first-team players to be prohibited from speaking to me? Come on, I'm still a human being. I did continue to go for a coffee with the lads after training, but it was hard. I felt distant from them, I wasn't part of it anymore. I think some felt a bit awkward around me, which is natural.

I have no problem with Paul Cook wanting to move me on. It's about opinions. I'll probably be a manager myself one day and they're lessons I have learnt. It was character building, a case I'll prove I'm not that guy. I was never that guy. It was so frustrating. He got me wrong, he knows that now, and that's why he's a massive part of my career. I almost have to thank him, because I wouldn't have played in the Championship with Wigan Athletic, Luton Town and Bristol City otherwise.

It gets strange because when I did have the chance to leave that summer, the gaffer wouldn't let me! Pompey agreed to cancel my contract, allowing me to depart on a free to Blackpool, which would have been perfect; only for Cook to now insist he wanted to think about it. I was confused, my agent was confused, as was Tangerines boss Gary Bowyer, who then offered a transfer fee to secure me. Pompey had paid peanuts for me 12 months earlier, so Blackpool offered the £40,000 that Accrington received — and it still wasn't happening. Then Leam Richardson rang, having not spoken to me all summer: "How are you getting on? The team coach is leaving Roko tomorrow for a friendly at Bristol City. Be there for 9am." I walked on to the bus, the lads shouted: "He's back," and were laughing and joking. It was brilliant to be there again. This was Pompey's final pre-season friendly and, in truth, I wasn't sure whether it was meant to be more punishment, making me watch the game and not bringing me on. As it was, I replaced Enda Stevens at left-back on 87 minutes in a goalless draw and received a yellow card for kicking someone. My head was gone, I was so angry. Still, from that moment, I was welcomed back into the changing room and everything was fine. It was like nothing had happened. Me and the gaffer never spoke about it again, and neither did the coaches.

There was one chat with Leam, actually. Just before I boarded that bus to Bristol City, he told me: "Strange things happen. At Chesterfield, the same thing occurred with Sam Hird and he ended up being the gaffer's captain." I have no idea whether the whole episode had been a test to see how I reacted, but I was never going to fold. Training with the under-18s, perhaps Mark and Mikey saw me for what I genuinely was — a hard-working lad — and presumably spoke highly of me whenever the gaffer and Leam asked for updates. Cook never explained it to me — and I have no idea if he ever took me off the transfer-list!

I wasn't in the squad for the August 2016 opener against Carlisle, which finished 1-1, but I was named at left-back 72 hours later for the trip to Coventry City in the EFL Cup. I scored a 25-yard free-kick in the 85th minute to equalise at 2-2 and send the match into extra-time. During my celebrations I took my top off and slid on both knees towards Cook, the culmination of all that frustration. I was definitely back. Off the field I also began to settle, meeting someone again in Lauren, and we moved in together in Locks Heath. She's from Glasgow, we've known each other since we were kids and reconnected during my Hartlepool loan when I'd return to Scotland at weekends. It started off as friendship — she was there for me when I was struggling, at a time when I thought I'd never share my life with anyone again — and it went from strength to strength. It's strange how people come into your life and that stability and happiness enabled my Pompey career to kick on during that second season. We are now married with two children.

In November 2016, I was warming up at half-time against Stevenage, kicking a ball around on the Fratton Park pitch with our other substitutes at half-time, when first-team coach Ian Foster came running over. He pointed to Adam May and Jack Whatmough and said: "You and you, get ready. You're coming on." The game was goalless, it was a match we needed to win, and they were bringing on a central midfielder and a centre-half. Why? We looked at each other and genuinely called it straight away, without knowing anything — Michael Doyle and Christian Burgess had been fighting. Doyler was always shouting in the changing room, being passionate, while Burge regularly piped up and said something. He could never sit there and stay quiet. If he disagrees with someone, he'll speak up. Well, we were right! That's what football's about, players demanding more from each other for the benefit of the team. In every changing room I've been successful in, players fall out and shout, but afterwards you shake hands and it's done.

Cook cancelled that night's players' Christmas party but we went out anyway, changing the venue to Southampton and having a few drinks, sticking together as a squad. Burge and Doyler were as good as gold, moving on. The following day, the management relented and Leam Richardson informed us we could go to Winter Wonderland in Hyde Park as previously arranged, without having a clue we'd gone behind their backs on the Saturday night. It wasn't a secret for long, however. Tom Davies, Adam Buxton and some others shared a house in Fratton and neighbours complained to the club about their noise in the early hours of Sunday morning after going out drinking. When we returned to training on Tuesday, we got wind of this and decided that, should these lads be disciplined, the whole group would take the punishment. Sure enough, Cook called a meeting before training and asked who'd gone out on Saturday night against his wishes

— and we all put our hands up. He then proceeded to run us into the ground, lap after lap of the training pitches. It went on and on and on. At the end of it we were sent home — yet it had now become us versus the staff.

It was a fortnight before our next match — at Grimsby Town in December 2016 — and I grabbed the winner from a free-kick four minutes from time after coming on as a substitute. The gaffer loved the goal celebrations, subsequently replaying the footage to us to highlight why that moment was the best part of the 1-0 win. And particularly how Gary Roberts, who I had replaced, was the first person on to the pitch to hug me when I scored. That reflected the team spirit among the squad — which Cook, either knowingly or unknowingly, had helped forge.

We travelled to Newport County on Boxing Day and what unfolded was the turning point for my whole career. I had been handed my first League One start in almost three months and was well aware that, should I not score or play well, then I'd be out of the team the following match. After 51 minutes, we were trailing 2-0, before Danny Rose reduced the deficit — then we won a penalty on the hour mark and I took it. With the chance to level, I was so nervous and decided to pass it down the middle, but not too hard in case the keeper stopped it with a trailing leg as he dived. Instead, I stuck it over the bar. I was doing well in the game but my Pompey career was over, done, finished. I was operating on the left of midfield, with the bench on the opposite side in that second half, and I'm thinking: "I know he's taking me off, I know he's taking me off. I need to somehow save myself here." So I ran all the way over to our bench and pleaded: "Gaffer, please don't substitute me." He said he wouldn't, which was a relief. It was 2-2 with 10 minutes remaining after Enda Stevens finished off Rose's pass. Then, on 87 minutes, I took a left-footed free-kick from the right, everyone in the box missed it and it entered the net for the winner! I still have the celebration picture on my phone, capturing my hand over my mouth and Adam Buxton around my neck. It looks like I've seen a ghost. It was relief, there was no joy — and I always look back on that moment of my football career.

We were positioned fourth for the visit of struggling Crewe Alexandra in March 2017, with Cook handing me my first start in seven matches, replacing Carl Baker on the right wing. We lost 1-0 to George Ray's 77th-minute winner, with the booing from the supporters pretty bad. On the Monday, before training, a players' meeting was called. We weren't getting on well with the staff or the fans and needed to sort this out. There was no bitching or blaming, it was more of a: "Can we sort it out together?" vibe. The more experienced lads stood up and said their piece, but not me. Then Amine Linganzi asked to speak — and his story was inspiring. He was a Christian and relayed his background about being born in Algeria and losing a family member as they escaped to France. He loved football and he loved the family feeling at Pompey. He was a guy who would make just one more appearance for the rest of the season, and it struck a chord. We left that meeting closer — and it was us against the world.

The following match was a 2-0 victory at Crawley, with Burgess and Bennett scoring. The travelling fans were right behind us that night and suddenly there was a feeling among the players that nobody would beat us during the run-in. I was in the best attacking form of my career and convinced I'd score every game, a feeling I've never had since. I was Accrington's 10-goal leading scorer in my maiden season, before suffering my family issues in the second campaign. Now I was playing with confidence once more. I was fearless. I can recall netting against Accrington in February 2017 at Fratton Park and some fans were booing me, so I cupped my ears at them. I was a young lad! I thrived in front of that crowd, and nothing fazed me. It helped having started my career at Ibrox, playing 21 times, with the Rangers supporters not liking me at some stages because I was a young kid and had some terrible games. Financial problems meant we'd been relegated into the Scottish Third Division and they were watching young lads who weren't ready. We drew 1-1 at home to Montrose and were being booed. I was fine with Fratton Park.

What also helped my form during that period was finally operating as a number 10, my best position and the one I enjoyed the most. The role under Cook involved him shouting at me to stand out on the right touchline, because he didn't like me in the centre if it was too tight. With the full-back occupied by our right winger, usually Carl Baker, I would find plenty of space so I could cut inside on to my left foot.

We headed to Notts County in April 2017 knowing we could be promoted to League One. On 14 minutes, I surged past Richard Duffy inside the box, took a touch, and he wiped me out. I couldn't understand why their players were complaining, but Gaz Evans was on fire with his penalties and broke the deadlock. Jorge Grant levelled early in the second half and, with 13 minutes to go, the score-line remained 1-1 — until Jamal Lowe intervened. He'd arrived from Hampton & Richmond in January and demonstrated one of her best attitudes towards training I have ever seen. This skinny kid from non-league was constantly in the gym, constantly grafting, working absolutely non-stop on things on the training pitch — and at Meadow Lane he came on to score twice and secure promotion with a 3-1 victory.

From Notts County until the final game of the season, it was dreamland. Just incredible. All the lads would go out together, we'd chill at Port Solent, having a drink with the sun shining. Then we'd play a match, win again, so go out and party once more. We were rolling — and that was the best three or four weeks of my life. I will never forget it.

I never thought we'd win the title on the final day against Cheltenham Town. Since Notts County it had been a case of let's stay unbeaten, win the remaining three games and see what happens. After all, we'd already achieved promotion and the fans were buzzing. At half-time we were leading 1-0 through Daniel O'Shaughnessy's own goal and the Gaffer wasn't happy about the performance. He had a right go at me, accusing me of taking a "screw you tablet" and purposely playing badly for him. When I put us 3-0 up in the 66th minute, I ran over to the bench and handed him a hydration tablet which I'd put inside my sock at half-time, which he found funny. We triumphed 6-1, I scored twice to take my season's tally to 15 goals, and we won the League Two title. It was such a party atmosphere. My mum, brother and girlfriend were at Fratton Park, as were Ashley's family on their first visit. Incredible. How did that even happen? It remains one of the best days of my career. Pompey winning the league will be hard to beat.

Footballers have journeys, and those opening two seasons at Pompey represented mine. My first year at Fratton Park was lonely but in the second season, the squad became incredibly close. It took 12 months for us to bond, along with the additions of Carl Baker, Danny Rose, Tom Davies and David Forde. In July 2015, when I had just moved down to live in Gunwharf and was struggling on my own, we flew to the Algarve for a pre-season training camp and I sat next to our chief executive Mark Catlin on the plane.

"I know it's hard moving away from home," he said. "Here's my number, take it. If you're lonely, we'll go for a coffee in Gunwharf. I live there too." He probably thought nothing of it, but it's the little things which stick with you. What a good guy; he didn't need to do that, although I never messaged him for that coffee. By my second season, there was a coffee club among the players and I'd join Michael Doyle, Enda Stevens, Kyle Bennett, Gary Roberts, Michael Smith, Forde and Davies, meeting up at the Garage Lounge one day and then The Tenth Hole the next. Every day, Doyler would shout at people and smash them in training, then join us afterwards for a coffee and nice chat. We were tighter, closer. I felt a greater part of the group, this fantastic bunch of lads.

I wasn't the only one among my teammates to come through the other side. When I first arrived, Adam Webster didn't play in the opening 12 league games, having featured just 18 times the previous season under Andy Awford. Yet he was that good in training, all the players would go up to him and say: "You need to ask the manager how you're not playing." He wouldn't, though, because he was a shy lad back then. Nonetheless, for the life of us we couldn't understand how this guy wasn't in the first-team. He was incredible, passing it left foot, right foot, and he could defend. Watching Webby in training, he was levels above. Serious levels above. You get players who look good in two or three training sessions – then you get players who, every day, are a level above anyone else. The latter was Webby.

On the flip side, it never happened for Adam Barton at Pompey, but in training he was the best player every single time. He was laid-back, it was like he didn't really care, but would run sessions at walking pace. No-one could get near him. When I first saw him at Pompey I thought: "When he gets in, he's going to go bang." He was a midfielder converted to centre-half and played everything at his own pace, saw everything, and could do plenty with the ball. I loved watching him. If I wasn't playing, the first name I'd look for on the teamsheet was Barts. I'd watch him in the game, the way he moved, the way he passed. He was incredible. Yet football was not everything to him; he was a cool character who played the guitar and was never into the football lifestyle. He'd train and then go home to his family.

Then there was Michael Smith, who signed permanently for an undisclosed fee in June 2016 following a successful loan spell the previous season. He soon learnt how Pompey fans could be harsh on their number nines. I'd be with Smudger on Southsea Common and supporters would be shouting at him, telling him how he was terrible — then, during matches, they'd boo whenever he missed a chance. He was brilliant in training and you wished you could speak to them and say: "Just give him a chance, wait until he scores a goal or two, then he'll kick on." It's almost like they judge you after a game or two, then it's hard to come back from. It never happened for him. You have to hit the ground running at Pompey.

In a fitting end to that League Two season, our chairman Iain McInnes paid for the players to spend three or four days in Marbella, although a few missed it having already booked family holidays. Benno was my roommate, but was only there for 45 minutes — he had to fly straight back after receiving a phone call telling him his daughter was ill! Still, it was a great few days with a fantastic group of lads and, little did we know, things were about to change at Fratton Park.

I had no idea that Cook would leave 26 days after winning the title. Nowadays, I know everything going on at the club I represent, but at Pompey I was young. I only trained and played and I never took any interest in anything else. We were on a high, despite losing free agents Enda and Michael Doyle in the subsequent weeks. The feeling was that Cook would have gone for another Blues promotion — not necessarily storming the league, but definitely overseeing a challenge.

Then he was gone, off to Wigan Athletic with Leam Richardson and, in June 2017, Kenny Jackett arrived as manager ahead of the 2017/18 season.

Playing the number 10 role under Cookie, I would take players on and drift around, whereas Kenny wanted me to play on the left wing and receive the long ball. I had just won the league as our top scorer and was now attempting to understand another way. I was meant to kick on in League One that season and was nowhere near it. My performance levels just weren't as high. It was nothing to do with the manager; my form simply wasn't as good as it should have been during what turned out to be my final Fratton Park season.

Although Kenny played me in a variety of positions, in fairness it wasn't his fault when I went in goal against Doncaster Rovers in February 2018. Our debutant keeper Stephen Henderson was forced off injured late on, and, having used all our substitutes, we were looking around for somebody to volunteer. I had already come off the bench to operate on the left-hand side of midfield and was playing terribly, so I told Kenny I'd take over. I had never played in goal in a competitive match before and the strip was hanging off me, but I did make one save with my feet. I'm always harsh on goalkeepers, but it's harder than you think! Just knowing where your goal is and the right position to take up at the right time, it's scary — yet what a buzz. I wanted to catch those corners. You can jump with your arms, you can punch it … why wouldn't you want to come and be dominant?

At the start of that 2017/18 season, I had a bit of interest from Wigan. At the time, they possessed great financial power in League One, Nick Powell had joined from Manchester United the previous summer and Paul Cook was now their manager as they sought an instant return to the Championship. I wasn't sure whether Kenny Jackett fancied me, while I had entered the final 12 months of my Pompey contract and there was no offer of a new one, with the club wanting to wait a few months. I wasn't on a lot compared to everyone else, having come from Accrington, and felt I'd done well enough to be rewarded. That summer transfer window passed, however, with me remaining a Pompey player, yet my contract negotiations were going back and forth. Jackett sometimes chose not to play me, my partner was pregnant, and Wigan were storming League One. That caught my eye, of course.

When it came to January 2018, I was able to speak to Cook — and they assured me they'd be lodging a bid. Pompey, though, didn't want to sell me to Wigan, which was their prerogative and, in Cook's eyes, were asking too much for a player available on a free transfer in six months — and I decided to wait for him and see out my Pompey deal. The Blues eventually offered me a new contract at the end of January. It was a respectful one, the three-year deal I'd asked for, but it was too late. I could see Wigan would be playing Championship football the following season — and wanted me to be part of it. Had Pompey offered me a new deal in the summer of 2017 following promotion, I would have definitely signed, but they took too long.

In fairness, Jackett was really, really good with me. He and Joe Gallen were extremely understanding. I told them of my decision to see out my deal and Kenny was amazing, asking: "Are you sure it's the right decision? You're having a child soon. There's a deal here for you." He later pulled me in and said: "You've obviously now made a decision, fair enough. Congratulations, all the best with your career, you have been a good servant here." Then he added: "Would you want to play the last games or do you prefer I protect you and not pick you?" Of course I wanted to play, to give 100 per cent to a club which had been good to me, to keep playing alongside those great lads — and I started 10 of the last 11 matches. It was great he let me do that and, after finishing eighth in our first season back in League One, I joined Wigan on a free transfer three weeks later on a three-year deal.

I'm not saying it because it's an interview about Pompey, I speak openly and honestly, and for me it's a special club, a special place. My partner loved it there. It's where we moved in together, our first house was in Locks Heath. She fell pregnant with our first son, Bran, and I won League Two. I loved that drive on match days more than anywhere else. It was incredible, the best thing ever. I'd get up early, put the suit on with the blue shirt, then drive to the Garage Lounge in Southsea and have my porridge, toast and eggs, with a coffee. After I'd drive to the stadium, people getting off the train would walk in front of your car, while other fans would bang on the bonnet, wishing you luck. What a build-up that was. It was amazing, so special. It's even better when you know you're starting at Fratton Park; you'd come out for kick-off and they'd play that Mike Oldfield tune, with the fans clapping along. I can still hear it now.

At Pompey I became a better player, a better person, and mentally tougher. I can deal with anything in life now, not just football. Pompey was character building — and what a six months, which culminated in capturing the League Two title. Pompey was the club where I experienced the hardest season of my life — yet it became the most rewarding time of my football career.

JOHN ARMSTRONG

86 games, no goals (February 1963 — May 1967)

Northampton Town 1
Pompey 1 (Wilson)

Second Division, County Ground, Saturday, April 24, 1965

Pompey: Armstrong, Wilson, Tindall, Gordon, Dickinson, Harris, McClelland, Portwood, Edwards, McCann, Barton.

Attendance; 20,660

EVENING NEWS, MONDAY, APRIL 26, 1965—19

RIGHT-BACK MOBBED AT NORTHAMPTON BY HIS TEAMMATES

Alex Wilson's goal saves Pompey with six minutes to go

SALUTE FOR SKIPPER

(By LINESMAN)

With just six minutes left to play in the last match of the season right-back Alex Wilson snatched the goal at Northampton on Saturday night which enabled Pompey to win their fight to avoid relegation.

Pompey's 1—1 draw against Northampton Town took them to safety, leaving Swindon Town and Swansea to go down to the Third Division.

Tragedy struck Pompey in the 77th minute when right-half Johnny Gordon headed a free-kick into his own goal.

But the Fratton Park men fought back magnificently, and Wilson's precious equalizer made it a memorable last match for Pompey's veteran skipper Jimmy Dickinson.

Pompey, who knew before the start that they needed one point to avoid the drop, rattled the usually composed and strong Cobblers defence with the fury of their attacks, and with sharper finishing they could have been at least two goals ahead by half-time.

But nothing was going to stop Pompey, and grand team spirit and determination saw them through.

Before the start, the First Divi-

sion-bound Northampton team trotted round the packed ground carrying banners which read: "Thank you for loyal support."

Fans who must have had a good head for height had climbed high up the two floodlighting pylons at one end of the ground to string a 20-yard banner: "Well done Cobblers" between the pylons.

Presentation

The teams lined up to clap Dickinson on to the field, and a presentation was made to the Pompey skipper on behalf of the Northampton club.

Albert McCann, who returned at inside-left quickly sent the ball into the Northampton penalty area, and Pompey went close to scoring in the first minute.

Centre-forward Dennis Edwards intercepted a pass which Mike Everitt intended for goalkeeper Brian Harvey, and lobbed the ball into the empty goalmouth. Right-back Theo Foley raced across to clear.

When Northampton centre-forward Bobby Brown got past Dickinson, John Armstrong raced out

of goal and got a hand to Brown's shot. Armstrong had to come out of the penalty area to clear, but the free-kick which followed was easily cleared.

Another scoring chance went begging in the fourth minute when Edwards ran through and lobbed his shot just too high.

Northampton right-half Derek Leck, off for nine minutes with an ankle injury, returned in the 13th minute and operated at half-speed on the right-wing.

Saved on line

Pompey, who stunned the Cobblers with their sharp, confident play, missed a third scoring chance. Inside-right Don Martin, who dropped back when Leck was injured, cleared a shot on the goalline from Cliff Portwood.

Right-winger John McClelland, whose speed was troubling the Town defence, had a shot saved on the line by Everitt, and Edwards and Portwood again went close to scoring.

Right to the end of the season Pompey were being plagued by that inability to round off excellent approach work.

Northampton, who had no chance of taking the Second Division championship from Newcastle, were very subdued. Their first real chance came shortly before half-time. Left-

More Pompey pictures
in next page.

half Joe Kiernan hit a free-kick across the Pompey penalty area and right-winger Harry Wolden's head turned the ball just wide of a post.

Lucky not to be two or three goals down, Northampton, the only Second Division club with an unbeaten home record, started to play with more purpose. Robson headed the ball through to Brown whose overhead shot hit the Pompey upright. But he was off-side and Pompey gained a welcome free-kick.

Gordon turned a shot from Martin behind for a corner and Armstrong dived at Brown's feet

Johnny Gordon (left) and Alex Wilson hoist Jimmy Dickinson on to their shoulders for the triumphant walk back to the dressing room after the match.—E.N. 1193.

Thirty seconds later Gordon was holding his head in anguish. When three Pompey forwards were trapped off-side Foley lobbed the free kick into the goalmouth. Up went the heads, and the ball flew off Gordon into the net, well out of Armstrong's reach. There was little applause from a shocked crowd who knew that they did not deserve to be so treated by fate.

With Gordon and Harry Harris desperately for an equalizer. It came in the 84th minute.

When McClelland took a corner Harris got his head to the ball, Portwood got a touch to it, and Wilson hammered in a shot which hit a defender on the way into the net.

Wilson also punching upfield pushing and jumped for joy when the final whistle sounded. Thanks to Wilson they had saved themselves with just six minutes to spare.

Teams :
Northampton Town: Harvey, Foley, Everitt, Leck, Carr, Kiernan, Walden, Martin, Brown, Hunt, Robson.
Portsmouth: Armstrong, Wilson, Tindall, Gordon, Dickinson, Harris, McClelland, Portwood, Edwards.
of York.

215

Jimmy Dickinson's 834th — and final — Pompey appearance was earmarked for the last game of the 1964/65 season. If that April 1965 trip to Northampton Town wasn't significant enough, it was also a fixture which would decide whether we would be relegated from the Second Division. Throw in the fact it was Jimmy's 40th birthday and this was quite the occasion. Thankfully, it generated the perfect ending.

Jimmy must come into the reckoning as the best footballer I ever played with. Operating at centre-half in front of me, I had a great view of his skills and he was an excellent player and an excellent gentleman. He was very quiet and unassuming, and I don't think I ever saw him touch a drop of alcohol. It never went near his lips, not even after victory when players would normally have a drink or two. Everything he did was extremely professional and the entire dressing room looked up to him.

It had already been announced this would be his final season, having spent an entire career at Fratton Park, yet we were fighting relegation to the Third Division and, following four straight defeats, I was recalled for John Milkins in goal for the last six matches of the campaign. We subsequently won three of the next four, including a 4-0 victory over Norwich City in which Harry Harris scored twice, but then rested Jimmy for the reverse game at Carrow Road the following day in our penultimate match. It was the only league game he missed all season, with Vince Radcliffe coming in, and we lost 3-1.

So we headed to Northampton on the final day, a side newly promoted to the First Division and unbeaten at home, while we'd won once on our travels in all season. The challenge was set — we needed to better Swindon Town's result to stay up. As it happened, the Robins were away at Southampton in an afternoon kick-off, whereas we were in action at the County Ground that evening. Sure enough, Southampton beat them 2-1 through Cliff Huxford and Terry Paine — which left us requiring a point to avoid relegation.

We were 13 minutes away from achieving that, with our match goalless, only for Johnny Gordon's own-goal to hand Northampton the lead. They had a free-kick and I came out for the ball and shouted: "Leave it," but he never did and it flicked off the top of his head and sailed over me into the empty net behind. We needed an equaliser to stay in the Second Division — and it came from the most unlikely of sources.

Our right-back Alex Wilson had, by that stage, scored just four times in more than 350 appearances for Pompey, but, in the 84th minute, following John McClelland's corner, he thumped home the finish to secure a 1-1 draw. We had stayed up and Jimmy was carried off the pitch by his teammates, marking a great ending to a fantastic career and a very happy birthday. Perhaps it was fitting that Alex scored the goal on that occasion because he and Jimmy were big buddies and similar personalities, both very quiet, unassuming people — and it proved to be his penultimate goal for the club. Afterwards, everybody was jolly and cock-a-hoop. I can't even remember getting home that night. What a finale and that remains the favourite Pompey game of my time at the club.

During almost five seasons at Nottingham Forest, I was never a regular and it reached a point where I needed to play football. At the age of 25, I had featured 23 times, including being named as 12th man in the FA Cup semi-final at Aston Villa in March 1959, which we won 1-0, although I wasn't included in the squad for the final. Instead, I was a spectator at Wembley as we beat Luton Town to claim the trophy — with Forest not having won it since. When Peter Grummitt broke his wrist in November 1962, I played eight successive First Division matches and, when he returned to the side, I handed in a transfer request. Then, in February 1963, Forest's manager Andy Beattie called me into his office. "I believe you want regular football?" he said. When I replied I did, he added: "How would you like to move to the south of England?" When I asked what it meant, he said: "Regular football with Pompey." Well, that would do for me. I didn't need any time to think about it.

I travelled to meet George Smith and his right-hand man and joined, with Pompey paying a £5,000 transfer fee. I was dropping down to the Second Division, but it didn't bother me one bit. I was joining a fantastic football club and finally had the opportunity of playing matches. I found Smith an excellent person. He was a big Army man, he used to bring it up sometimes, and his knowledge of football was impressive. He spoke very well about it, I found him interesting and he was a really good coach. I later played for Fourth Division Southport under a young, upcoming manager called Billy Bingham and I would put them both in the same bracket. Billy was such an enthusiastic guy and later managed Northern Ireland twice, as well as Everton.

I arrived at Fratton Park during the Big Freeze, one of the coldest winters in the 20th century, which had devastated the 1962/63 season. That, coupled with being initially ineligible for the FA Cup, meant my February 1963 debut against Luton came 16 days following my transfer — and it was still Pompey's first league fixture of the calendar year! We won 3-1 through goals from Johnny Gordon, Ron Saunders and Albie McCann and my Blues career was up and running.

However, my second appearance was a 4-2 defeat at Southampton and I played a stinker that day. I wasn't on my game, which brought me straight back down to earth after an encouraging debut. It was my first south-coast derby and, being from Scotland and seeing the Glasgow Rangers and Celtic matches, this one was just as much of a rivalry. There was a different level of hostility, but not much, and it was brilliant to experience, but the score wasn't enjoyable. As a consequence of my performance at The Dell, John Milkins was preferred for an FA Cup third-round replay against Scunthorpe United — and so began our goalkeeping rivalry which spanned the next five-and-a-half seasons.

Milky was seven years younger than me, a very good goalkeeper, and the battle between us was very good, but I think he won it! We were competitors for the same spot, but we also liked each other. He was a nice lad and very talented. I don't know how true it was but I heard Arsenal were interested in him at one time. With Peter Shearing also competing with us for the number one spot, it wasn't until April 1963 before I established myself as a regular, playing the last 13 matches as we finished 16th. That included a 3-0 victory over Leeds United, when I saved Jack Charlton's penalty five minutes from time, with the likes of Norman Hunter, Paul Reaney and Gary Sprake also in their team. It ended a run of nine league matches without a point, yet results continued to be inconsistent for the remainder of the campaign.

The 1962/63 season ended with a 7-0 defeat at Chelsea, who needed victory to win promotion to the First Division. They absolutely caned us and were excellent that day, with 54,558 packed into Stamford Bridge. It was like being inside a cauldron. All these years on, I still remember that day — even though I want to forget it! I started the following year as first-choice goalkeeper under George Smith and we were picking up some good results, but, following a 3-2 win at Southampton in February 1964, I found myself dropped in favour of John Milkins for the remainder of the season.

We had some very good players and that campaign saw Ron Saunders score 33 league goals — a post-war record — and 34 overall as we came ninth, which was the highest finishing position I ever had at Pompey. Ron lived three doors down from me in Fortune's Way, Bedhampton, and we took turns driving to training. He was a very good striker, powerful, excellent with his head and scored a lot of goals. He was also a great guy, very dedicated to football. I never saw him have a drink and he was always the first in for training. Such a smashing bloke. Ron got on really well with Tony Barton, who was previously with me at Nottingham Forest and a right winger, although not a flying machine like others. They would later work together in management at Aston Villa, winning the First Division title in 1981 before Tony took over and led them to the European Cup a year later.

Albie McCann was a little buzzer, he was into everything, featuring on the inside left and buzzing all over the place. He was a smashing little fella and, when on form, a very good player. John McClelland was another buzzer: just put the ball in front of him and he went like hell, very quick, whereas Tony on the other flank was a more thoughtful player. Then we had Johnny Gordon, a Pompey lad, who played at right-half and fancied himself as a singer — and was very good too. I can remember him getting up at Fratton Park to give the players a song and he also appeared on Southern Television's talent show *Home Grown*, where he finished second. I socialised a lot with Roy Lunniss, who arrived at Pompey a few months after me and played left-back. He was very competitive on the pitch, although I wouldn't say he was a hard man — more a gentle giant.

Having survived on the final day of the 1964/65 season at Northampton and now without Jimmy Dickinson, three days later George Smith announced he was scrapping the reserve and youth-teams. The club was nearly bankrupt, so it was the chance to save money, while our Tamworth Road training ground was sold off. George had some fantastic ideas as a manager — whether that was a good one or not, I don't know — but this is what he came up with and, in April 1965, a squad of 16 was chosen, with 21 other players handed free transfers. It was particularly unfortunate for goalkeepers because, if you weren't selected, then you had no chance of any games so had a bit of a job to get back in. There were no reserve matches — we didn't have any reserves — and you wouldn't have a goalkeeper on the bench, so I spent my time watching us from the stands, sometimes in the directors' box.

Initially, George told me and Milky that he'd play one of us for two matches, then the other would come in for two matches, but that was never going to work. So I started the opening three games of the 1965/66 season, then came out for two, then returned for one, then John was selected for three and that's how it worked until February 1966, when he established himself as first-choice. George saw his mistake in that selection policy and mentioned it to me afterwards. Now he would be playing the best goalkeeper — and I found myself out of the team.

Smith was right to scrap that, the better player simply has to be picked. Maybe it's okay for a centre-forward or someone in midfield to be in and out of a side, but a goalkeeper has to be on the ball all of the time. You need a consistent run in the team, you play better and feel better with regular appearances. John was performing better than me at the time so George stuck with him. You've just got to cope with that; there's nothing else I could have done. I respected John, he was a cracking guy as well, but there wasn't much difference in ability between us. Goalkeepers are more or less the same anyway.

John Milkins was Pompey's regular keeper from that point onwards and, over the next 12 months, I would feature on just four occasions as my time at Fratton

Park neared its end. In October 1966, he sustained a shoulder injury, which saw me handed a first league appearance of the 1966/67 season in a trip to Wolverhampton Wanderers. Despite playing well in a 3-1 defeat, I found myself out of the side the next game, so I put in a transfer request because of my lack of opportunities, which was accepted by George Smith. However, I stayed for the remainder of the campaign, ending it in the first-team. With Milkins breaking his arm in the corresponding fixture against Wolves in February 1967, I featured in the final 11 games of the season as we finished 14th in the Second Division.

Our last match was a 1-1 draw at Huddersfield Town and, days later, Ray Potter was signed from First Division West Bromwich Albion. When that happened, I knew leaving was on the cards — and, subsequently, I was told in May 1967 that my contract would not be renewed and I was being handed a free transfer. The following day, I faced Kilmarnock in a Fratton Park friendly which ended in 1-1 draw, played in front of a crowd of 9,294, which turned out to be my farewell performance for Pompey.

I had long been frustrated about being in and out of the team and now, after 86 appearances, my Pompey career was at an end. Left without a club in the summer of 1967, Southport manager Billy Bingham called and asked whether I would be interested in a move following promotion to the Third Division. Bingham left in February 1968 during my first season, taking up the Plymouth Argyle job, yet we finished 14th and I remained there until the summer of 1971, when I retired through a back injury.

I enjoyed my time at Pompey, although it should have been a First Division club at the time rather than mid-table in the Second Division. I haven't been back to Portsmouth for a while, but I was settled in the area, sometimes you just like a place, you feel right at home. It's an excellent club and gave me the best times of my career, especially in my early years.

MARK CHAMBERLAIN

198 games, 22 goals (July 1988 — May 1994)

Pompey 4 (Taylor OG, Quinn, Connor, Chamberlain)
Leeds United 0

Second Division, Fratton Park, Saturday, September 3, 1988

Pompey: Knight, Neill, Hogg, Gilbert (72 mins, Whitehead), Hardyman, Chamberlain, Horne (90 mins, Kelly), Dillon, Sandford, Quinn, Connor.

Attendance; 15,263

18—THE NEWS, MONDAY, SEPTEMBER 5, 1988

News Sport

SUPER POMPEY SOUND WARNING

POMPEY 4, LEEDS UTD 0

WATCH OUT Division II – Pompey are back in business and will take some stopping in their bid to make an immediate return to the top flight.

Pompey pulverized Leeds United in the Fratton Park sunshine on Saturday – and Leeds, like Monday's visitors Leicester City, were rated a better promotion bet than Alan Ball's side in the pre-season call-over.

Manager Billy Bremner must have accepted that on the day his side were ruthlessly outclassed by a team who had all the slick hallmarks of the man who put it together.

Some of the football which signed Leeds apart

● GOALBOUND . . . Terry Connor (right) gets the better of Leeds defender Jack Ashurst on his way to Pompey's third goal at Fratton Park on Saturday. Looking on is Mick Quinn whose pass set up the chance. Picture by MURRAY SANDERS. Photo sales no – CO480-5.

● Pompey picture special – Page 17.

WE DID IT

No excuses

Top of the table

DIVISION II
	Home Goals					Away Goals					
	P	W	D	L	F	A	W	D	L	F	A	Pt
POMPEY	3	2	0	0	7	0	1	0	0	2	1	9
Watford	3	1	0	0	1	0	2	0	0	3	0	9
Bradford	3	1	1	0	1	0	0	0	3	1	7
Oxford	3	2	0	0	4	2	0	1	0	1	7
Blackburn	2	1	0	0	3	1	1	0	0	2	1	6
Barnsley	3	1	1	0	2	1	0	1	0	1	1	5
Plymouth	2	1	0	0	2	1	0	1	1	1	5

It was while filming ITV's *Harry's Heroes: The Full English* in 2019 that I finally uncovered the truth about Ronnie Whelan. "He was going to do you, Chambo," admitted John Barnes, confirming what I had long suspected. Whelan's tackle five minutes into our FA Cup semi-final against Liverpool in April 1992 was rubbish. It was naughty, and he meant to injure me. To this day, people come up and say: "That tackle was awful. Whelan shouldn't have been on the pitch to equalise. We should have won the game." For me, it was a sending off — yet he wasn't even booked. I tried to carry on for a little while, but that was it, my involvement over after 10 minutes. My season ended with knee ligament damage.

It emanated from me intercepting the ball inside our box and then winning a tackle as I tried to drive out into space. At that moment, Whelan came in and caught me high, nowhere near the ball, taking me on the right knee. It was horrible. I recently watched it back on YouTube — I like to see some of my old games now and again — and, strangely enough, that knee started to hurt as I did so. To this day, Whelan has never apologised. Whenever I went to Anfield to watch my son Alexander play, I never saw Ronnie at the games. My son had a box, with our seats behind the Liverpool players involved in corporate hospitality, such as Bruce Grobbelaar, John Aldridge, Steve McMahon and Phil Babb, but not Ronnie. I don't know why. Maybe he's back in Ireland?

I have no ill feelings towards him, because that's the way tackling was back then. As a winger, I was used to it and I didn't mind a bit of physicality. Graeme Souness wasn't the nicest guy in the world on the pitch and Bryan Robson was strong but fair. They competed, they wanted to win. I had faced Liverpool for six seasons in the old First Division and there were good games against them. They would have known my qualities and no doubt said: "We'll sort him out." That's what football's like and it's exactly how my managers approached facing John Barnes. For our Villa Park semi-final replay, my wife Wendie walked past Liverpool's team bus just as Whelan stepped off and had a go. "You kicked my husband," she said. "Why did you do that? You didn't even say sorry." Apparently he just shrugged his shoulders.

When assessing the extent of that Highbury injury, I was sent for an MRI scan which identified I had nicked my ligaments — thankfully I'd be back for the start of the following season. Then the doctor added: "How's your broken foot, though?" It turned out I had fractured my right foot earlier in the season without realising! It could be traced back to a 2-0 defeat at Middlesbrough in August 1991, when I attempted to clear the ball and instead kicked an opponent's studs as he put his foot in to block. For months afterwards I was struggling, with the foot locking up after an hour of training and leaving me limping. Jim Smith once pulled me in and asked what the problem was, yet I didn't know. Now, seven months later, everything was explained. I had a go at our physio Neil Sillett: "Tell the boss I've been playing with a broken foot. I wasn't taking the mickey!" Still, despite the ligament damage caused by Whelan, I was back for the start of the following campaign, just as the doctor predicted.

Life at Fratton Park began in July 1988 following a £200,000 switch from Sheffield Wednesday, where I had endured a frustrating time under Howard Wilkinson. His game plan involved playing the ball as far forward as possible and running after it, earning corners and winning free-kicks. It wasn't about people with ability and didn't suit my game. Upon deciding to join Pompey, Howard asked the reason. My response was: "Well, I want to play on a Saturday. I deserve to play." Recently he had started playing me in the number 10 role, so Howard replied: "But I've just found your best position." My answer was: "Yes, you have — and it's on the pitch!" He genuinely wanted to keep me, although I've no idea why as he only seemed to use me as a substitute. I played 66 games and scored eight times in the First Division for the Owls, yet 34 of those appearances came from the bench — and I couldn't stay there any longer. When Howard asked why I'd chosen Pompey, I explained it was simply because I wanted to play football. "You'll never leave there," he warned. "It's so far south that no scouts will go to watch you."

Pompey represented the chance to work with Alan Ball, an England World Cup winner who, as a kid, I'd watched playing for Arsenal and Southampton. Growing up, I read everything about football, so the opportunity to play under him was a massive draw. Leaving the First Division to drop down a league for Pompey wasn't an issue and it wasn't even a big gap financially in those days, unlike the modern game when you just wouldn't consider it. I actually received £200 a week more to join Pompey. Having been with the Blues for a month, the lads asked why I had decided to leave the top flight. When I explained how Bally was the main draw, they dropped the bombshell that he wouldn't be my manager for long. It was the worst-kept secret in the dressing room that our first-team coach John Gregory would be replacing him. Most of the lads knew.

Still, my Pompey career got off to a good start, with a debut 4-0 win over Leeds United in September 1988 taking us to the top of the Second Division — and I netted our fourth, with a left-footed shot from outside the box. We battered a Leeds side which contained former Blues players Vince Hilaire, Noel Blake and Ian Baird, with our other goals scored by Mick Quinn, Terry Connor and a Bob Taylor own goal. It's my favourite Pompey game, while the crowd must have been thinking: "We've got some player here!" Mind you, they'd waited a little while to see me play competitive football, having damaged my knee in a pre-season friendly against Charlton Athletic in a 2-2 draw at their New Eltham training ground. As a consequence, I missed Pompey's opening two matches of the 1988/89 season, but certainly enjoyed myself when finally let off the leash against Leeds.

I liked Bally's training, although one of the issues at the club was we didn't have great facilities. We used Moneyfields, which was horrible, the worst I came across in my entire career, so it was very, very disappointing. The shower room consisted of a pipe positioned above, with holes drilled in for the water to pour out. We had one-and-a-half pitches to use, while the bowling green at the front would host Bally's keep-ball sessions. It was so flat and beautiful that the ball pinged around, but that lasted a month before we were turfed off it. The training ground is where you develop your teamwork and skills, yet Moneyfields was rubbish. That wasn't all. In the previous season I was part of an Owls side which won 2-1 at Fratton Park in October 1987. I returned to the south coast to become a Pompey player and discovered the roof had been knocked off the Fratton End, while the lower section was no longer in use. Where had that nice full-up ground gone? Instead it was dour, flat terracing, while crowds had dropped to around 6,000 on some occasions. It was painful.

Under Alan Ball, we'd finish training and I wasn't even tired, so I'd ask: "Is that it, are we finished? We're not doing any more?" The lads responded: "It is. We're off to the pub." The level of work wasn't what I was used to at previous clubs, so I'd return to Fratton Park to carry out more running, completing laps of the pitch. I was a 400m runner when younger, Staffordshire champion, and my county record stood for quite a while before being broken. Not that I was that keen on running; I preferred football and would turn up for meets in my football shorts and the school would provide the correct gear. As a winger, running was important. You had to keep going at the full-back knowing he'd tire sooner rather than later. Mind you, my extra training at Pompey probably only lasted a couple of months. The enthusiasm for it wears off, I suppose.

John Gregory, as expected, replaced Bally as manager in January 1989, almost five months after my Fratton Park arrival, although, like a lot of young bosses, he didn't have the experience of handling footballers and went down the route of attempting to forcibly assert himself, alienating some of the senior players. During the 1989 pre-season, we were instructed to come into training dressed smartly, wearing a jumper, shirt and tie, yet the weather was red hot. Gregory and assistant Steve Wicks would also spy on the players when we were out on the town.

We'd go for a drink on certain nights, which was our prerogative. At the time it was standard practice in football, yet we certainly weren't going to misbehave. On one occasion, we were in a pub down Guildhall Walk and one of the boys spotted our management looking at us through the window! Why are you doing that? It was very strange.

Gregory tried to be the strong man, but we didn't need that. We just required guidance, someone to set the team up and get us to play, to trust his players. He obviously learnt and became a better boss, as you'd expect, going on to manage Wycombe Wanderers, Aston Villa, Derby County and Queens Park Rangers. I believe lads who want to get into football management should start by working with someone who is really experienced, learn how to manage men, work out how to handle different characters, recognise when some need a rollicking and others an arm around the shoulder like any human being.

I actually got on well with John. We were in the same England squad against Denmark in September 1983 and faced each other in the First Division on occasions, so there was a bit of mutual respect. I didn't have an issue with him. He was a bit different and would give the lads massages after training, although, as I sit here now, I cannot actually remember much about him in terms of being Pompey manager! For me, it wasn't a great period at Fratton Park in terms of starting the season so well, then Bally getting sacked and eventually finishing my first campaign in 20th — and Gregory was later dismissed just short of a year in charge.

I know he has since criticised the club's drinking culture, yet while some of the lads liked a drink, it would be done at the right time — a Wednesday night — and formed part of the fabric of the footballing environment we grew up in. I won the first of my eight England caps in December 1982 against Luxembourg. I had spent the summer as a Fourth Division player with Port Vale, watching these guys on TV in the 1982 World Cup finals. Then I moved to Stoke City and, within 18 games, had been called up by England boss Bobby Robson at the age of 21. On my first England camp, we went to a country pub near the team hotel in Barnet and all the squad were drinking. Bryan Robson, Ray Wilkins, Peter Shilton, Paul Mariner; these were my heroes and constantly had a pint in their hand. When the barman called time, Mariner was on a fruit machine with four pints of lager on top of it. That's the way football was, everybody was doing it, yet on a Saturday we possessed the same level of fitness. Regardless of the drink.

At Pompey, a group of us would drink on Wednesdays, including Steve Wigley, John Beresford, Kenny Black, Graeme Hogg and Warren Aspinall. Alan Knight never joined us because he was a goody-two-shoes. I had no idea he was actually a heavy drinker. We'd come in on a Thursday morning for training and it was: "Knightsie, you should have been out with us. It was a good night." He would respond dryly with: "Well done." It was only after I retired that I discovered he was an alcoholic. I didn't have a clue.

The summer of 1989 marked John Gregory's first pre-season as Pompey boss. We were being worked particularly hard at HMS Mercury, near Petersfield, so one day we afterwards went for a few beers in Port Solent. I had a house there overlooking the Solent, and still do, and there was a 35-foot motor boat on my berth. Not that it was mine — it actually belonged to a friend. I let him keep it there, without charge, and as a thanks I was allowed to use it whenever I wanted. We were having a few beers and the idea came about to take the boat out, even though I kept insisting to the lads that I was unable to drive it. They got their way, we stocked up with beers from an off-licence and — although Hogg declared himself out — me, Wigley, Beresford, Aspinall and Black were on board, following a ferry to the Isle of Wight so we wouldn't get lost. I actually got told off for going too fast into East Cowes harbour, but we arrived safe and sound. No problem.

Now it was about finding somewhere to have a drink, so we asked someone in the nearest pub where the action was, with the advice being to catch a taxi to another part of the island. Sure enough, we had a good time. At the end of the night, we got a taxi back to East Cowes harbour, only to discover the driver had dropped us on the other side of the water — West Cowes. We asked if he could take us around to the marina we could see in the distance, but the driver insisted he was now off duty and left us there. So how were we going to get back to the boat? Firstly, one of the lads discovered a wooden pallet: "This will float," he said. "Perhaps we can sit on it to get us across the water?" It sank as soon as we put it in.

Then Steve Wigley found a rowing boat in somebody's back garden. We were climbing into it when we heard a siren and flashing police lights. "What are you doing, lads?" asked a policeman. We explained how we needed to get across to our boat, then they questioned where we got the rowing boat from. Thankfully it didn't escalate and we were told to put it back where we had borrowed it from. Then we asked for a lift and, upon the promise of some Pompey matchday tickets, the policeman drove us round. Thank goodness we didn't get on that rowing boat, because we probably would have drowned! Now reunited with the motor boat, I was obviously in no condition to drive, so we slept in it — or tried to. Kenny Black had contact lenses in and they'd dried up, so he couldn't shut his eyes. "If I'm not sleeping, neither are you lot," he insisted and kept us awake all night with his moaning. He wouldn't shut up. We returned to Port Solent the next morning — and headed straight into training!

Players don't do that now, of course. I never see my son Alexander drinking. At Liverpool they'd win games and go home without having a drink, instead spending the evening on the PlayStation. How boring is that? Times change, though, and nowadays when kids join a football club they're educated about their diet and the importance of stretches and recovery. So, by the time you become a professional footballer, it's entirely normal.

John Gregory was sacked in January 1990, days following a 3-2 defeat against Leicester City which left us 23rd in the Second Division. He was replaced by his assistant Frank Burrows, who was brilliant and able to communicate well with the boys, commanding total respect. The best thing Frank did was work with Alan Knight, effectively becoming the first goalkeeping coach I ever saw. He would stay behind after training and go through routines with Knightsie, one-v-one focused, and, in 14 months as manager, improved him no end. Usually, coaches would hold a shooting session with the goalkeepers, throwing a few crosses for them to catch and that was it. Frank introduced a specialised programme, working loads with our 'keeper. Ultimately, he was sacked in March 1991 and replaced on a caretaker basis by Tony Barton, who had stepped up from reserve-team manager. Everyone loved Tony, but unfortunately he didn't have the respect he deserved from the boys and we all knew he wasn't going to be there long. He wasn't interested in making any enemies, so was very soft on us. We finished 17th and Pompey were searching for a new manager. They chose Jim Smith.

Now I was to marry Wendie in the summer of 1991 and, after getting the pre-season dates off Pompey in advance, we'd planned our honeymoon in Jamaica around them. Then Jim arrived in June 1991 — and drew up an entirely new schedule which clashed with our wedding plans! Obviously I was aware of his reputation for being fierce and having the capability to get angry, so I went in to see him, introducing myself before explaining the problem. He responded: "Don't worry about it. You go away and enjoy yourself." I returned to Wendie and said: "He's nice, the new boss." Well, we returned from our fortnight-long honeymoon, which saw me miss the first week of training, and when the 14 names for the opening first-team friendly at Brentford were announced, I wasn't among them. It became a familiar pattern during pre-season. I'd play against the non-league teams but, when it came to Football League opposition, wasn't anywhere to be seen, including a 1-1 draw with my old club Sheffield Wednesday.

I never asked Jim why I wasn't in those squads. I'm not like that, I'm not confrontational. Instead my style was focused on doing my best to turn things around. Perhaps Jim had been listening to manager talk and heard there were older pros at Pompey earning a good living out of the game, but not putting it all in — and classed me in that category, pre-judging me. He never actually told me that, yet having been a regular for three seasons to all of a sudden not making the squad, it was clear what was going on — people had spoken to him. Not that it took long to get back into the team when the 1991/92 season got under way. I was a substitute for the first game at Blackburn Rovers. I trained properly as I always did, carried on as normal, didn't moan, didn't complain. I'm no troublemaker. I was probably a bit casual in training, but that's how I was. I'm no madman, and Jim soon realised I was all right.

A key part of Jim Smith's time at Pompey was how the young lads were given the opportunity, in particular that opening match at Ewood Park in August 1991. It takes an experienced manager like Jim to possess the bravery to do that. Undoubtedly he was trying to make a point to some of the older pros, prompting him to put Darryl Powell, Kit Symons, Darren Anderton and Andy Awford in against Blackburn. If you're unsure about a kid at 18, put him into a first-team training session and you'll soon find out if he's got what it takes. If he can't handle it, you either say: "No" or: "Give him a bit more time." As players, you aren't going to suffer a kid who's not up to it. You'll say: "He shouldn't be here with us, boss. He's going to get hurt, he gives the ball away every time." It's called a "session wrecker" because they can't work with him, he needs to be of a certain standard. However, on the flipside, there are the others, like that group at Pompey. Kit was calm in his defending and decision-making, better in the air than Awfs, and the step up into the first-team was easy enough for him. Yet Awfs was quicker, calm in possession. Whenever balls were delivered down his side for the opposition striker he wouldn't jump in, staying on his feet. They did things right and complemented each other as a central-defensive partnership.

You know a good player when you see one, which was also the case with Anderton — and he could run as well. The first time I noticed him was during one pre-season at HMS Mercury when he was an apprentice. We were challenged to run laps of this cricket ground with the pros going first and, while recovering our breath, we watched the kids, spotting this lad well in front of the rest. Considering the distance, he'd started too quickly, so, as he ran past, we shouted: "You need to slow down, you've got another five minutes to go yet." But he just carried on. "Stupid boy," we thought. Little did we realise that Anderton was an excellent cross-country runner who represented Hampshire as a schoolboy. He was a level above in everything he did at Pompey, with that quality on the ball and his decision-making. He was a very, very good footballer, as he later proved with Tottenham Hotspur and England.

Towards the end of that 1991/92 season, we suffered defeat in the FA Cup semi-final replay to Liverpool and, being injured, I watched from the Villa Park stands as we lost 3-1 on penalties. However, the following year we should have reached the Premier League. Anderton and John Beresford had now gone, but Jim recruited Paul Walsh from Spurs, who was a level above the new Division One. Not only was he a quality player, but he worked his socks off and ran and ran and ran, challenging defenders when in possession. Guy Whittingham possessed that same work-rate and they were superb as a partnership, while Martin Kuhl was still there, establishing a bit of stability in the midfield with his physicality and a good range of passing. We had a good team, with good lads. There wasn't a bad egg among them, and Jim was exceptional at managing men.

Towards the end of my time at Pompey, he pulled me and Walshie aside and said: "You're too old for this, you don't need to train all week. I want you both available for Saturdays, so either train at the beginning of the week or the end. Let me know and we'll go from there." I picked the end of the week and would carry out my own fitness routine in the meantime, but Walshie being Walshie still pounded away, working really hard. Jim was looking after us and we appreciated that. When he arrived as Fratton Park manager, his reputation was Mr Combustible, but he wasn't like that with our group and was actually one of those bosses you could have a beer with. When stopping over for away matches, he'd often come into the hotel bar. Normally that was the signal for players to find somewhere else to drink, but you'd want to stay with Jim and listen to his stories. He was good company and he'd talk to you, like one of the boys. Although he was still the boss and you wouldn't take liberties!

In May 1994, just five days after our Division One campaign had ended, we competed in a post-season tournament in Greece called the Thrace Trophy, which also included Coventry City, AEK Athens and Xanthi. After our first match, ex-Everton manager Howard Kendall, who was in the process of becoming Xanthi boss, told us: "Come down to the beach tomorrow, we'll have a good drink. This is a lovely place." So we did — and got drunk with Howard, who could drink forever. On the fourth day, Howard said: "When are you lot going home?" When we questioned why, he added: "Make sure you take Jim with you, I can't keep up with him!" For away trips during the season, the lads took it in turns sitting with Jim, who loved a red wine. Genuinely, there was a rota detailing who was going to keep him company and stay up drinking. In January 1994, we spent a week in Lancashire with successive matches against Blackburn in the FA Cup and Manchester United in the Coca-Cola Cup. On the day of the United game, which was midweek, physio Neil Sillett warned us the manager was still feeling it from drinking the night before — and was about to take a 1pm team talk. Then, during his briefing, Jim said: "Sill, those chips we had at dinner last night must have been off. I feel terrible." We fell off our stools laughing. We knew exactly why he felt like that, and it was nothing to do with chips! To be fair, he was laughing as well.

I previously mentioned how we should have won promotion in 1992-93, especially having been top of Division One with two matches to play as we headed to Sunderland in May 1993. Unfortunately we lost 4-1, with Guy Butters and Walshie sent off in a season where goals scored was used rather than goal difference. Ultimately, we were pipped by West Ham United to the second automatic promotion spot, then lost in the two-legged play-off semi-finals to Leicester. The main reason we failed to go up, however, was a 5-5 draw at Oxford United in November 1992, who were always a difficult team, especially at the Manor Ground.

That evening we absolutely battered them, leading 5-3 with three minutes to go and playing so, so well. The next thing I know, I look around and Warren Neill wasn't on the pitch. Jim had replaced him with Stuart Doling, and I thought: "What's he done that for?" Jim Magilton pulled one back in stoppage time and it was panic stations. I asked the referee, Jim Rushton, how long was left, and he replied: "Kick the ball out and it's over." So I told Martin Kuhl: "I'll take kick-off and will play it back to you, so just put it into touch. The game will then be over." Yet he screwed his kick straight to their 'keeper Paul Reece, who knocked it down the pitch. Joey Beauchamp connected and Chris Allen finished it to make it 5-5! It's probably the first time I've been angry after a game of football — and I voiced it in the dressing room. You've got to say that cost us promotion, two points we threw away from a position where we should have won. Otherwise we would have reached the Premier League.

The following season was my last at Pompey — Jim killed me. I was certainly worth another two years at Fratton Park, but that's football and I didn't bear a grudge. In the aftermath of our May 1993 play-off semi-final defeat to Leicester, he had us in for a meeting and said: "Whittingham's scored 47 goals, Walshie is *The News/Sports Mail's* player of the season, but my player for the year is Mark Chamberlain." With that, he presented me with a reggae cassette in front of all the lads as a reward. Then he made me captain for the start of the 1993/94 campaign. By the end of it, I was left without a club after my contract expired.

During the second match of the season, I ruptured my groin in a 2-1 defeat to Charlton Athletic at Fratton Park. It required a trip to Harley Street to see Jerry Gilmore, who eventually operated on me, putting a mesh in there and sending me away with instructions to carry out six weeks of rehab. After three weeks, our physio Neil Sillett asked how I was. I told him I was fine, apart from being unable to run at that stage. Then he added: "And what would you say if Jim asked you to play now?" Sure enough, our manager came to see me: "Look, we need you in midfield to settle us down and play passes." As a stupid footballer, I agreed! I started against Tranmere Rovers and Middlesbrough, both of which resulted in league wins, while I also turned out in two cup matches. It went well, except I couldn't move — and was soon injured again. In December 1993, six weeks into my next rehab, Sillett came back: "How are you? Jim's going to ask you again." Well, I still couldn't move, yet ended up back in the team and finished the season well, including a worldie goal in a 3-0 win over Wolverhampton Wanderers in March 1994. Despite being 80 per cent fit by the campaign's end, I had managed 24 appearances as we finished a disappointing 17th.

With my contract up, Jim dropped a bit of a bombshell: "I cannot offer you a deal. You can't run." I know I couldn't run, I had twice come back early from a groin operation to help the team! I shouldn't have been playing for many of those games, but we all did it. As a professional footballer you play with injuries at times. I was among seven players released in May 1994, informed just before our final match against West Bromwich Albion, with Brian Horne, Chris Price, Mark Kelly, Shaun Gale, Roy Young and Michael Birmingham also departing. After 198 games and 22 goals, West Brom represented my Blues farewell and, while it finished in a 1-0 defeat, I completed the full 90 minutes. Regardless, I attended that post-season tour for the Thrace Trophy and started both matches as we beat AEK Athens on penalties after coming back from four goals down to claim a 4-4 draw, then defeated Coventry 1-0 in the final to claim a bit of silverware.

I was on the lookout for a new club in the summer of 1994 and, in the meantime, Jim allowed me to train with Pompey to maintain fitness. Despite being 32, I was still quick, leading the sprinting sessions, with the lads encouraging me to approach the manager and see if he'd change his mind about a deal. I never did, though. If he was interested then I was right in front of him. Nonetheless, I understood where he was coming from. When I started out at Port Vale, lads aged 30 were finished. Whenever you ran past them they'd say: "You go past me again and I'll break your legs." They hated the fact you'd shown them up because they weren't fit. Jim was looking at everything I'd gone through physically, the injuries, and no doubt asked whether he should be offering a 32-year-old another contract. I suppose I could have gone to him in the hope of a change of heart after watching me train every day, but I didn't want that rejection. Besides, I wouldn't have wanted to put Jim on the spot like that either. Jim did, however, offer me a player-coach role, involving succeeding Kenny Todd overseeing the youth team, while still being available for the first-team. Although coaching would later be my future, at that stage I wanted to continue playing full-time and couldn't really see how I could combine both roles at Pompey.

Still, not having an agent at the time, I wrote to all Division One clubs letting them know about my availability. The only one to respond was John Rudge at Port Vale, who'd also had my brother Neville pestering him on the phone. He was interested and said he'd be back in touch — yet I never heard from him again. Then one day I was contacted by the PFA, who enquired if I had managed to find a club. I explained the Rudge situation and it turned out he'd done the same with a few lads and hadn't followed it up, with the PFA insisting they "needed to have a word" with him over it! As it was, I trialled at Brighton & Hove Albion for two weeks, subsequently signing for them in August 1994 in what turned out to be the worst move ever. They were a very cliquey bunch — apart from Steve Foster, who was nice — but the rest of them weren't, which is very unusual in football. I then finished my Football League career with Exeter City.

Despite having left Pompey, I still kept in touch with some of my old team-mates, including Gerry Creaney, which led to me being on the receiving end of a beating in April 1995. Now Gerry wasn't a well-liked person, a big head who had scored plenty of goals for Celtic and represented Scotland under-21s, which he often let the lads know about. He didn't have a great relationship with many in that dressing room, but he didn't boast like that with me as he was aware I'd played eight times for England. Still, I felt he needed somebody on his side, even if he did have a big mouth. I did the same when David Hirst arrived at Sheffield Wednesday from Barnsley, looking after him, including invitations to come to the house where I'd cook for him. While at Pompey, a lot of people didn't like Warren Aspinall, but I did, although Steve Wigley once warned me about Gerry: "You go into town with him, don't you? Be careful."

Anyhow, it was a Thursday night, Gerry's 25th birthday, and with me unhappy at Brighton and not part of the squad, I went out with him in Southsea and we ended up at The Pyramids Centre for a few beers. Now I've no idea if he did anything in there, or said something he shouldn't, but we ran into trouble outside. We were halfway into a taxi from the rank across the road when a group of four or five lads appeared and this big bruiser shouted: "That's my taxi." I replied how as we'd got there first, but he repeated himself: "That's my taxi." With that, the taxi driver drove off, so now it was nobody's taxi! Then the lads confronted us: "You're Gerry Creaney, aren't you. You think you're all that. Come on, let's have it." Well, I've never been in that situation before, I'm not a fighter, and this big lad went for Gerry. Somebody may have hit me from behind, I don't know, I can't re-member, but when I came to I picked up Gerry off the floor and we headed in the direction of The Queens Hotel. About a minute later, I spotted another group of people, this time girls and lads, who asked what had happened, so we explained. Then I felt something hit me from behind again and I rolled over on the floor. I've no idea if it was the original group of lads who had returned and I didn't want to find out, so I sprinted towards The Queens Hotel.

I don't know what happened to Gerry but I wasn't staying around any longer. Sorry, I'd taken enough! The hotel's doors were shut but I could see the porter inside, sitting in the hallway. With my face now a mess, I made sure he couldn't see it as I banged on the doors and, sure enough, the porter came over to see me. "I've got these lads chasing after me, can I come in? My mate's still there, can you also call the police?" Thankfully I was let inside and later went to Queen Alexan-dra Hospital with a broken nose and a few scars. Gerry was far worse than me, having a fractured cheekbone which required an operation and ruled him out of the remaining five games of the season. As it turned out, Pompey advised us not to proceed with finding those who attacked us, while the group of people who witnessed the second attack were warned off by those responsible and told not to testify, so it never went to trial. It wasn't a good period and still affects me now. I struggled with it psychologically and even today don't go into certain places. Experiencing something like that was awful.

I've continued living in Port Solent, with my sons Alexander and Christian born in the city, although with the surname Oxlade-Chamberlain, in tribute to my wife's late brother, David, who died in a car accident. They represent the third generation of professional footballers in our family, although, of my sons, only Christian was on Pompey's books. My coaching career began with a part-time role with Southampton academy under-11s, including helping out at develop-ment centres in Hamble, Eastleigh and Havant. After gauging the standard of players, I asked if I could bring my Alexander, who was half decent. He was aged eight, yet had never really played for a team. Instead we'd cycle over to the playing fields in Port Solent and train. Alex would turn out for a Paulsgrove side where his friend Bobby Scott played, featuring in some summer tournaments, but that was it.

Alex went on to play for Southampton before moving to Arsenal, Liverpool and Besiktas, scoring seven times in 35 England outings — but Pompey did try to get him to switch to their academy. Steve Martin, from the Fratton Park youth set-up, once saw me out and about and mentioned how he'd seen Alex and asked whether I'd be interested in bringing him to Pompey — which I wasn't. Then, in

2011, Paul Hart, the Blues' director of youth operations, rang and offered me a full-time job as under-16s coach. That appeared a great move for me, working full-time for an academy, although I later wondered why he had employed me. He never picked my brains about Southampton's successful academy practices.

Then one day Hart said flippantly: "Your son should come here." I replied: "No, he's not for you, Paul." From working at Pompey, I had learned Paul Hart was a very pragmatic person. When he came to watch sessions, you had to make sure the lads played in a different way. In front of him, the kids had to control the ball with the inside of the foot, not the outside, and there could be no flashy stuff or flicks. He hated seeing that. Considering the way Hart worked — and how my son likes to play — I didn't want him to move to Pompey.

My youngest son Christian, however, did come to Fratton Park after being spotted at the age of 12. He was rejected by Southampton a couple of times and ended up attending Pompey's development centre under Paul Hardyman. On one occasion, they played the academy and were the better team, so three or four of them were taken on, including Christian, who ended up earning professional forms at the same time as Alex Bass and making a living from football. Alex has won the FA Cup three times in his career, all while at Arsenal under Arsene Wenger, while I lost in two semi-finals, the first with Sheffield Wednesday in April 1986. And we all know what happened on the second occasion — thanks to Ronnie Whelan.

ADAM WEBSTER

81 games, five goals (July 2011 — June 2016)

Accrington Stanley 1 (McCartan)
Pompey 3 (Bennett, Pearson OG, Doyle)

League Two, Crown Ground, Tuesday, March 8, 2016

Pompey: Fulton, Davies, Burgess, Webster, Stevens, Doyle, Hollands, Evans, Roberts (77 mins, Naismith), Bennett (83 mins, Freeman), Smith (73 mins, McNulty). Subs not used: Bass, Clarke, Barton, Chaplin.

Attendance; 1,841

I had to be realistic. I always thought I was going to play in the Premier League — it's what I wanted — but when you're struggling in League Two and not playing, that ambition was so far from reality. I was preparing myself for the worst. Pompey would have released me, without a doubt. I'm always telling people that. My contract was expiring and my career was heading for non-league at the age of 20. When you can't even get into a Pompey team finishing 16th in League Two, there aren't many places to go next.

I needed a back-up career should football not work out, so I started a level-two personal trainer course along with around 10 of my Fratton Park teammates. A few of the older boys like Ryan Taylor and Andy Barcham had been talking about it and it was arranged for a company to visit the training ground during the afternoons to teach us. It made sense as I could soon be left searching the non-league game for a club, while requiring another job to supplement part-time wages, but I wasn't enjoying the course. It occurred to me I actually needed to put all my energy into football rather than getting so stressed about coursework, so I made the decision not to finish it. I had to sort myself out and give this everything. As it was, I got a bit of luck. Had Andy Awford remained as Pompey manager, I wouldn't have played centre-back in those last four matches of the 2014/15 season and my time at Fratton Park would have been over. I knew our caretaker boss Gary Waddock liked me, as did his temporary assistant Paul Hardyman — and between them they saved my Pompey career.

Born in Chichester and raised in West Wittering, I was scouted at the age of 10 while playing for East Wittering Community Primary School and asked to attend Pompey's Advanced Training Centre (ATC) at Chichester College, before being recommended to the Elite Training Centre at Miltoncross School, overseen by Hardyman. I must have caught the eye because Hardy organised a trial with Pompey's Centre of Excellence, as it was then, but I wasn't at that level at that time. I was too nervous, so they turned me down and I returned to the ATC.

One morning in pre-season, I was scheduled to train at Cowplain School on the Astroturf, yet I refused to leave my bed because I fancied playing cricket with my mates instead. Thankfully mum made me get up and drove me there. I'm so glad she did, otherwise that could have been the day I walked away from football. At that time I didn't enjoy football but loved cricket, even though I was never good enough to play professionally. I started too late, beginning in year seven at Chichester High School, and would bat at three or four and bowl a bit of medium-pace swing, line and length. I represented Stirlands Cricket Club in Birdham, Chichester, sometimes being involved in first-team matches, playing on Saturday and Sundays. I was a great batsman in the nets, incredible, then, when it came to being out in the middle, I was too tentative and safe, not playing the shots because I was too worried about getting out. Yet I loved it and it was so much fun.

My following season at Pompey I had a growth spurt, filled out a bit more, and was physically no longer gangly or uncoordinated. Everything clicked. I was always tall from primary school age and technically good, but I couldn't keep up with the strength and running power of some of the boys because they were like men and I wasn't. I was a little boy. Now I was one of the best players, I felt comfortable with my under-16s group and enjoyed it a lot more, earning a two-year scholarship.

By the summer of 2011, I had been a first-year scholar for a month before being invited by Steve Cotterill to train with the first-team. Then, in August 2011, we had an afternoon behind-closed-doors reserve friendly against Swindon Town. As I had trained in the morning, I was told several times I wouldn't be needed to play, instead merely sitting on the bench for the experience. Jed Wallace was on trial, with Benjani Mwaruwari, Jason Pearce and Joel Ward also featuring. During the second half, Cotterill turned to me and said: "You did really well this morning, son. Do you want to go on?" I wasn't expecting it — I was tired after training and didn't even have time to eat — so I replied: "I do feel a bit lethargic." Andy Awford was also on the bench and Cotterill turned to him and said: "What did that idiot just say to me?" before returning to me and saying: "Well, you're going on now!"

I played the last 15 minutes and following a 4-0 win, with Benjani scoring a first-half hat-trick, Cotts was walking away, chatting to Jed's agent, when I overheard him saying: "You'll never guess what somebody has just said to me?" It soon went around the first-team and, from that point, I was nicknamed "Lethargic." Ricardo Rocha always called it me. The following week, I was included in Pompey's first-team squad which travelled to Real Betis for a rearranged pre-season friendly. It finished in a 5-1 defeat and I was brought on in the 70th minute for Lewis Stockford. I made another slip up on the morning of the game when I went to return the manager's offer of a handshake and said: "Morning, Steve." He snapped: "What did you call me?" I didn't know the protocol was "Gaffer." I was so naive, I didn't have a clue!

Cotterill left Fratton Park to join Nottingham Forest in October 2011, with Michael Appleton appointed as his replacement, yet I was sidelined with ankle ligament damage, which was gutting. Instead Sam Magri, a second-year scholar on a pro contract who had captained England under-17s at the World Cup, was training with the first-team under the new manager, with much expected of him. Whereas scholars are normally given Christmas off to go home and see their families, I spent the whole of the festive period training with the first-team, and loved it. Appleton kept telling me: "I don't care how young you are, if you're good enough then you'll play." Sure enough, for the first-team's FA Cup third-round trip to Chelsea in January 2012, I was named on the bench, unused, but watching in awe at John Terry spraying balls everywhere. I was also among the substitutes seven days later when we hosted West Ham United at Fratton Park in the Championship — and this time I made my debut, aged 17 years and 11 days. Losing 1-0 and down to 10 men following David Norris' sending off, I came on for Greg Halford at right-back with 15 minutes left. I remember Liam Lawrence wobbling this ball to me for what would be my first touch and thinking: "Please, just control this" — thankful it was a perfect touch. It could easily have gone under my foot. He shouted: "Sorry, mate," but, if anything, it probably helped me settle into the game.

However, four weeks later Pompey entered administration for the second time in two years and were heading out of the Championship following a 10-point deduction. In the summer of 2012 we travelled to Benahavis, Spain, for a 10-day pre-season tour, with the squad made up of academy players and triallists, having left behind all our senior players to be sold to prevent the club's liquidation. The opening match of the 2012/13 campaign saw us under a transfer embargo, so we faced Plymouth Argyle in the Capital One Cup with nine teenagers — and just me, Ashley Harris, Simon Eastwood and our assistant manager Ashley Westwood having first-team experience. We lost 3-0 but held our own until the final three minutes when they scored twice.

Days later the club were allowed to sign players again but it wasn't until September 2012 before we picked up our first win, a 3-0 victory at Crawley Town who had been reduced to nine men. I came on as a substitute and zinged a left-footed cross from the right which Ashley Harris headed in at the back post for my first career assist. Harris was so highly thought of at that stage and I remember Jason Pearce and Joel Ward buzzing about how good he was in training. He was incredible. A joke. Then two years later, in the summer of 2014, he had left Pompey and was out of the Football League.

My early Pompey outings alternated between playing at right-back or left-back and, while I was never a full-back, I was enjoying it. At the age of 17, I was regularly featuring in first-team football and the position didn't bother me. I had previously played a bit at right-back in the under-16s and under-18s, so I knew it. To be truthful, I wasn't ready to play centre-back at that stage. I didn't have the physicality, the know-how or experience. Not that I cared, I just wanted to play. However, when Michael Appleton walked out to join Blackpool in November 2012, my appearances dried up under caretaker boss Guy Whittingham as we slipped into League Two with successive relegations. We used 54 players that season, which will never bring you success.

Just five days before the start of the 2013/14 season, Whittingham approached me following a Pompey XI friendly at Gosport Borough and told me I was off to Aldershot Town on loan. We had lost 4-1 at Privett Park, our first-team coach Alan McLoughlin went mental at us at half-time and I hadn't played very well, being substituted in the 58th minute — now I was heading to the Skrill Conference, initially until January. I didn't get a say and I was gutted. I thought I'd have a chance to play for the first-team in League Two. Yet that loan turned out to be the best thing for me.

I was handed regular football and played at centre-half against proper men, which helped me massively. Having been a central defender asked to play full-back for Pompey, obviously there comes a point where you're not thriving and aren't playing that well — it wasn't my position. I was always natural on the ball, right footed but able to use my left. My dad, Richard, helped run a club called West Wittering FC and, from the age of 11, every weekend I'd go along with him, practising kicking the ball, working on both feet. Not every centre-half is comfortable on the ball, but technically I was fine. Physically, though, I had to learn the trade and do the dirty side. I probably wasn't very good at winning headers and the hard parts of the game, so I needed to be educated. Aldershot manager Andy Scott paired me in the centre of defence with Jake Goodman, an old-school centre-half on loan from Millwall, with me on the left side finding the passes, while he did the dirty work. I'd been around Pompey's first-team for a long time, but now actually felt part of a side, playing regularly, growing up. Without doubt, I improved as a player.

In my absence, Guy was sacked as Pompey boss and replaced by Richie Barker in December 2013. Richie was keen on getting me stronger, which involved me training at Aldershot in the morning and coming back to Fratton Park in the afternoon for a gym session. It was too much on my body and, on Boxing Day, I pulled my hamstring in a Shots match against Forest Green Rovers. I had never before suffered that injury and that was definitely down to the workload initiated by Barker. He was proper old school and I knew I wouldn't get a chance under him because of the way I played as a centre-half. He also wasn't liked by the boys and it wasn't a nice place to be. The atmosphere was terrible before Andy Awford replaced him.

Once recovered from my injury I returned to Aldershot, who had extended my loan until the end of the season, but, for whatever reason, couldn't get back into their team, and, with Pompey's regular right-back Daniel Alfei picking up a hamstring injury in training, they invoked a 24-hour recall clause in April 2014. We were 21st in League Two and I was in against Hartlepool United at right-back — and scored the winner after 82 seconds! Ricky Holmes' free-kick was headed back across goal by Ryan Taylor and, when the keeper parried it, I finished from close range. It was my first Pompey appearance in almost a year — and my first goal for the club had given us a vital 1-0 victory in the battle to avoid non-league football. I missed the following game against Dagenham & Redbridge, a 4-1 win, with a little knock before returning at home to Bristol Rovers, when I scored again, this time from outside the box in a 3-2 success. We stayed up with three matches to spare, eventually finishing 13th, as I featured in four of the final six matches, scoring twice.

Awfs had been my academy manager, he liked me, and, having been appointed permanently as boss, that summer I was informed I was his first-choice right-back for the 2014/15 season, accompanied by the number two shirt. I started our first match at Exeter City in a 1-1 draw and thought I would play every game, yet it didn't turn out like that. In our second league match, I was sent off in a 2-1 win over Cambridge United for two bookable offences, but the first yellow card wasn't even me! It was the first sending off in my career and I would lose my place to Crystal Palace loanee Alex Wynter. If that wasn't bad enough, when I came on against Northampton Town in the Johnstone's Paint Trophy in October 2014, I went up for a header and landed badly, damaging the meniscus in my right knee and putting me out of action for 10 weeks. I returned to the line-up on Boxing Day against AFC Wimbledon, representing my first league start for more than four-and-a-half months, and we lost 2-0 to leave us 15th. Fratton Park was toxic. It was a bad, bad place at the time.

Off the pitch, Awfs had had a falling out with David Connolly, who was a very angry man. This was someone who had played international football for the Republic of Ireland and in the Premier League, his standards were so high and he was such a good finisher, yet he found it difficult to accept that not everyone had the same motivation and ability levels that he possessed. Nick Awford probably knew he wasn't good enough but his dad was the manager, and someone like David Connolly wasn't going to tolerate that — although Nick wasn't the only one he had a go at. I actually thought Connolly was all right, although one day during pre-season training at St John's College Playing Fields, we were about to do some running and he walked away and drove off — it turned out his son was in the car! Michael Doyle was the same. He was horrible on the pitch but off it, he was sound. He'd sometimes accidentally kick the ball out of play, turn around and swear at me — yet he was the one who had played the bad pass. When he came to us on trial in June 2015, we were training at the Mountbatten Centre and he was swearing at everyone. I was thinking: "Blimey, who's this?"

There were periods in my Pompey career when the team was struggling and I was getting pelters from the fans. They were killing me, with the 2014/15 season the worst. When you come through the academy, some players are loved, but I was never one of those. I would hear it in games and I'd get tweets about it. At Leyton Orient in March 2013, when Dan Butler's poor back-pass gifted the hosts a 1-0 victory, I was on the bench and didn't come on, yet after the match I found myself copied into tweets which read: "Don't worry Dan, you'll never be as bad as Adam Webster." I didn't play and was still getting killed! That was awful and I hated it. You don't want to see those sorts of things but I was still only young, at 18, and it was tough. I remember seeing similar things directed at Ben Close. He's a good footballer, but also used to get a lot of stick, despite being from Fratton and a proper Pompey boy.

In my case, that was probably the consequence of not playing in my natural position. Obviously I wasn't performing that well, but it's still not nice to hear, especially when you aren't even playing and are still getting killed. You're a teenage lad, not in the team, low on confidence, and being copied into stuff said about you on Twitter. Seeing that was another kick in the nuts. When a young lad makes it through into the first-team, he's going to make mistakes. That's how he learns, so back him. Don't destroy his confidence. This was a period in which the team was struggling, everyone was moaning at everyone and it's easy to point the finger at a youngster. Booing won't improve players. It might rile them a little, but it's not going to help in the long run.

During the opening two seasons after coming out of administration, Pompey didn't recruit well. They weren't good characters, they all thought we'd win promotion without working for it — and it was never going to happen like that. There was a lot of conflict in that dressing room. While Awfs did well as caretaker manager, when he became permanent he didn't really have a way of playing and the bigger characters had quite a lot of influence. I was nowhere near the first-team and he never explained why. If he did I certainly cannot recall it. In April 2015, we lost 3-1 at Morecambe, I came off the bench for the final seven minutes after Josh Passley suffered concussion — and it proved to be Awfs' last match in charge. I wasn't buzzing over the decision because he gave me my chance in the academy, but it occurred to me this could be an opportunity to get back into the first-team — and it was.

It was a massive moment in my career. If I didn't play well in those final four games, that was it. Out of contract, I would be heading to non-league, probably going down the personal trainer path again. Then our caretaker boss Gary Waddock told me: "You're playing in my first match." Stevenage was do or die, all or nothing, the biggest game of my career. What's more, it was in my favoured position of centre-half. I was never that confident and I always had that impostor syndrome which, when you're not playing, is easy to feel. I lined-up as the left-sided central defender alongside Nyron Nosworthy and, despite a 1-0 defeat, I was buzzing with how I played, while *The News* made me Pompey's man of the match. Prior to that, the fans probably didn't have much faith in me, yet I hadn't been playing in my best position. In fact, Stevenage represented only the third time in my 47 Blues appearances that I had featured at centre-half. Hopefully, once they saw me there, it began to change a few minds.

I stayed in the side for the last three weeks of the campaign, totalling four outings, as we finished 16th. As it turned out, the incoming Pompey manager had watched the games ahead of his appointment. I thought I had done well, I was certainly hopeful I could win a new deal, and thankfully Paul Cook liked what he saw — so five weeks after his arrival from Chesterfield, I signed a new two-year contract. I owe Gary Waddock and Paul Hardyman so much. They could easily have not played me. I had started one game in almost three months, but they put their faith in me. I haven't bumped into Gary since, but texted him at times. I'm so very grateful for what he did and have sent some nice messages over the years thanking him. I recall Gary texting me when I got my £20m move to Brighton & Hove Albion in August 2019. My response was: "A lot of this is down to you."

Paul Cook was massive for Pompey. He was one of the first managers I came across who actually possessed a playing identity. We had good players, great lads, and should have gone up in the 2015/16 season, because it was in our hands for so long. It took a while for me to break into his team and I didn't start the opening 12 league games, but eventually I had the rhythm of playing and his management style suited me down to the ground. We'd face each other in head tennis on this makeshift court outside his office and although he was very good at it, particularly using his left foot, he would also dream up rules as he went along to ensure he won. Me and Conor Chaplin had so many games against him and he didn't like it when either of us beat him. It was so funny and those days were class.

Following his appointment as manager he took us to Vale do Lobo, in the Algarve, for a team-bonding trip and it was like a stag do. With so many new faces, it helped everyone get to know each other, creating a good team spirit. We didn't do much training, probably two sessions on a pitch and a couple of early morning runs on the beach. It was mental. We were encouraged to go out at night and get drunk together, with everybody obliging!

That summer, Christian Burgess had been bought from Peterborough United and Matt Clarke arrived on loan from Ipswich Town and they started the season as Cook's preferred centre-half pairing. I was training well and handed starts in the Capital One Cup and Johnstone's Paint Trophy, but remained on the bench in League Two, with the manager telling me: "I've got to find a way to get you into my team." That moment finally arrived in October 2015 — Pompey's 13th league game of the season — when we travelled to Newport County and I lined-up alongside Burgess in the centre of defence. From that point, I was a regular, starting 27 of the next 30 games in all competitions.

My favourite Blues match was the trip to Accrington Stanley in March 2016, our biggest fixture of the season at that stage. Positioned fifth in League Two, we faced a John Coleman side who were one place and one point ahead of us with a game in hand. We turned up to the Crown Ground really late after deciding to change at the hotel because the Accrington dressing rooms were so bad. Coleman felt that was disrespectful and fell out with Cook over it. They were also arguing over Romy Boco being on the hosts' bench, despite a gentleman's agreement that he wouldn't face Pompey after we'd cancelled his contract to let him join them on a free transfer in January. We were 3-0 up at half-time, through Kyle Bennett, a Matty Pearson own goal, and an incredible Michael Doyle left-footed volley from 25-yards — he never scored goals like that in training!

Then, in April 2016, I ruptured ligaments in my right ankle during a 3-1 defeat at York City, ending my season prematurely. I should have had surgery, but the hope was that by holding it off I could make a potential League Two play-off final at Wembley. I was pushing really hard, but it would have been stupid because I wouldn't have been right, not even for a one-off game. As it was, we lost in the semi-finals to Plymouth — and I'd played my final Pompey match.

I didn't know I'd be moving on at the end of that season, although I was hoping for a Championship switch. We had faced Derby County and Reading in the Capital One Cup and they were matches I felt I'd performed well in, almost finding them easier than some of the League Two games. There had also previously been interest in the January transfer window from Ipswich following the FA Cup third-round encounter between the clubs. We had drawn 2-2 at Portman Road — I still can't believe we didn't win that game — then beat them 2-1 at our place in the replay — and I had caught their eye, having started both matches. That same month, Mick McCarthy tried to buy me, but Pompey rejected it as they wanted to win promotion. Not that I wanted to leave. As soon as the season ended, we had our individual player meetings with Cook and he advised me I needed to take the step. "You are ready," he said. "You've got to go and do it."

Ipswich came back in. I don't actually think there was interest from anyone else, and it happened so quickly. In June 2016 I became their player in a £750,000 move, which also involved Pompey receiving Clarke and cash in part-exchange. I was still injured at the time, which they obviously knew as the scan results on the ankle wouldn't have been very good. Still, they got me right for pre-season, although, despite playing regularly for the Tractor Boys until January in my first season, the ankle was so lax having not been repaired properly and went again, requiring surgery. I still made 53 appearances in two seasons at Portman Road, before joining Bristol City and then Brighton.

Maybe I ended up proving some Pompey managers wrong, but it's very easy to say: "I should be playing." In reality, there probably were times when I shouldn't. I'm not sure some of them would have expected me to progress to play more than a century of Premier League games, but they had their reasons for not selecting me and I also have to look at myself for those performances. If I could go back and give advice to myself as a kid, it would be to back myself more, because no-one else is going to do that for you. You have to be completely confident in yourself and your ability. At Pompey, Jed Wallace would give the ball away every single time he had it – and then put one into the top corner. He didn't care if it might go over, he'd shoot because he thought it would go in. I wish I could be a bit more like that but I was never that confident, which is the thing that has held me back, I've not had enough self-belief. Never enough: "I am here, now I'm going to show you." I don't know why. I honestly don't know.

Pompey was a rollercoaster, I loved a lot of it and obviously there were also tough times because it was such a rocky period for the club. It was difficult, but my last year at Fratton Park was so good. The adversity I suffered definitely helped my career. At the time it's hard, you don't know how you can get out of it, but those tough times make you. We have it so good at Brighton in terms of facilities and the club's stability, yet it's annoying because the young lads don't know how good they've got it — or the rubbish some of us have been through in the past to arrive at that stage. Accrington away on a Tuesday night is an experience — but I wouldn't change any of it. It has made me who I am.

From the age of 16 or 17 at Pompey, I wanted to play in the Premier League and genuinely believed I could. I just had to go the long way around and earn my stripes. I worked hard and emerged through a lot of adversity and setbacks. If you can do that, then you'll get the bit of luck you deserve.

PAUL HALL

216 games, 42 goals (March 1993 — August 1998)

Pompey 2 (Creaney, Hall)
Nottingham Forest 1 (Collymore)

Division One, Fratton Park, March 26, 1994

Pompey: Knight, Neill, Awford, Gittens, Dobson, Stimson, Hall, Powell (75 mins, Russell), Chamberlain (67 mins, McLoughlin), Boere, Creaney. Sub Not Used: Flahavan.

Attendance; 12,578

If Paul Walsh was the best footballer I played alongside, Jim Smith was the angriest manager I ever experienced. The Bald Eagle was an eccentric, a great man who wore his heart on his sleeve — and the person responsible for bringing me to Pompey as a 20-year-old, for which I'm eternally grateful.

My first full season was 1993/94 and, being pretty early into my first-team involvement, I was often a substitute, watching with fascination at Jim's explosive half-time rants at my teammates. You'd always know when he was angry because he'd come in, take off his jacket and then head to the toilet, with everyone thinking: "Oh no." Well, his bladder must have been a massive balloon because he'd take ages in there, creating an uncomfortable wait for the lads ahead of the inevitable ticking-off.

Now there was a bench in the Fratton Park dressing room which the physio Neil Sillett used to rub down injured players — and there was also a space beside it. I had wondered why nobody sat there, and also why my playing colleagues always covered their shirt and trousers with a towel for some reason. Anyhow, being new to the dressing room, I needed a spot, so I grabbed the only vacant one I could find — next to the bench. On one occasion, Jim exploded: "You lot are a waste of space. I'm telling you now, you are a waste of space. When are you going to start learning?" His head went beetroot red and then, with one fell swoop, he swept aside these paper cups full of hot tea. A couple of cups flew into my face, my clothes were drenched, and I could see the lads sniggering — they knew precisely what would happen to the person in that seat! Alan McLoughlin came up to me afterwards: "I don't think you'll sit there in the future, will you?"

I had come to Pompey's attention while at Torquay United, where I made my debut at the age of 17, having been scouted in Smethwick, near Birmingham, by John James, the person who discovered Lee Sharpe and Darren Moore. After almost 100 appearances for the Gulls, I was sent off for punching an opponent off the ball in an FA Cup first round defeat against Yeovil Town in November 1992, and, during my two-week ban, it was fixed for me to go on a week's trial at West Ham United, where Billy Bonds was manager. He decided against a deal, with his assistant Harry Redknapp explaining how they wanted me but couldn't do anything, so I spent my second week at Pompey, with Jim Smith prepared to pay £70,000. It was arranged for me to sign on deadline day in March 1993, involving catching the train from Torquay to Exeter, then Bristol, then Newbury, and then to Portsmouth & Southsea station, where my agent would pick me up — and it had to arrive before 5pm!

That same day I was also offered to Bristol City, managed by Russell Osman, with my Torquay boss Neil Warnock offering me the choice but, having already spent time at Fratton Park, establishing relationships, that clinched it. Besides, they were third in Division One and looking like making the Premier League. So there I was on the train, this kid with his Walkman and two sponges on his ears listening to reggae music, heading to Pompey not knowing what to expect. The deal went through five minutes before the deadline, with Jim lighting up a big cigar in celebration, as did my agent — one each side, puffing away and giving me second-hand smoke inhalation. I had gone from £175 a week to four figures. Earlier that season, Torquay's chairman Mike Bateson told me they couldn't afford a £5-a-week rise!

I must have looked like a scared kid when I entered that Pompey changing room, but Alan McLoughlin was the first person to welcome me and totally defused my anxiety. "You've got all the club's money now, have you?" he said. "You're the reason why I can't get a raise on my contract." That was Macca's humour, he made me feel at ease straight away. Whenever the manager asked for the squad to get into pairs in training, he'd always make a beeline for me. He showed me how to treat people and, when I became a senior pro, I carried it on with other young kids coming into the changing room. When Deon Burton broke through at Fratton Park, myself and Fitzroy Simpson put an arm around him, took him out for coffee and tried to provide a bit of schooling to help with his grounding. Aside from Macca, Kit Symons and Andy Awford took me to a Chinese restaurant on Palmerston Road called Stranded At Lees and I couldn't believe how they were so young, yet so good. They were such a brilliant central-defensive pairing, with Awfs a good footballer technically and Kit an excellent man-marker who could pass the ball.

Just eight weeks after leaving the bottom division of the Football League, I was handed my Pompey debut in a Division One play-off semi-final second leg against Leicester City. It was May 1993, we were trailing 1-0 following Julian Joachim's goal in the first leg and, for the Fratton Park return, with Mark Chamberlain out injured through knee ligament damage, I was named on the bench alongside Darryl Powell. I had never seen anything like it before or since. There was ticker tape everywhere and we even had to delay the kick-off for it to be removed from the pitch. The atmosphere around the place was incredible.

I had come from Torquay and was now playing in front of these supporters who would still be shouting, screaming and chanting if you were 4-0 up or 4-0 down. They never stop. I came off the bench at half-time, replacing Chris Price in midfield, yet we drew 2-2, which meant elimination 3-2 on aggregate. When you live in the city and integrate with the people, you play with a lot more heart. You win, lose and draw together as people and I understood that. I lived in Hilsea, my neighbour was staunch Pompey and would sometimes tell me when I was brilliant — and also when I had a stinker — and you have to take that. I was once interviewed on TV by Lindy Delapenha, who, like me, played for Pompey and Jamaica, and he told me all the players of his era lived in the city. It's the only way you can truly connect with an area, and for five-and-a-half years, I played for Pompey and lived among the fans. I understood.

Jim Smith could be brutal and at times I thought he was going to burst a blood vessel. He wanted to get the best out of you, and that was usually delivered by shouting, yet he taught me so much. July 1993 marked my first pre-season and we travelled to Finland for the Mypa Tournament, where we faced an Ajax team consisting of Jari Litmanen in the opening match. We lost 2-0, yet I came on at half-time for John Durnin and ripped their full-back to shreds. I murdered him, to the point where their manager, Louis van Gaal, afterwards asked Jim if they could buy me. His response was: "I'll tell you what, we'll do a swap. I'll take Litmanen and you take Paul Hall." Jim was quite cheeky like that! One evening over there, Jim gave us permission to go out and, as a newly-turned 21-year-old, partying and dancing was on my mind. The following morning, the lads were chatting and saying: "Hally can really dance, you know." So Jim took me aside and said: "Son, you need to make up your mind whether you want to be a footballer or a disco dancer." It was a little reminder that I didn't have to follow the older players. I possessed talent and could have a good career in the game, but I needed to understand where my priorities were — and I never, ever forgot that from Jim.

Tactically, he knew what he was doing, he knew when to make his changes, and was able to mix young players with old, an alchemist like Harry Redknapp. He relied on coaches such as Graham Paddon and Mike Bailey on the training pitch, yet picked the team and was meticulous in his planning. Jim knew what he wanted and you never messed with him. The following summer, in May 1994, we had a post-season trip to Xanthi, Greece, for the Thrace Trophy, a four-team tournament in which we faced AEK Athens before beating Coventry City 1-0 in the final, with me getting the winner. Former Everton boss Howard Kendall was on the verge of becoming Xanthi manager and spent every night drinking red wine with Jim. They'd be telling stories, drinking the bar dry, while we'd sit there listening, fascinated by the tales they came out with. It also allowed us to run around the hotel and do what we like because they were downstairs — it was like your mum and dad being out so you could do what you wanted!

The 1993/94 campaign represented my first full season with Pompey and, three games in, I was handed my first start for the visit of Luton Town to Fratton Park in August 1993. I was shocked when Jim Smith relayed the news, but marked the occasion by grabbing the only goal of the game — and I'm getting goosebumps thinking about it now. On 41 minutes, Mark Stimson dispossessed Kerry Dixon and pulled it back from the byline, which I met with a left-footed finish at the near post to put it past Hatters 'keeper Juergen Sommer, a former Torquay teammate. What a Pompey dressing room that was — and Paul Walsh was the finest footballer I played with by a mile, yet also the best teacher. He really was that good. I was blessed to play alongside somebody of such talent. I watched him and learnt so much. When the ball went into him, I knew to get on my bike and he'd put it on to my big toe.

Walshy left for Manchester City in March 1994, but returned to Pompey 18 months later to renew our partnership. Later that season, however, he went down in the first half against Leicester with a cruciate ligament injury to his right knee and never played again. He was a total professional, although Walshy confided in me that it wasn't always the case at Liverpool and Tottenham Hotspur, which killed him at that level. For a kid from Manchester, he was the best coach, but they all were — Alan McLoughlin, Alan Knight, Mark Chamberlain, Warren Neill, Guy Whittingham, all those guys. It was Chambo who taught me how to play in between the lines, how to be a playmaker from the wing, which was wonderful knowledge. At one point, I thought he was lazy because I'd run up and down, yet he never did — then I had an epiphany. I recognised that everything slowed down when he was in possession. He moved the ball to where he needed to go at the right time with the right pass. It was such a skill. Chambo would say: "All of you, slow down. You're running around too fast, you're wasting energy," and he was right. You had to control the game.

The 1993/94 season served as my breakthrough, with 36 appearances and six goals, including my favourite Pompey game — the March 1994 visit of Nottingham Forest to Fratton Park. Being a right winger, I was up against England left-back Stuart Pearce and, as it turned out, I scored the winner in a 2-1 victory. I ripped Pearce to shreds that day, with their manager, Frank Clark, later mentioning in his autobiography *Black & White And Red All Over* that I was the only player he saw taking Pearce to the cleaners! Before the match I wanted to size up Pearce, but he didn't come out for the warm-up. It was something I took offence to, and what followed was one of the best games of my life. I was going past him, putting crosses in, nutmegging him. I was embarrassing Pearce so much, he was also smashing me. In the end, with Jim fearing for me, I was switched to the left wing up against Des Lyttle for my own protection, which is where I added to Gerry Creaney's opening goal, cutting across the area and finishing right-footed. Stan

Collymore pulled one back for Forest, but we held on to beat a side challenging for promotion.

We also claimed a famous scalp the following season when drawn against Everton in the Coca-Cola Cup. Following a 3-2 first-leg win at Goodison Park, through goals from Creaney (two) and Bjorn Kristensen, we met on the south coast in October 1994. The Toffeemen handed a debut to Duncan Ferguson, who had joined on-loan from Glasgow Rangers, and, when Dave Watson opened the scoring after 17 minutes, the match appeared to be heading for extra-time at 3-3 on aggregate. I was introduced on the left wing as a half-time substitute for Preki and, two minutes from time, found myself in front of goal, putting a left-footed finish through Neville Southall's legs to level the tie and win overall. Scoring against someone like Southall was a feather in my cap — what a fantastic keeper — but there were other great players in that Everton side too, such as Watson, David Unsworth, Vinny Samways and Andy Hinchcliffe.

Jim Smith was sacked in February 1995 following a 1-0 home defeat to Leicester in the FA Cup fourth round, although I wasn't surprised. We were 19th in Division One having lost nine of our last 15 matches in all competitions and, when that happens, people start questioning what you are doing. Jim was known as a winning manager, but unfortunately he couldn't withstand the growth of us younger players, with our performances up and down. His replacement was Terry Fenwick, who named me on the bench for his maiden game in charge, a 2-0 victory over Stoke City, and after that I was a regular in his starting line-up, something I had never been under Jim.

He also converted me into a striker, unlocking my belief. Until that point, I'd spent my career as a right winger, yet often would get to the byline and put it into the stands. Now this new Pompey manager was telling me: "You're going to play up front. How do you feel about that?" Pompey fine-tuned me, they taught me how to play football, and Fenwick made me a much more effective player by employing me as a striker. He was very influential, he gave me the opportunity to really improve myself, and, for the rest of my career, other clubs utilised me in that position on occasions, with the outcome a total of 139 goals in domestic and international football. Fenwick had faith at a time when Jim had probably stopped believing in me. He recognised I regularly scored goals from the wing in training, so, from the start, played Preki wide and put me up front. He was pivotal for my career, seeing something in me that Jim Smith, Cyril Knowles and Ivan Golac couldn't — operating as a striker.

That became my role for almost two years at Pompey, featuring in 49 matches of the subsequent 1995/96 season, starting all but two of them, as I netted 10 times from a forward position. However, by May 1996 we were in the Division One relegation zone as we headed to Huddersfield Town for the final game of the campaign. Should we achieve victory — and Millwall collected no more than a point — we'd leapfrog above them and be safe courtesy of goal difference. That's exactly what unfolded as Deon Burton's early goal handed us a 1-0 triumph, while Millwall were held to a goalless draw at Ipswich Town.

Having narrowly stayed up, we finished seventh the following season in 1996/97 and I'm particularly proud of our FA Cup run, which saw us win 3-2 at a strong Leeds United in February 1997. We travelled to Elland Road to face a George Graham side positioned 11th in the Premier League and containing Nigel Martyn, Carlton Palmer, Brian Deane, Lee Bowyer and Gary Kelly, with Ian Rush among their substitutes. Yet goals from Alan McLoughlin, Mathias Svensson and Lee Bradbury handed us victory in front of a 35,604 crowd, with Fitzroy Simpson also missing a penalty after Macca had gone off injured. Afterwards there was a spontaneous conga from some of our team, so, with my shirt off, I also got involved — I was pretty proud of my body back then! We'd just achieved something unbelievable; Leeds were expected to roll us over and reach the quarter-finals, but instead were beaten like Wolverhampton Wanderers and Reading before them. As for that photograph, that goes down in Pompey folklore. What a fantastic day.

Ruud Gullit's Chelsea were now the obstacle between a place in the FA Cup semi-finals, visiting Fratton Park for a televised game in March 1997. The previous month, Terry Venables had become owner of the Blues after joining as director of football in July 1996. We barely saw him on the training ground, probably about four sessions in total and, bearing in mind we'd just won at Elland Road without his input, he was now involving himself in preparations for Chelsea, suddenly appearing and announcing: "Right, this is what's going to happen." His message was Frank Leboeuf cannot pass it, so to let him have the ball whenever possible. The match gets underway, Leboeuf receives the ball, attempts a pass and loses it — and we're all thinking: "Terry Venables is a genius."

Then, on 25 minutes, Leboeuf is on the ball once more, we let him have it, no problem, then he produces this long pass from his own half which bounces twice in front of Mark Hughes, who unleashes an unbelievable right-footed half-volley from just inside the box to give Chelsea the lead. I'm now looking at the bench thinking: "Gaffer, are you sure?" We ended up losing 4-1, with Deon Burton coming on to grab a late consolation. That was the first time Venables had got involved and, while I don't live with regrets, you do think what might have been. We had beaten Leeds and kept the same starting XI for Chelsea, but Venables changed things tactically. We were instructed to leave Leboeuf alone. Come on, man. You don't do that. Venables was a superb coach who taught me a lot of things, including how to play efficiently, but he got involved in that FA Cup quarter-final and it just didn't work. Still, we ended up one place below the play-offs, three points adrift of sixth-placed Crystal Palace, with Bradbury, Svensson and myself scoring 39 goals between us.

In the summer of June 1997, I was handed my Jamaica international debut against Cuba, with one eye on potentially our maiden appearance at the 1998 World Cup finals in France. My dad was from Jamaica, and, while mum was born in Manchester, her parents were part of the Windrush generation, so I comfortably qualified to play for the Reggae Boyz. However, in those days there was no international window, which meant that, on occasions, commitments with my country saw me miss Pompey matches, at times sparking a backlash from supporters and the manager. There was myself, Deon Burton and Fitzroy Simpson and I suppose when you take three prominent players out of your team and the club are unable to call the match off, then you'll struggle a little. The Blues fans would ask: "Where were you? You are supposed to be here," and I can see their point, but their frustration wasn't that we were playing badly for Pompey. We simply weren't available because we were off to El Salvador in the World Cup qualifiers or Miami to play Brazil in the CONCACAF Gold Cup.

I always got on with Pompey fans, but that was a difficult time for me. You'd read things in the newspaper, hear them on the street, sometimes from your own teammates. Things like: "What are you going out there for? Are you going on holiday?" I don't think they appreciated how hard we were working and what was at stake for us. We'd fly back from playing for Jamaica on the Wednesday night, land Thursday morning, acclimatise and then turn out on the Saturday for Pompey. It wasn't ideal for anyone, yet the World Cup finals don't come around often. I made 48 appearances for Jamaica, scoring 14 times, and whenever I return to Fratton Park I'm proud knowing my name is on that international honours board alongside the likes of Jimmy Dickinson.

Ahead of the 1997/98 season, Lee Bradbury had been sold to Manchester City for £3.5m, with John Aloisi replacing him, as Venables began to use his influence as manager of Australia's international side to bring some of their players across to Fratton Park. The campaign kicked off at Manchester City, with Bradders lining-up for the Maine Road hosts and the Gallagher brothers also present. I was more into reggae and hip-hop, but still liked Oasis. I can appreciate good music, and they were the flavour of the month at that time. All the lads were listening to them, and now they were on the pitch before the game — and I immediately hated them. They were in the tunnel beforehand, then were winding up the Pompey fans ahead of kick-off, which really angered me. I hated seeing that and took of-fence. They had no right being on the pitch, overstepping the mark by gesticu-lating to the travelling Blues support — and I don't mind admitting it increased my motivation. When I scored an 80th-minute equaliser to give us a 2-2 draw, I went mad. I was thinking of the Gallaghers when I went over to celebrate with our fans. That showed Oasis!

I was disappointed when Fenwick was dismissed in January 1998, but we weren't on a great run and sitting bottom of Division One. I really liked him, he wants to play the game a certain way and wears his heart on his sleeve, which sometimes can be the undoing of you when results start to deteriorate. It affects people's patience. His replacement was Alan Ball, a World Cup winner who sent me to France six months later with the message: "You're a lucky lad, going to the World Cup finals … don't let it pass you by." However, Alan didn't really fancy what I was doing, starting me twice in the final 19 matches of the season as we battled relegation. I actually scored the first time he named me in his line-up — a 2-1 defeat at Sunderland — while I came off the bench to grab a late point in a 2-2 draw at Tranmere Rovers in April 1998, but I wasn't part of things. I was an unused substitute on a three-man bench for the final two matches of the season, including the last-day 3-1 win at Bradford City which kept us up, through goals from John Durnin (two) and Sammy Igoe. These are the little microaggressions aimed at you to make you doubt your future at a club. As a player, I believed I could help the team, but now I was out of it.

Straight after that Valley Parade victory, myself and Fitzroy Simpson flew to France to meet up with the Jamaica squad for a friendly with Saudi Arabia, then it was on to the World Cup finals, where we finished third in a group containing Argentina and Croatia, so failed to qualify for the knockout stages. Still, we were back on Pompey duty by mid-July, joining the squad for their pre-season tour to the Republic of Ireland and five friendlies in eight days, yet a lot of things hap-pened during that summer and it was probably the only time I didn't feel welcome at the club. I knew I was no longer part of the story — and it didn't need to be like that.

For a start, Fitzroy and myself were put into a totally different part of the Done-gal hotel compared to the rest of the squad, immediately making us feel as though we didn't belong. Then Bally began picking on little things, which I recognised as obvious attempts to get under my skin, whereas should other players in the team do the same thing, he wouldn't say a word. If he had told me I wasn't playing be-cause Pompey were looking to sell me, I'd have gone, no problem. Anything for this club. But to initiate it in the manner he did left a sour taste in my mouth. This was their way of trying to get me out. Everything comes to an end, nothing is permanent in life, but I had been a good enough servant to the club. I felt I deserved more and the way it finished left a void, a feeling of unfinished business with the Blues. I never held the club responsible for that, it was the people in charge.

In August 1998, Bally informed me a bid had been accepted from Coventry City, so I told him I didn't want to go — but I had to, the club supposedly wanted to balance the books. Then they used the money to buy Steve Claridge from Wolverhampton Wanderers, who would have been on more money than me! In a previous season, I had rejected the chance to join Southampton after being asked to consider it. I lived in Portsmouth, everybody around me were staunch Blues supporters. I understood the rivalry, I lived it, plus I'd been warned many times: "You'd better not play for them!" It was not something you did as a Pompey player — no amount of money could have made me join them. I remember going to a nightclub in Southampton with Fitzroy and Deon Burton and being chucked out because we were Pompey! All I wanted to do was come in for a dance, so we'd instead go to Bournemouth.

I was happy at Pompey, living in Hilsea with my girlfriend at the time. It's a lovely part of the world, sunshine, great friends, where I spent my most successful years as a footballer. I didn't want to go. Coventry were in the Premier League under Gordon Strachan and had just finished 11th, but it was almost a step back. Their fans were good, but not as connected as Pompey, which is a real family club. Put it this way, my career didn't go the way it should have gone with the Sky Blues, probably because my heart was still at Pompey. I wanted to come back; I was homesick. If you look at my Coventry career, I didn't really have one. It wasn't because I wasn't good enough, I knew I was. I'd played in the World Cup finals, in the Championship. But it wasn't Pompey.

I was emotionally invested in the club and remain a Pompey supporter even now. They were the greatest days of my football career.

DANNY ROSE

64 games, five goals (June 2016 — January 2019)

Pompey 6 (O'Shaughnessy OG, Bennett, Naismith 2, Lowe, Evans)
Cheltenham Town 1 (Dayton)

League Two, Fratton Park, Saturday, May 6, 2017

Pompey: Forde, Evans, Burgess, Clarke, Stevens, Rose (71 mins, Aborah), Doyle, Baker (60 mins, Lowe), Naismith, Bennett, Chaplin (61 mins, Roberts). Subs not used: O'Brien, Whatmough, Kabamba, Linganzi.

Attendance; 17,956

CELEBRATIONS David Forde and Enda Stevens are held aloft by the Fratton faithful after the 6-1 triumph over Cheltenham paved the way for a remarkable title success

I had been to Fratton Park before, of course, but that May 2016 evening was different. It was spine-tingling, hairs standing on the back of your neck. Absolutely incredible. Pompey had plans to do transfer business early for the following season and, as a target, their chief executive Mark Catlin had invited me to attend a League Two play-off semi-final first leg against Plymouth Argyle. It finished 2-2, with Marc McNulty and Gary Roberts scoring, yet the atmosphere left a real impression — nothing like I had ever experienced before other than attending Old Trafford. In League Two at that time, Pompey was the best club you could represent and that evening was so profound that, even if the contract wasn't great, I still would have joined. Imagine playing in front of that crowd week in, week out. That night I decided to become a Blues player.

My maiden Fratton Park visit as a player was in August 2013 on the opening day of the 2013/14 season, when I featured for Oxford United. We won 4-1 and Johnny Ertl was sent off in the second half after catching me on the right temple with his elbow while we went up for the ball, although it wasn't intentional. Years later, I returned as part of Northampton Town's title-winning team on the final day of the 2015/16 League Two campaign, where Pompey gave us a guard of honour as we entered the pitch. We won 2-1 and I had a decent game, playing the full 90 minutes, apparently that day also convincing Paul Cook to follow up his interest.

Having arrived at Sixfields three-and-a-half months earlier from Oxford on a short-term deal, I was playing some of the best football of my career under Chris Wilder when I began to hear whispers of potential interest from the Blues. My teammate Ricky Holmes, who previously played for them, had held a conversation with Mark Catlin along the lines of: "You've got to sign this lad I play with." I was contracted to the Cobblers until the end of the season and, following 15 appearances in their title success, they tabled a decent offer to extend my stay. However, after that Fratton Park trip, my mind was made up as long as the deal was adequate. I would happily sacrifice League One football to join Pompey.

There were other potential signings also present among the 17,622 crowd that night, including Hallam Hope, who I later played alongside at Swindon Town. I was present with my agent and we were scheduled to meet Cookie after the game. However, he'd been sent off in the first half so the timing was no longer right, not that I needed any convincing. I actually flew to Marbella with the Northampton lads early the following morning, who were well aware of where I had been the previous night, urging me to stay. Although Ricky's words struck home: "Rosey, if Pompey want you, then go."

Following Pompey's elimination after the second leg at Home Park, I drove from our Swindon home to the training ground with my wife and children to meet Cookie and Robbie Blake, who made us feel so welcome. With two offers on the table, negotiating went backwards and forwards, but once we agreed terms at Pompey, it didn't matter what Northampton did, and I signed a two-year deal in June 2016 — becoming Paul Cook's first recruit of the summer.

Northampton didn't have a training ground at the time and it was a case of getting changed in the stadium and travelling to different locations to train at, whereas Pompey was a much more professional environment. The balls were out straight away on the first day of pre-season training, the standard among the players was very good, and everyone was on it. I was aware of the play-off semi-final defeat to Plymouth the previous season, but there was no hangover and I don't remember a single conversation among the players about it. They focused on the challenges of 2016/17 pretty quickly. The need to look ahead was probably behind Cookie taking the lads away to the Republic of Ireland on tour in July 2016 for a week of work hard, play hard in a great environment to bring us together, particularly us new additions. I remember immediately getting really friendly with Kyle Bennett and Christian Burgess, two completely different characters, while there were also two new physios in Nick Meace and Andy Procter for everyone to get to know.

Our first friendly over there was a 3-3 draw at Sligo Rovers, where Seamus Coleman, who they had sold to Everton years earlier, was a guest of honour, personally putting money behind the bar at a nearby pub, with karaoke also organised for after the match. It represented the first time the lads were able to let their hair down, although when the team coach had to leave for the two-hour trip back to the Johnstown Hotel in County Meath, the majority of the older players opted to stay out — so were left behind! I ended up catching a taxi back in the early hours along with Kyle Bennett and Adam Barton, with Benno and myself kipping on the hotel room floor of the gaffer's brother. We weren't alone, there were lads asleep in the hotel lobby and I remember Jack Whatmough snoozing with his head on a table. It's probably frowned upon a bit now, especially the higher up the leagues you go, yet it was important to get to know each other and have a laugh.

Our second match was a 2-0 win over Bohemians, in which I scored our opener, and afterwards it was into Dublin for some drinking in the local pubs, where we also met Pompey fans, although it was more casual than the Sligo evening and definitely not as much alcohol. It's up there with the booziest pre-seasons I ever experienced and certainly provided the foundations for creating a team bond which, ultimately, would drive us to the League Two title.

Pompey possessed a distinct way of playing and everyone was well-drilled in their roles and responsibilities, which was the strength of Cook. We worked so much on shape and patterns of play that it became second nature. On occasions, there were cries from supporters to operate with two strikers when drawing 0-0 at Fratton Park, but our play was always about patience, grinding down the opposition, getting them tired, taking their legs away. And, more often than not, it worked. We lost 11 times that season, yet certainly weren't outplayed. Stevenage were the only side which did the double over us and the first game, at Fratton Park in November 2016, was a particular low point. Although, in a weird way, it galvanised the lads.

It was goalless at half-time, we weren't playing great and Darren Sarll's men were making it difficult for us. There were a few boos at half-time, understandably. I was among the first to return to the dressing room and it was quite calm, with nothing much said, until David Forde came in, shouting and bawling about how we needed to pull our fingers out and start doing the business. I was unsure whether he was referring to the defence or the team in general. Then Burgey piped up. He always had something to say for himself, which is fine and healthy in that environment, in the heat of debate. He commented on a defensive mix-up with his goalkeeper towards the end of that half and the pair of them exchanged words — then Michael Doyle got involved, siding with Fordey. All of a sudden, Doyler and Burgey were grappling with each other, with the skipper falling back and using his feet to defend himself.

Fights aren't uncommon in the dressing room or at the training ground. You get scuffles, like wrestling someone to the ground after a bad tackle, but drawing blood is very rare — and that afternoon Burgey had it dripping down his face. Paul Cook substituted them both and losing two massive players for the second half didn't help the team as we went on to lose 2-1. Afterwards I was asked to speak to the local media, who had found out about the fight, but I couldn't give too much away.

As it so happened, the players' Christmas party had been arranged in Cardiff that night, with a coach scheduled to drive us there after the game — only for Cookie to demand it was scrapped. Yet on the players' WhatsApp group it was clear there was no bad love. It was heat of the moment stuff, certainly nothing personal, and the general consensus was: "We've still got to go out lads," so we instead met up at a Whiteley pub and then headed into Southampton. Importantly, everyone attended, the team were as one, while the respect between Doyler and Burgey grew.

It was pre-planned that we'd go in fancy dress to Winter Wonderland in Hyde Park on the Sunday, with each player having been allocated a letter of the alphabet and challenged to find a costume which it began with. I had P so chose *Pirates Of The Caribbean* and Captain Jack Sparrow. It wasn't clear whether the lads were still going after the fight, but me and Kyle Bennett definitely were, meeting up at 10am and catching the train to London, although definitely not in fancy dress! We actually bumped into Northampton's squad so joined them, with Benno, being the character he is, grabbing their kitty and volunteering to order the rounds, which included us. Then, around 3pm, we received a group message from Cook's assistant Leam Richardson declaring Monday training was now off and we were given permission to have a drink and enjoy ourselves. Well, some of us already were!

Still, that gave the green light for the rest of the lads to jump on a train and meet us, with some of us staying over in a London hotel and having a great night. Irrespective of having gone against the manager's wishes, that weekend was important, showing team unity despite the dressing-room incident — and we probably came together as a result.

I'm not sure how Cook found out, but, on the Tuesday morning, he ran us into the ground. It was ridiculous, running around training pitches for 90 minutes, which was unusual, especially at that stage of the season. We rarely did running and fitness drills mid-season, it was usual football running. Our next match was at Grimsby Town in November 2016, when substitute Kal Naismith scored a match-winning free-kick four minutes from time in a 1-0 victory, sparking a fantastic celebration, with everyone piling onto him. That was team spirit.

By March 2017, we were fourth in League Two ahead of Crewe Alexandra's visit to Fratton Park. I found myself on the bench for a seventh successive match, with Amine Linganzi preferred alongside Michael Doyle in the two holding midfield roles. It's funny, sometimes your stock can go up when you don't play and it was clear the subsequent 1-0 defeat was not a good performance. Crewe were struggling, it was a game we expected to dominate and win, especially having drawn 1-1 at home to Morecambe the previous match, but it didn't turn out like that. Understandably, Cookie was fuming afterwards. I try to think back on how my Pompey managers reacted in situations like that and, while Kenny Jackett didn't lose it often, he certainly did in a 3-0 defeat at a wet Blackburn Rovers in October 2017.

With a trip to Crawley Town 72 hours later after Crewe, before Monday's training session, Doyler called us into the meeting room for a team chat. The group had been through ups and downs and it was now or never for us to be successful at Pompey, so the lads voiced their thoughts on the situation and what was needed to turn it around. It was not a meeting where players were digging each other out but as a group we needed to stop having sloppy moments in games which had been costing us, and more of a focus was required to achieve our ambition. I had my say on a few things, but I don't remember anybody picking out certain individuals and their professionalism. It was about getting back to doing what we did best and sticking to that, no matter the outside noise. At the time, I didn't believe that meeting was really important but obviously it was. It wasn't uncomfortable to hold open discussions and fortunately we had that chemistry where. Should people say something, you'd listen.

I was recalled for Crawley, alongside Carl Baker, and we won 2-0 through second-half goals from Burgess and Bennett — starting a run of 31 points from a possible 36 as we claimed the League Two title on a dramatic final day of the season. Before that, in April 2017, we headed to Notts County in the knowledge that victory — and helpful results elsewhere — would see us promoted, although I wasn't involved. The previous match against Plymouth, I had jarred my right ankle after kicking an opponent's foot, so at Meadow Lane I stood with fellow injured teammates Matt Clarke and Noel Hunt among Pompey's fans. With around 10 minutes remaining and leading 2-1, we moved to the away dugout and fed the Luton scoreline to Cookie. Ultimately, we won 3-1, with Jamal Lowe netting twice, prompting a pitch invasion at the final whistle. Although it was massively gutting not to be in the team that day, the celebrations afterwards were amazing. Notts County's manager Kevin Nolan brought a load of beers into our dressing room, which was top class.

Some players don't achieve success. It must be great to perform in the Premier League and have everything which comes with that, but an average footballer at that level won't win any silverware. During my career, I secured five promotions — Newport County, Fleetwood Town, Northampton, Pompey and Swindon — while also featured in Oxford's promotion season before leaving them for Northampton. Pompey was the best of them all. The challenge was the most demanding, coping with huge expectations, the pressure, the size of the fanbase, which made the achievement that much more special. Better was to come, however, with a 6-1 victory over Cheltenham Town to clinch the League Two title on the final day — which is head and shoulders the favourite match of my career.

Having subsequently beaten Cambridge United and Mansfield Town following promotion, it was set up for the last match at Fratton Park. We knew we could beat Cheltenham — and by a good margin — yet it was at the back of your mind that either Plymouth or Doncaster Rovers would still claim the title. Regardless, an own goal from Daniel O'Shaughnessy got us up and running and we became

League Two champions, having topped the table for 32 minutes all season. It was surely unheard of, and the trophy wasn't even at the ground!

With the campaign now over, the majority of the players headed to Marbella for three days of beer, music, celebrations and laughter, which was a great way to cap a fantastic year. However, not long after we returned, Cookie left to join Wigan Athletic. It was definitely a surprise — I don't even recall any rumours circulating within the players' WhatsApp group — and it came as a blow. We had momentum, we could have challenged to get out of League One, but now he'd gone. I was gutted. He never said goodbye to me personally, there was no phone call — and Kenny Jackett arrived as our new manager in June 2017.

With Cook, you'd arrive for training in the morning and he'd invite you into his office for a chat and a cup of tea, while, on other occasions, he'd share a beer with you. At the same time, you wouldn't want to get on the bad side of him. He's still the favourite manager of my career. Obviously Cook was chalk and cheese with Kenny in terms of personality and style of play, yet both were very professional. However, you probably couldn't enjoy yourself as much under Kenny with his tunnel vision.

When Pompey reached the Checkatrade Trophy final in March 2019, being a Swindon player at that point, I did co-commentary at Wembley alongside Andy Moon for *BBC Radio Solent*. Having played in the opening four matches of the competition that season before leaving, Ashleigh Emberson at the club later organised a winners' medal for me, without me asking, which I thought was a lovely touch. Anyhow, Pompey were losing 1-0 to Sunderland when Gaz Evans crossed from the left and Nathan Thompson headed home an 82nd-minute equaliser. I've since watched the highlights and, when that moment arrives, the camera panned to Kenny — and he's emotionless. I completely understand that — as a manager he'll be thinking: "Right, do I make a sub?" or some other tactical decision to affect the game — yet Cook would have reacted so differently in that situation.

I never had a relationship with Kenny. On one occasion, I noticed a new face watching training wearing Pompey gear so I asked how he was, being polite. It turned out to be Kenny's son, who's also a coach — I didn't even know he had a son! Whereas Cookie's wife would get involved with the players' wives and kids and he also had a younger daughter, so my kids got to know her at games. With Kenny, there really wasn't a relationship. It was strictly player and manager. I wouldn't say that's wrong, because every manager has their own methods and ways. Some like to keep their distance from the players, which is fine. Some are really involved, some are too involved in certain stuff, and Cook got the balance right.

Jackett was ultra professional, but most players want something more from their boss, a bit of personality and that was the difference. In his managerial career he obviously achieved success, including winning that Checkatrade Trophy at Pompey and reaching the League One play-offs in successive seasons, with professionalism a strength of his. Certainly his messages in terms of how he wants a team to play are quite clear. However, that player/manager relationship just wasn't there for me, particularly when you're left out of a squad with no chat to explain why. Not a single word. I remember having one or two analysis meetings with him which weren't necessarily great. I'd never say he would make you feel on top of the world, whereas Cook could. You might feel 10 times bigger. That's what I missed going from Cookie to Kenny; the highs of winning League Two on the last day to him within 28 days.

Now with a new manager at the helm for our return to League One, I started the opening four league games, then, in an August 2017 trip to Wigan, I was partnering Adam May in midfield only to be brought off for Ben Close after 53 minutes, which was really disappointing. I was playing against Cookie and knew some of their players, such as Sam Morsy and Chey Dunkley, and wondered why I'd been taken off in the 1-1 draw. I didn't get it. Perhaps he had seen something he didn't like, which was fine, so I went to see him and discovered that, in his mind, there were four in the pecking order for the centre of midfield — and I was fourth. Stuart O'Keefe had arrived on loan from Cardiff City, so Kenny had an obligation to play him, while Close and May, who never made a league appearance between them the previous season, were now ahead of me. I didn't receive any information about what I could do to climb this pecking order — and now I was struggling to even make the bench.

Our form had become poor, losing four successive goals, including 1-0 at Luton Town in the FA Cup first round, and I was wondering whether Kenny could be sacked, or at least may choose to recall me. Regardless, something had to change. We travelled to Charlton Athletic in the Checkatrade Trophy in November 2017 and I was partnering May in the centre of midfield. With O'Keefe suspended for the following match against Blackpool, it was a straight shoot-out to see who would replace him and line up alongside Close. What a mindset to head into a game, but Kenny's assistant Joe Gallen came to me at half-time to reassure me I wouldn't be substituted — as they had Bloomfield Road on Saturday in mind for me. Sure enough, I was back in and we subsequently won eight of the next 10 matches in all competitions.

I was back in the team and in the best form of my Pompey career, starting 11 successive games, and we shot up the league into sixth, with Brett Pitman on fire.

At that moment, I felt I was at the peak of my career. I was aged 29, competing in League One for the first time, performing well, winning matches and suddenly Kenny's mindset had changed from: "Here is a player I don't want to keep" to: "Right, we'll talk about a new contract." My deal had six months remaining, discussions had started and my agent had gone back and forth. We were really receptive. This team wasn't as good as the one which won League Two, but we were getting results and playing decent football. Then arrived the moment which changed my Blues career.

It was December 2017 and we were facing my old club Northampton at Fratton Park, looking to end the year on a high and cement our place in the top six of League One. On 29 minutes, referee Lee Swabey awarded a drop ball which I contended with John-Joe O'Toole. I ended up breaking my left leg — and never played another league game at Fratton Park again. It was so surreal. I don't think it's naive wanting to go into a drop ball; at the time it was part of the game. There's no blame attached to O'Toole, none at all. It was just as much my fault. The laws of the game subsequently changed 18 months later, with drop balls no longer contested, albeit not directly because of what happened to me. The game evolves and it's something which had to change. I went in hard with my inside foot — and O'Toole had gone in hard too. He actually won the ball, kicked it and the follow through caught my follow through. It could have happened to him.

Initially, it never occurred to me that I'd sustained a broken leg. I knew I was in trouble and was taken to the physio room just before half-time with an aching pain in that area. It was horrible. There wasn't an ambulance around, or one that was going to arrive quickly, so kitman Kev McCormack carried me and put me into the club doctor's Jaguar, parked in Frogmore Road. He drove me to Spire Portsmouth Hospital in Havant and, on the journey, I was lying across the back seat, feet up, not seatbelted, feeling every bump in the road, and thinking: "Please don't be a break, please don't be a break." Following a scan, I was informed it was a fractured tibia, a clean break, with thankfully my fibula being fine. I had a bit of a cry, trying to come to terms with my season being over and in the middle of contract talks. Naturally at that point you're fearing the worst. It was never a case of thinking I wouldn't play again because I knew I would and didn't for one minute consider it career-threatening. I don't know why. I was more concerned with the here and now, thinking about negotiations for probably the biggest contract of my career.

During my period on the sidelines, Pompey extended my contract in March 2018 for another season, which I was grateful for. Other clubs wouldn't have backed an injured player like that but there was definitely an element of loyalty, which allowed me to concentrate on rehab throughout the off-season. Admittedly, it wasn't the same contract we'd been negotiating because my injury had changed circumstances and instead it was an extension of the existing deal. Incentives and bonuses had improved, but, in terms of salary, there was no pay rise, which was fine. Before injury, my form and number of games had given me negotiating power — now I was unavailable for four months and missing the remainder of the season. Being realistic, I'd have been lucky to receive a new two-year deal on improved terms.

Still, I returned to fully feature in Pompey's 2018 pre-season programme, with a host of new faces now around, including Craig MacGillivray, Lee Brown, Ronan Curtis, Louis Dennis and another central midfielder in Tom Naylor. I was flying too. I was fit and at the front of running with Gaz Evans, which was always a good benchmark. That summer we spent a week at Fota Island in Cork, a resort with three beautiful golf courses — not that the players were allowed to use any of them by Kenny Jackett. In fact, other than working hard in training, he wouldn't let us do a lot. We weren't allowed to enjoy ourselves and, considering there were new players in the group, we'd have all benefited from team bonding. That's something Kenny doesn't regard as important, but every manager has his own methods.

England were playing Columbia in the 2018 World Cup finals in Russia and senior members of the squad asked the manager if we could head into town and have a drink while watching the game. We were told we could see it at the golf club — and strictly no drinking. Come on, we thought. Let us have a few pints. Ultimately we're football fans as well. It wouldn't have any effect on the season physically, and could actually strengthen the bond of the group. It's little things like that. In the end, some lads had a couple of beers anyway while watching England's 4-3 penalty shoot-out win. Whether Kenny found that out, I don't know. I shared a room with Dion Donohue and after the game we snuck out. We just wanted to see Cork and enjoy ourselves a bit. We weren't out too late either, back home for one or two in the morning, nothing too silly, then trained fine the next day. On another day, Gaz Evans and Christian Burgess snuck out to attend an Alanis Morrisette concert, which was in Cork. Towards the end of the week, around five of us went to the 18th hole on a boiling hot day, having a couple of beers, watching the golfers and enjoying each other's company. No doubt it would have been frowned upon by the management had they ever discovered.

The opening match of the 2018/19 season saw me fail to make the 18-man squad against Luton at Fratton Park, despite being fit and featuring in seven of the pre-season friendlies. The late Anton Walkes was instead in the centre of midfield alongside Tom Naylor and, while a lovely guy, to me Anton was clearly better at right-back. The following match was a trip to Blackpool, with Walkes restored to right-back, while I was back involved, coming off the bench for Ben Close in the 66th minute in a 2-1 win. I would never again play in League One for the Blues. From that point, I was solely used in Checkatrade Trophy matches and, with the team now long-time leaders at the top of the table, deep down, I knew it was over for me at Fratton Park.

My Pompey League Two title-winning teammate Noel Hunt got in touch and, now being assistant manager at Swindon, asked whether I'd be interested in dropping into League Two to join them. Me and Pompey amicably came to an agreement to cancel my contract by mutual consent in January 2019 and I signed a six-month deal with the Robins, with an option for an additional year. I had played just five more times for the Blues after breaking my leg.

Looking back, that 2016/17 title-winning season is head and shoulders above any success I've had. The experience, the scale of celebration afterwards, the fans, the group of players with that chemistry . . . there was nothing like it at Swindon, Newport County, Fleetwood or Northampton. To play a small part in getting Pompey out of League Two, and being able to have a profound effect on fans' lives, makes me very, very proud.

ACKNOWLEDGEMENTS

The strength of the *Played Up Pompey* books centres on those who contribute. These are willing participants, generous with their time and possessing a genuine affection for Portsmouth Football Club. Over the course of the four *Played Up Pompey* books, a total of 92 former Blues players have been interviewed. None went through the motions or required financial inducement, they spoke because they wanted to, not because they had to.

I would also like to thank my wonderful wife Emma and children Abi and Greg, who have been extremely patient and understanding during the writing process.

My parents, Keith and Daisy, have offered a lifetime of guidance and advice, while Tony Parratt, former editor of the *Heartland Evening News*, is responsible for unleashing me upon the newspaper industry.

Thank you to my faithful proofreaders consisting of Roger Holmes, Paul Boynton and Steve Bone, while Gareth Edwards, from Portsmouth Central Library, has been a tremendous help sourcing photographs and archive copies of *The News*, going beyond all duty. Thanks, too, to Phil Kelly for his proofreading help.

Former club photographer Joe Pepler and *The News'* snapping legend Steve Reid have again supplied many of the excellent photographs contained within this book, while Chris Gibbs, from the Pompey History Society, has also dug into club resources to locate some older pictures. Any other photographer whose work is involved is invited to contact the publishers in writing providing proof of copyright.

I would like to thank Bishops Printers managing director Gareth Roberts and designer Andy Sanders for their support for the opening three *Played Up Pompey* books before passing on the baton. And finally to Danny Hall, from publishers Vertical Editions, for his boundless enthusiasm and immense passion for the project, always willing to humour me and indulge in a late night WhatsApp conversation about the progress of *Played Up Pompey Four*.

ROLL OF HONOUR

Vince Abela
Colin Adams
Stefan Aldred
Stephen Alexander
Carl Allen
John Allen
Christopher Alton
Colin Amey, *RIP*
Phil Andrews
Steve Andrews
Meg Argyle
Paul Argyle
Richard Atkins-Greig
Rick Austin
Steve Ayling
David Ayling
Peter Ayling
Leon Aylmer
Thomas Giles Babb
Thomas Edward Babb
Joshua Michael Babb
Christian Bailey
Pat Bailey
Steve Bailey
Des Baines
Nigel Baker
Dave Banbury
Matt Barber
Stuart Barber
Tom Barker
Billy Barrett
Andy Bartholomew
Liam Batchelor
Dean Battley
Mark Beavis
Sean Bebee
Paul Beckett
Lee Bennett

Christopher Bentham
Steven Ross Benzeval
Nolan Bishop
Trevor Bishop
Elias Blachford
Graeme Blackford
Carolyn Lucy Blake
Alan Bloxham
Mike Blythman
Graeme Bosbery
Iain Bosbery
Christopher Bousher
Dave Bowers
Sam Bowers
David Bowers
Stephen Bowles
Darren Box
Jack Bridgen
Brian Briggs
Tony Brooks
Ian D Brown
Jake Brown
Greg Brown
Arnold Bryant
Matt Buck
David Burch
Dave Burch
Steve Burghard
Stuart Burnett
Mark Adam Burnett
Nigel William Burr
Michael Burridge
Steve Byrne
Mark Callaway
Stacey Campbell
Simon-Paul Campbell
Nicholas Campbell
Stewart Carnegie

Edward Carter
Derek Challis
Steve Chambers
Tracey Childs
Greg Choppen
Robert Churcher
Paula Clark
Simon Clee
Alan Clements
Mark Coates
Richard Coates
Jon Cobb
Terry Collis
Lee Colvin
Anthony Conway
Tony Cook
Rich Cooksley
Martin Cooper
Malcolm Cooper
Steve Cope
Steve Cornell-Davis
Martyn Cornish
Jonathan Coupe
Nick Court
Paul Crage
Trevor Crowe
Anni Crowhurst
Roy KW Cullen
Lee Culshaw
Neville Dalton
Robert Daly
Joshua Daly
Finley Daly
Jack Dando
Lloyd Davey (*in loving memory of Alan Davey*)
Glenn Robert Davies
Stewart Davies

Bryan Davis

Phil Dawtrey

Stephen De Mellow

Malcolm Deathers

John Denney

Sean Derwin

Jack Dewing

Mark Disberry

John P Dolden

Elaine Dore

Tom Drees

Dennis Duncan

Derek Durant

Aaron Easson

Chris Ebbens

Gareth Eddington

Alan Edney

Steve Edwards

Tim Edwards

Timothy Egleton

Joakim Ellingsen

Andy Ellis

Rob Ellis

Liam Emerson

Ryan James Empson

Toby Evans

Ant Evans

Steven Ewins

Steve Ewins

Richard Eyre

Graham Eyres

Lee Farndell

Clare Farnell

Robert John Fawdry

Brian Fenwick

Peter Fields

Billy Fitzjohn

Paul Fletcher

Graham Fletcher

Simon Flood

John Flood

Ashley Fookes

James Foot

Tim Foote

Andy Ford

Lou Formby

Paul Fowling

Stuart Richard Franklin

Ed Fulda

Simon Gale

Oliver Gates

Chris Gibbs

Ken Glanfield

Ashley Glover

Mark Goodyear

Matthew Graham

Myles Grainger

Mel Grant

Nicholas Grant

Tarren Gratwick

Kevin Gray

Chris Greasley

Bob Gregory

Laurence Griffiths

Steve Groves

Will Hahn

Robert Haines

Dave Hallett

Sean Hamilton

Mark Hancock

Ray Hards

Shaun Hardy

Kevin Paul Harland

Terry Harris

Trevor Harvey

Steve Hatch

Steve Hatcher

Chris Hatter

David Hatter

Aaron Hatton

Phillip Hawkes

Jeremy Hawkins

Clive Hawkins

Jax Hayes

Robert Hayward (Talkington)

Ashley Headon

Graham Heeps

Anthony Hesse

Robert Hewett

Lee Hewett

Noah Hicks

Michael Hills

Matthew Hills

Karl Hoey

Alfie Holt

Stephen D Hooper

Chris Hosier

Paul Houghton

Tony Howe-Haysom

Sasha Howe-Haysom

Matt Hoy

Simon Hunt

Malcolm Hunt

Andy Hunt

Iris Huntington

Brian Huntington

Harvey Huntley

Paul Hutchinson

Keith Jacks

Nick Jacobs

Charlie James

Chalton James

Jake Jeavons

Arthur Edward Jeffery

Colin Paul Johnson

Steve Jones

Carol Jones

Andy Jones-Show

Michael Jordan

Graham Kendall

Jeremy Kerswell

Stuart King

Neil Kirkpatrick

David Kitson
Tracy Kneller
James Knibbs
Kevin Knight
Jamie Knott
Eric Laming
Ian Laming
Ali Lance
Paul Langford
Kjeld Lauridsen
Ciaran Lea
Peter James Lee
Karen Lewis
Steven Lewis
James Lewis
Derek Lewry
Ian Limb
Dan Limb
George Limb
Jacob Littlefield
Peter Longyear
Paul Lucas
Min Luk
David Macaskill
Kipper MacRae
Steven Maidment
Paul Maidment
Stephen Main
Alex Main
Robbie Main
Andy Maitland
Kevin Marden
Jacob Marsh
Nick Marshallsay
Rich Marwood
Sean Mason
Mark Maspero
Wayne Matthews
Danny Matthews
Leslie R Matthewson
Tom May

Tim May
Dave Maynard
Mark McCann
Dylan McClafferty
Peter McGreal
Ian McKelvie-Seth
Alan McKinlay
Connor McMain
Ian McTeer
Grace Melton
Linda Methven
Lee Middlebrook
Keith Middleton
Lawrence DW Miller
Mark Miller
John Terence Patrick Miller
Stephen Mills
Stuart Milne
Oliver AW Mitchell
Yvonne Moore
Lee Morby-Bagley
David Morey
James Morgan
Jack Morrison
Rufus Mowatt
Callum Munro
Jonathan Murray
Matthew Need
Glenn Nicholls
Mark Nicholls
Gareth Nowell
Joshua Older
Daniel Older
Keith Oliver
Stuart Orford
Jack Osmond-Smith
Chris Owens
Antony Parham
Ben Parish
Derek Parnell

Dan Parr
Harry James Parsons
Steve Parsons
Geoff Paul
Charles Pearce
James Penfold
Lee Penny
Phil Penteney
Peter Perdoni
Claire Perry
Anthony Perry
Phil Phillips
Charlie Phillips
Samuel Polden
Trevor Port
Andy Porter
Brian Portet
Robert Powell
James Powers
Steve Pratt
Dean Preston
Graham Price
Derek Priddle
David Proud
Alex Radice-Gomm
Darren Stuart Raffan
Gemma Raggett
Nigel Ralph
Theo Rattue
Tim MJ Rawding
Jordan Rayment
Rich Raymond
Chris Redman
David Stephen Reed
Adrian Reid-Robertson
John Reid-Robertson
Paul Renouf
Tom Rhodes
Lee Richards
Anne Ricketts
Iain Rider

Adam Rider	Andrew RH Smith	Simon Tyrrell
Simon Ridge	Louis Smith-Merstham	Robin Tysoe
James Roberts	Matthew Snow	Gary Underwood
Mark Gordon Roberts	Craig Southam	Bryony Vine
Lewis Robinson	Mark Spencer	Paul Voden
Glen Roskilly	Paul Spencer	Tony Walder
Eddy Ross	Peter Stanworth	Neil J Walker
Martyn Roy	Andy Stevenson	Michael Wallace
Simon Russell	Dan Stevenson	Mike Wallace
Derek Russell	Arthur Steward	John Walters
Josh Russell	Ciarán Steward	Elaine Ware
Kevin Ryan	Neil Stock	Christopher Waterman
Ricky Ryan	Paul Stokes	Roger Watling
Davey Sadler	Rob Stokes	Rhys Watson
Tim Sanders	Graham Stone	Gary Wearn
Jason Saunders	Graham Stout	Dan Webb
David Saunders	Den Strange	Kevin Weeks
Stuart Saunders	Dan Strophair	Roger Welch
Matthew James Saunders	Ben Stroud	Matthew Wells
Barry Savage	Martin Sutherland	Ben Whelan
Jim Sawyer	Andrew Tanner	Steve White
Samuel James Scott	Scott Taviner	Alan White
Olly Searle	Darren Taylor	Paul Whiteaway
Terry Sells	Phil Templeman	Stephen Whitewick
Warren Sharman	Wesley Thomas	Shaun Whitmarsh
Clive Sharman	Mark Thompson	Jim Whitmarsh
Kelvin Shaw	Adrian Thompson	Matt Wigman
Graham John Shaw	Matthew Thomson	Scott Williams
Kevin Shelley	Matt Tice	Trevor James Williams
Peter Sheppard	Bethany Tiller	Stephen Mark Wilson
Robert Shimbart	Steve Titheridge	Richard Wilson
Barry Shotton	Lee Todd	Scott Wilson
Paul Simmons	Glyn Tookey	David Martin Winter
Tony Simms	Trevor Tovey	Shawn Woodward
Daniel Sloman	Frank Tracey	Paul Wright
Jim Smalley	Glenn Turnbull	Bob Wright
Steve Smethurst	Keith Turnbull	Mike Yeatman
Jake Smith	Elliott Turnbull	John Young
Toby Smith	Chris Turner	Steve Young
Clive Malcolm Smith	Mike Tuttiett	Alan Young